PRINCIPLES OF
GROUP SOLIDARITY

PRINCIPLES OF
GROUP SOLIDARITY

MICHAEL HECHTER

UNIVERSITY OF CALIFORNIA PRESS

BERKELEY   LOS ANGELES   LONDON

University of California Press
Berkeley and Los Angeles, California

University of California Press, Ltd.
London, England

© 1987 by
The Regents of the University of California

Library of Congress
Cataloging-in-Publication Data
Hechter, Michael.
Principles of group solidarity.
(California series on social choice and
political economy)
Bibliography: p.
Includes index.
1. Solidarity.   2. Social groups.
3. Social choice.   4. Social control.
I. Title.   II. Series.
HM126.H43 1987   303.3'3   87-5074
ISBN 0-520-06102-0 (alk. paper)

To Debra
Segui il tuo corso, e lascia dir le genti

We shall discover the laws of social forms only by collecting such societary phenomena of the most diverse contents, and by ascertaining what is common to them in spite of their diversity.

Georg Simmel

We are not students of some subject matter but students of problems.

Karl Popper

CONTENTS

TABLES AND FIGURES

PREFACE

The impetus for this book was born on a chilly summer Parisian day in 1975. In the course of a long discussion over lunch at Recamier, Fernand Braudel inquired about my future research. I had been flirting with the idea of applying my just-published theory of nationalism to the history of the French regions of Brittany and Occitania. Braudel listened politely to these thoughts and then chided me avuncularly, *"Ne vous répétez pas!"* Something in his tone tugged at me, and when I walked back to my hotel, these words were still echoing in my ears. If I had then had the vaguest premonition of the difficulties to be endured in following his injunction, this book never would have been written.

Almost all of the institutions in the American academic world conspire to keep scholars engaged in the spinning of variations on previously enunciated themes. The division of labor is as firmly ensconced in the university as it was in Adam Smith's pin factory, and its justification rests on much the same rationale. Specialization breeds greater productivity. Not only are scholars housed in departments that are surrounded by thick disciplinary walls, but our identities are bound up in smaller enclaves of these selfsame departments. It is often said that scholarly expertise, like good French wine, does not travel well.

My own desire to loosen the bonds of the academic division of labor was spurred by a realization that the problems in which I had come to be interested could not possibly be resolved within the confines of any single subspeciality, let alone any single field. Yet colleagues, journal editors, academic think tanks, and granting agencies all tend to look askance when someone shows signs of hankering "to hunt in the morning, fish in the afternoon, rear cattle in the evening, [and] criticize after dinner."

In the face of these very real constraints, the support I received during the early stages of this project was crucial in strengthening my commitment to it. Douglass C. North enabled me to penetrate into the inferno of contemporary rational choice theory without abandoning all hope. I am particularly grateful to Herbert L. Costner and Arthur L. Stinchcombe for their expressions of faith that this book was both feasible and worth doing. Former students and colleagues in the University of Washington's Seminar in Macrosociology were a constant source of enthusiasm and hard-headed criticism. (The existence of this remarkable seminar owed much to the quiet but firm support of Frederick Campbell, chair of the Washington Sociology Department.)

The book began to take its present shape during an extended stay in Norway during 1984. The last several drafts were written at the University of Arizona. Gradually I have come to appreciate that the quality of any finished scholarly work is due largely to the quality of the criticism that is levelled against its initial formulations. In this respect I have been fortunate indeed. The early drafts of this work elicited such searching criticisms—at the hands of Brian Barry, James S. Coleman, Herbert L. Costner, Debra Friedman, Oscar Hechter, Douglass C. North, and Karol Soltan—that I was forced to rethink the entire argument.

In addition, the comments of Malka Appelbaum-Maizel, Yoram Barzel, Mary C. Brinton, Richard Curtis, Kenneth Dauber, Roger Gould, Roberto Fernandez, Edgar Kiser, Edward Lawler, Gary Libecap, David Moore, Margaret Levi, Tony Maier, Doug McAdam, and Michael Sobel made this a better book than it would have been otherwise. While this version probably does not fully satisfy any of these critics, what is clear is that it has been improved substantially by their efforts. Carol Diem and Lisa Rosenthal have been perspicacious research assistants. Naturally, I take responsibility for all remaining shortcomings of argument and evidence.

Several groups also have played a role in the evolution of this book, and I am happy to acknowledge their contributions here. Seminars held at the Universities of Tokyo (arranged by Yasusuke Murakami) and Chicago (arranged by Gary S. Becker and James S. Coleman) raised important issues. I am grateful to the Institute for Comparative Politics at the University of Bergen and to its director, Stein Kuhnle, for offering me a visiting professorship. One of the chapters was written while I was a guest at Iowa House, at the University of Iowa. Finally, a good part of the insight I have gained into the dynamics of intentional communities I owe to membership in PRAG during 1974 and 1975 and to friendships with various members (and ex-members) of Seattle's Love Family.

Writing books usually strains ideal patterns of family reciprocity, and the writing of this one did so perhaps more than most. From my wife

Debra, my son Joshua, and my parents I beg forgiveness for being a pre-occupied husband, father, and son for a longer period of time than any of them deserved to bear.

M.H.
Tucson, Arizona
November, 1986

CHAPTER I

INTRODUCTION

A S SOCIOLOGY begins to resemble a congeries of distinct substantive areas, the intellectual coherence that it once possessed has virtually disappeared. That the field has always had its share of dissension is indisputable. Every few years someone publishes a book about the impending crisis in sociology, but these dire warnings routinely fall on deaf ears. Meanwhile, most sociologists continue to march to the sounds of different drummers.

Along with their colleagues in the other social science disciplines, modern sociologists are dubious of the prospect of a unified approach to the explanation of social phenomena. Too many of the theories that were promoted by the sociological pioneers have not withstood the harsh glare of empirical verification.[1] In consequence, skepticism has gained at the expense of credulity. Surely this state of affairs is cause for some celebration. Yet a surfeit of theoretical skepticism also has its liabilities. One not so auspicious result of the decline of theory is that scholars often have no compelling intellectual rationale for selecting their research problems, and other criteria—the availability of grants and the political considerations of the day chief among them—become popular justifications.

In the face of reigning confusion, many prefer to bypass theoretical concerns entirely and go directly to the evidence. To these sociologists, the

---

[1]In contemporary sociology there is precious little consensus about the proper meaning of the terms *theory* and *explanation*, let alone about the adequacy of rival theoretical perspectives. Sadly, Robert Merton's (1967: 39) complaint still holds true: "Like so many words that are bandied about, the word theory threatens to become meaningless. Because its referents are so diverse—including everything from minor working hypotheses, through comprehensive but vague and unordered speculations, to axiomatic systems of thought—use of the word often obscures rather than creates understanding." Since it is not my intention to enter into the epistemological debates that are currently so fashionable in some sociological circles, I should clarify my own position on these matters. I take theories to be *causal* explanations that provide *intelligible* answers to why-questions about *empirical* facts (for amplification, see van Parijs 1981: 1–25). This conception rules out much (but certainly not all) of what passes for theory among sociologists.

field need not have a consensual theoretical foundation because its progress depends on cumulative discoveries of fact. What is important is to observe things that have not been observed before. The body of sociological knowledge will develop as a result of generalizations derived from known facts. Moreover, the production of these facts is something that can easily occur independently of any theory.

Misgiving about the state of sociological theory is by no means confined to empiricists. One can admire and appreciate the contribution that theory has made to the development of a science like physics, yet still doubt its utility in contemporary sociology. After all, sociology might not be ready for scientific explanations. Given incessant theoretical squabbling, perhaps the best that can be done is to accept the distressing fact that there is an enormous multiplicity in current social science and to renounce all hope of developing a general theoretical orientation for the time being (Geertz 1982: 31). Admittedly, sciences mature at different rates and in different historical periods. Those sociologists who take the achievements of physics as the standard for self-appraisal ignore the fact that between twentieth-century physics and twentieth-century sociology stand billions of hours of sustained, disciplined, and cumulative research (Merton 1967: 47). From this point of view, it may follow that sociologists should begin to lay the groundwork for theoretical development by doing the most careful research that current methods permit.

Though evidence is necessary to test the limits of any theory, radical empiricism is unlikely to provide sociology's salvation. In the first place, most research is covertly theoretical. Because all descriptions are partial, investigators tend to rely on implicit theories to guide their collection of facts. This procedure introduces unknown (and often unknowable) assumptions, setting the stage for Alfred Marshall's admonishment that the most reckless and treacherous of all theorists is the one who professes to let the facts and figures speak for themselves. In the second place, this kind of empiricism fails to suggest long-term research agendas. Without explicit theories, there is no way to decide on the relative importance of facts. A democracy of facts too often degenerates into anarchy. Without explicit theories, there is little prospect of arriving at a body of cumulative research. Even the great inductivist Francis Bacon once admitted that truth emerges more readily from error than from confusion.

Although the field is in theoretical disarray, the disarray is hardly complete. There is a distinctively sociological way of looking at the world. It holds that the key to understanding social life lies with the analysis of groups, rather than individuals. This belief is founded on the premise that the behavior of any group is not reducible to the actions of its individual members. Instead, groups are irreducible entities that deserve study in their own right. In order to explain social phenomena, therefore, it is necessary to renounce methodological individualism—the view that all social phenomena are in principle explicable only in terms of individuals—and to replace this unsavory doctrine with a sociological alternative.[2]

The first sociologists arrived at this conclusion by finding fault with economic theories that regarded social order (that is, security of persons and their property) as an unintended outcome of the interaction of selfish actors. If individuals freely pursued their own selfish interests, the sociologists reasoned, chaos would be a much more likely outcome than order. Marx argued that the free market results in an anarchy of production; Durkheim was concerned about its effects on anomie; Weber complained that it undermines all systems of fraternal ethics. Since a relatively high degree of social order has existed throughout history, a key problem is to explain just how it has been achieved. Few contemporary sociologists address the issue head on. Yet whenever they seek to explain why certain people respect the law, give to charity, and act on some moral basis, while others engage in crime, act opportunistically, and commit suicide, they implicitly raise the question of social order. To a large degree their hopes of providing an answer are pinned on either normative or structural explanations.[3]

Proponents of the normative basis of social order (hereafter referred to as *normativists* in order to distinguish them from those scholars—largely philosophers and economists—who are concerned with the optimal design of social institutions) hold that the maintenance of social order depends on the existence of a set of overarching rules of the game, rules that are to some degree internalized, or considered to be legitimate, by most actors.[4] Not only do these rules set goals, or preferences, for each member of society, but they also specify the appropriate means by which these goals can be pursued. Without such rules social order would be precluded, for everyone would be compelled to participate in an unceasing war of all against all. Yet the content of these rules is less important than the fact that some rules exist at all, for it varies widely from one group to another and from one historical era to another.

When I entered graduate school in the mid-1960s, normativism was still the dominant perspective in the field. Soon after, however, its popularity

---

[2] "If, then, we begin with the individual, we shall be able to understand nothing of what takes place in the group" (Durkheim [1895] 1938: 104).

[3] Readers are advised that the following critique is couched at a metatheoretical level. No major sociological theorist's oeuvre fits comfortably into the procrustean bed provided by these somewhat oversimplified categories.

[4] The most important works in this tradition remain Durkheim ([1912] 1961a) and Parsons (1937).

began to wane in the face of persistent criticism. My own reservations were both conceptual and empirical. That norms may be responsible for preference formation is entirely plausible. Yet if they are also responsible for the individual's selection of means, then all action must be socially determined. Since norms promote consociation at the expense of antisocial behavior, the problem of order rather neatly disappears in this formulation. But this solution is only satisfactory if it sheds light on the genesis and enforcement of norms. When it comes to these critical issues, normativists have had conspicuously little to offer.

Normativist explanations also have serious empirical failings. It is impossible to measure accurately the salience of a norm to an individual apart from observing that person's behavior.[5] Yet normativists are among the first to admit that individual behavior is not solely determined by internalized controls: sanctions, habits, and individual preferences all are recognized as having their due. Disentangling the effects of internal norms from those of external sanctions, habits, and preferences, however, is a Herculean task that normativists have too frequently chosen to ignore.[6]

For reasons of this kind, I, along with many other sociologists of my generation, began to explore the merits of structural explanations in sociology.[7] In these, individuals are portrayed as being subject to particular sets of social relations (such as an historically specific stratification system or a particular social network) or environmental conditions (such as fluctuations in political regimes). Both social relations and environmental conditions have the effect of narrowing the individual's choices, and, hence, actions. This amounts to an implicit claim that when all the members of a given group are in the same boat, their individual differences do not significantly affect their behavior. Variations in social order are readily expli-

[5] This statement holds notwithstanding the heroic attempts of survey researchers to do just this. Since a norm is (by definition) something that we are all obligated to honor, survey respondents often have an incentive to affirm their support of it whatever their true attitude about the norm might be. Is their response to the questionnaire item due to this (positive) sanction, or is it due to their acceptance of the norm? No survey instrument is capable of revealing whether a respondent would actually honor a given norm in the absence of potential sanctions. One may reasonably suspect that respondents themselves may not be able to *know* if they would actually abide by a given norm that they believe to be internalized. How can I ever know if, as a passenger on a rapidly sinking ship, I would allow women and children to proceed me into the lifeboat, as the norm bids me to do?

[6] This problem is not inherently insoluble. There is no reason why one cannot construct deductive theories on normative premises that yield falsifiable propositions (a tactic parallel to that employed by rational choice theorists; see Chapter 2). Unfortunately, normative theorists have not availed themselves of this strategy.

[7] Marx ([1867] 1965) and Simmel ([1922] 1955) are the progenitors of this kind of sociological structuralism. Contemporary examples include Laumann (1973); Wallerstein (1974); Tilly (1978); White, Boorman, and Breiger (1976); and Marsden and Lin (1982).

cable for structuralists: they are determined by the set of social and environmental constraints that are currently in force. Naturally, when these constraints change, so do the resulting behaviors.

Some historical and contemporary situations are undoubtedly amenable to analyses couched in these terms. Because patterns of social relations and environmental conditions—the causal factors in such arguments—often can be objectively measured, specific structural explanations also tend to be readily falsifiable. This affords them a great advantage over normative explanations.

Indeed my own first book (Hechter 1975), which attempted to explain the course of Celtic nationalism in modern British history, was heavily indebted to structuralist reasoning (see also Hechter 1978). Its central theoretical claim was that the cause of nationalism lies in the existence of a stratification system that gives cultural distinctions political salience by linking them to individual life chances. I argued that when individuals perceive that their life chances are limited merely by virtue of membership in a particular group, they will either leave that group or come to see that they share vital interests with its members, thereby giving them reason to engage in nationalist political activity.

Subsequently, however, I became increasingly aware of the limitations of the structural approach. While it does a good job of predicting those areas that have the potential to develop nationalist movements, it is virtually mute about the conditions under which nationalism erupts, rather than lying dormant. *Internal Colonialism* presented evidence that the basis for a nationalist coalition had remained roughly constant in Wales and Scotland from 1885 to 1966. The apparent reason for this constancy was that the inhabitants shared material interests deriving from their common position in the social structure. There was little reason to believe that the stratification of Celts relative to non-Celts had changed substantially from 1885 to 1966. Yet the actual numbers of members and voters supporting the nationalist parties fluctuated wildly during these years. Popular support for nationalism was moderately high from 1885 to 1914; it diminished from 1914 to 1964 and rose again, precipitously this time, from 1965 to 1978. Since then it has declined once more.

These fluctuations suggested the possibility that the variation in nationalist voting was due to factors other than purely structural ones. Whereas patterns of intergroup stratification may have created the possibility of nationalism, they were insufficient to account for actual swings in political mobilization. This had been recognized in *Internal Colonialism*, which offered an ad hoc explanation for the rise of nationalist party activity after

1965. But this explanation evaded a more fundamental question: why do the individuals in any group develop solidarity with other members in order to pursue their collective interests?

I began to appreciate that structural explanations are not appropriate for every kind of sociological problem. At best they reveal why specific agents come to share common circumstances and interests. But they are less helpful in explaining just how these agents will react to their circumstances. Individuals typically have some choice-making discretion in all groups and societies. To the extent they have such discretion, their behavior will confound expectations derived from theories that countenance only aggregate-level causal factors. By ignoring individuals entirely, structuralists are left with two serious problems.

On the one hand, the causal factors in their explanations are contextual, like those of the normativists, and must always be treated as exogenous in their models. Hence, structuralists have not succeeded in explaining the rise and fall of social structures or environmental conditions from their own theoretical premises. This leads to a demand for historical studies, which—though informative—tend to produce new data to be explained rather than any satisfactory explanations themselves.

On the other hand, the claim that structurally imposed commonalities are sufficient to account for group behavior is rather easily challenged. If collective action is facilitated when the individual members of a group share common interests, then why does it occur so rarely? How can structuralists account for the fact that some people in a given structural position free ride, whereas other similarly situated actors do not? Marxists, for instance, long have faced the uncomfortable fact that the proletariat doesn't always (or even very often) change from a *Klasse an sich* (class in itself) to a *Klasse für sich* (class for itself). Although structuralists profess no need to countenance individual behavior, for many kinds of problems it is hard to see how the issue can be avoided.

Over two decades ago a small band of sociologists, led by George Homans and James Coleman, reached a similar conclusion about the shortcomings of normative and structural explanations. They argued that the field would advance only on the basis of some consensus on individualistic first principles, like those used by economists and behaviorist psychologists.[8] The impact of their profoundly revisionist work was blunted, however, by its

[8] The earliest statements were American—including Homans (1961); Emerson (1962); Blau (1964); and Coleman (1966)—although Blau has subsequently recanted in favor of a version of structuralism. More recently, the individualistic influence has travelled across the Atlantic; see, among others, Boudon (1981); Opp (1982); Lindenberg (1983); Raub (1982); and Banton (1983).

frequent failure to directly address sociology's traditionally macroscopic concerns. As a result it could be relegated easily to fields, like social psychology or methodology, distant from the macrosociological mainstream.

Dissatisfied with normativism and disillusioned with structuralism, I continued searching for an adequate theory to guide my research.[9] It seemed that the best place to start was with the original sociological critiques of individualistic theories of rational choice.

The early sociologists found fault with these theories on several counts. They argued, in the first place, that no rational choice theory can account for the genesis of individual wants, for these are determined through socialization processes. For many sociologists, the individual is an abstraction created by society itself. This is a basic reason why groups should take analytic precedence over individuals. In the second place, socialization not only determines the individual's ends but also limits one's choice of means. In consequence, much behavior is simply not amenable to rational analysis; motives such as altruism, duty, and guilt have to be considered as well as that of pure self-interest. Whereas individuals sometimes do engage in rational calculations of benefit and cost, much of their behavior is not readily understandable in these terms—it is nonrational and ritualistic. Finally, rational choice theories cannot explain why so much social order has existed throughout history. From a rational choice view, the only reason that people do not commit crime is out of their fear of the consequences, rather than from any innate sense of civic duty. It follows that the only guarantor of social order in complex societies is the police. Since policing is expensive, however, the attainment of social order should be highly problematic.

Though these objections appeared to be damaging, rational choice explanations rapidly gained popularity in allied social science disciplines, notably in economics and political science. Why should other social scientists find so much utility in the very same kinds of explanations that sociologists have resoundingly dismissed?[10]

---

[9] It is a heartening sign that many of these problems in classical theory have begun to be appreciated by a new generation of sociologists. One of the indications of this trend is that work on the so-called micro-macro problem is receiving greater attention. Indeed, in a recent symposium on the current state of the discipline in the *American Journal of Sociology*, two of three papers (Coleman 1986 and Collins 1986) explicitly point to the need for more such research. Some of this kind of work has already begun to appear (Blalock and Wilken 1979; Collins 1981; Hechter 1983; Granovetter 1985). Giddens (1979) and Habermas (1983) claim to address the micro-macro problem, but their anti-positivist epistemological commitments set their work apart and prevent them from joining in a concerted attack on the issue.

[10] Naturally, answering this question requires an investment, for contemporary rational choice tends to be written in a language that is quite its own. Although the pioneering works in the literature (written by the likes of Anthony Downs, James Buchanan, Gordon Tullock,

To determine how adequately rational choice logic can account for a fundamental sociological problem like that of social order, I devised a new theory of group solidarity on rational choice foundations. To my surprise, far from being dismissible, the theory was more suggestive than I had been led to believe on the basis of the conventional sociological critique. The more I explored the theory's ramifications, the more suggestive it appeared to be. I could only conclude that in their rush to establish a new social science discipline, the founders of sociology had dispensed with rational choice theories a bit too hastily. Far from being immiscible, sociology and rational choice are mutually complementary.

Chapter 2 begins with a definition of group solidarity and then proceeds to survey alternative explanations of it. Although sociologists insist on the overriding importance of the group in social analysis, definitions of this term are few and far between. For sociologists groups are more important than individuals because they substantially determine their members' behavior. At least some part of any given individual's behavior is therefore due to group affiliations. Clearly, however, membership in some groups has a greater potential for influencing behavior than membership in others. Another way of putting this is that "groupness"—that is, the group's capacity to affect the member's behavior—is itself a variable. Following Emile Durkheim, the "groupness" of any group may be referred to as its solidarity. The more solidary a group, the greater the influence it casts upon its members. Groups influence their members by subjecting them to a variety of obligations to act in the corporate interest and by ensuring that these obligations will be fulfilled.

What then accounts for the varying solidarity of groups? There are two principal sociological solutions to the problem. The first is normativist. Normativists argue that some groups, such as families, are more solidary than others, such as choruses, because the members of families have internalized more extensive norms. Whereas internalization is a perfectly plausible mechanism of solidarity, it suffers from two liabilities. In the first place, it is difficult to measure the effects of internalization apart from anyone's actual behavior. In the second place, this explanation begs a fundamental question—why are some groups more effective socializers than others? At this critical juncture, normativist theory has little to offer.

---

and Mancur Olson) are readily accessible to lay readers and richly substantive, the most recent research tends to be mathematical, laden with jargon, and highly abstract. Still, at the core of the literature one can often find some simple and compelling ideas.

The structuralist solution to the problem is quite different. Individuals are seen to coalesce into solidary groups (such as classes or ethnic groups) not because they carry group norms within them, but because they share common individual interests. These interests derive from each person's location in specific networks of social relations; thus, most of the workers on the Ford assembly line have common interests with respect to their supervisors and bosses. Since the workers' individual interests on the shop floor tend to converge, every worker's pursuit of his or her interests vis-à-vis management is in line with the interests of the group composed of all similar kinds of workers. In this way, the greater the commonality of individual interest, the greater the resulting solidarity of the group. This solution predicts far more group solidarity, however, than the historical record reveals.

If neither of the sociological theories of solidarity is wholly adequate, what can be said for rational choice theory? Although there is no rational choice theory of solidarity per se, much can be learned about group dynamics from a consideration of the theory of public goods. A *public good* (like social order) is a good that, once produced, cannot be denied to all relevant persons, whether they contribute to its production or not.[11] (Even thieves can profit from other people's tendency to uphold private property rights.) This characteristic of the public good has an important implication, for, according to the theory, rational actors will choose to free ride, that is, to consume the good without contributing to its production. But if everyone does so, then clearly too little of the public good will be produced, or none at all. If so, then how are public goods (like social order) ever produced? Only by solving the free-rider problem. But how can this problem be solved? Unfortunately, rational choice theorists have done a better job of posing this question than of resolving it.

Three kinds of answers have been proposed. The first answer is coercion: the state enforces social order by threatening to imprison anyone who violates it. This solution, however, raises two ancillary problems. On the one hand, there seems to be more social order than can be explained by coercion alone. On the other, since the state is itself a public good, how does it ever arise? The second answer is selective incentives: a professional association (like the American Medical Association) sustains itself by supplying various goods (like magazines or liability insurance) selectively, to members alone. But why shouldn't members free ride on its services and

---

[11] The degree to which social order is a public good is discussed by Michael Taylor (1982: 39–94).

obtain similar goods at less cost in the marketplace? And if selective incentives are necessary to attract members, how are they ever produced? (Consideration of the third answer, repeated exchange, which is also inadequate to the task, is deferred to Chapter 4.) Whereas there is no satisfactory rational choice explanation of the production of pure public goods, this is not the case for the production of *collective* (or quasi-public) goods, which are, to some extent, excludable from noncontributors.

Using this insight, Chapter 3 develops a rational choice theory of group solidarity. The starting point of this theory is the assumption that actors initially form groups, or join existing ones, in order to consume various *excludable jointly produced* goods—goods whose attainment involves the cooperation of at least two (but usually far more) individual producers. The survival of any group therefore hinges on the continuous production of such goods.[12] But this is a highly problematic outcome. It requires the establishment of several different kinds of rules—rules about how to make rules, rules that serve to coordinate members' productive activities, and rules that govern each member's access to these goods once they have been attained. If all these kinds of rules cannot be agreed upon, either an insufficient supply of joint goods will be produced or none at all. Since actors join groups in order to consume joint goods, the failure to provide such goods will lead to the unravelling of the group. Yet once these rules are agreed upon (or otherwise adopted), why do rational members actually abide by them? There are two possible reasons. On the one hand, members can comply with the group's rules because they are *compensated* to do so. Since this does not cause them to contribute to the production of the joint good, this solution involves no solidarity. On the other hand, members can abide by group rules out of a sense of *obligation*. Compliance then entails solidarity, for these obligations can only be fulfilled by expending some of the members' private resources on the group's behalf. In fact, solidarity can be best understood as compliance in the absence of compensation, or a quid pro quo.

The theory of group solidarity treats these group obligations as a tax that is imposed upon each member as a condition of access to the joint good. The more *dependent* a member is on the group (that is, the more costly it is to leave the group in terms of opportunities forgone), the greater the tax that the member will be prepared to bear for a given joint good. However, while dependence increases the extensiveness of corporate obligations, it

---

[12] The nature of the joint goods that are produced in groups may change over the course of time. Whereas a group may form to consume one particular joint good (say, protection from invaders), the group's very existence can stimulate the production of new joint goods (say, social rewards) as an unintended by-product.

does not insure compliance with these obligations. Compliance requires formal *controls*. Some agency of the group must have the ability to monitor the members' behavior and to provide sanctions to reward the compliant and punish the noncompliant. Only then can free riding (or deviance) be precluded. If the group has the capacity to control the relevant behaviors of their members through monitoring and sanctioning, the probability of compliance will vary with their dependence: the less the dependence, the less the compliance, and vice versa. But groups without any control capacity cannot achieve high degrees of solidarity even if their members are highly dependent. More formally, dependence and control capacity are each necessary but insufficient conditions for the production of solidarity. Individual compliance and group solidarity can be attained only by the combined effects of dependence and control.

Whereas the role of dependence in social life is uncontroversial, the same cannot be said of control. Chapter 4 asks whether formal controls are indeed necessary (as the theory holds) for the production of joint goods and the attainment of solidarity. (Readers who are mainly interested in applications of the theory therefore may prefer to proceed directly to Chapter 5.) The necessity of formal controls is challenged by two different kinds of arguments about prosocial behavior. The first argument is that prosocial behavior—such as altruism and helping behavior—is likely to emerge in the absence of *any* controls at all. This conclusion follows from the assumption that most people are not free-riding individualists, but already socialized actors who enter into groups both ready and willing to do the right thing.

There is nothing in rational choice that denies that individuals can pursue altruistic or prosocial ends. Indeed, the theory tends to be mute about the genesis of individual ends. Note, however, that it is far easier to account for social order by making the assumption that individuals are already predisposed to produce it than by assuming the ubiquity of rational egoism. The problematic nature of social order is underscored in the face of rational egoism. To be persuasive, rational choice theorists cannot rely on extra-rational motivations to account for harmonious social outcomes. Since a consideration of the literature reveals that the efficacy of socialization rests, to a large degree, upon the existence of formal controls in groups, much of the force of this argument is dispelled in any case.

Although they do not hold humans to be naturally prosocial, population biologists and game theorists argue that prosocial behavior can spontaneously emerge, and be sustained, either on the basis of selection mechanisms or repeated exchange. Whereas selection theories may account for prosocial behavior among the closely related kin of many animal species, they offer little prospect of explaining its evolution among non-kin. The argument about repeated exchange, however, does not suffer from this liability. As game theorists have shown, prosocial behavior (cooperation) can emerge spontaneously in iterated two-person Prisoner's Dilemma games (Axelrod 1984)—and may even constitute a self-reinforcing equilibrium—but the common knowledge base needed to sustain this cooperation is unlikely to be available in large groups. The upshot of Chapter 4 is that the theory's conclusion—that formal controls are necessary for the attainment of solidarity in large groups—is sustained.

The remaining chapters flesh out the empirical implications of the group solidarity theory in several quite different kinds of groups. Chapter 5 focusses on the role of dependence by considering the causes of differential solidarity among legislative political parties. Whereas the leaders of some parties forever lament their colleagues' lack of party discipline, the parliamentary representatives of other parties seem to be kept in line effortlessly. When these representatives are dependent on party leaders for reelection and career advancement, party solidarity is enhanced. But when these legislators become more dependent on alternative bases of support (such as those provided by interest groups), party solidarity will decline. Although the quality of the evidence is far from ideal, the theory's claims about the relationship between dependence and solidarity are lent some support. The case of legislative party solidarity is unusual, however, in that the roll-call voting procedure (which is an institutional given in all these legislative systems) enables party leaders to monitor their members costlessly. Few groups are blessed with such an ample, ready-made control capacity.

Since the formal controls necessary to produce solidarity are themselves a collective good, why would rational members ever consent to establish them in the first place? Chapter 6 attempts to answer this question by considering the evolution of formal controls in two nonhierarchical groups, rotating credit and insurance groups. It argues that members institute these controls when this is their only means of gaining access to some joint good. Thus, new entrants to capitalist labor markets often find themselves bereft of goods like credit and insurance that had previously been supplied by membership in primordial groups like the extended family, lineage, or village community. These migrants form rotating credit associations and insurance groups in order to obtain such goods. Their access to credit and insurance is limited, however, by a variety of hazards that threaten the production of these goods, including default and fraud. Recognizing that unless these hazards are reduced, their investments will disappear, members willingly institute formal controls.

Unfortunately, the mere existence of these controls offers no guarantee that rational members will abide by them. Whereas the enforcement of production and allocation rules is generally inexpensive in small groups, the costs of enforcement rise exponentially in large ones. These costs are the major obstacle to the attainment of compliance in large groups and in society as a whole.

Chapter 7 highlights the issue by examining the costliness of controls in the capitalist firm, a compensatory group that produces commodities for maximum profit. One of the threats to the maximization of profit is low labor efficiency. Although the firm compensates its workers to comply with production rules, the workers' interest may lie in shirking rather than in full compliance. In order to reduce the risk of shirking and to attain full compliance with production rules, firms must resort to costly formal controls. Since many different types of controls may be selected, what then determines which of these types is adopted? The drive to minimize control costs has been one of the most important factors in the evolution of management systems in the capitalist factory. The firm is often faced with a choice between the strategies of direct supervision and scientific management. Each entails its own benefits and costs. Direct supervision typically leaves employers vulnerable to high agency costs. Yet scientific management and other piece-rate schemes are ineffective when it comes to compliance with nonroutine and complex tasks that are difficult to monitor. In the face of tasks that involve costly monitoring, compensation offers a limited basis for compliance. To remedy this problem, some firms turn to quasi-obligatory strategies designed to increase the solidarity of the firm: they establish internal labor markets.

If the maximization of profit is the firm's joint good, the intentional community seeks to provide a joint good that is far more subtle as well as more difficult to produce: corporate unity in all spheres of community life. The fundamental by-product of this unity is insurance against the vagaries of nature and human relations. Like all joint goods, production of this one is threatened by members' egoistic behavior. Unlike party control of the government, credit, insurance, or profit, however, the production of corporate unity is threatened not only by egoistic behavior in a specific range of activities but also by egoism in thought as well as deed. To attain unity, members of communes agree to adopt controls designed to root out egoism in all of its forms (Chapter 8). But how can such compliance with such extensive obligations ever be produced? Normativists have a ready answer to the question: while controls are needed to produce solidarity in the *Gesellschaft*, they are practically superfluous in the *Gemeinschaft*, where compliance to group directives is voluntary, rather than coercive. In contrast, the group solidarity theory proposes that relatively large groups can attain high levels of solidarity only by adopting specific practices and institutions that economize on control costs. These issues are explored in a discussion of the determinants of the longevity of nineteenth-century American intentional communities. That institutional arrangements yielding control economies are found disproportionately in long-lived communities is consistent with the expectations of the group solidarity theory and inconsistent with its normativist alternative.

Finally, Chapter 9 assesses the overall strengths and weaknesses of the group solidarity theory and discusses some of its implications for further research.

CHAPTER II

THE PROBLEM

A social fact is to be recognized by the power of external coercion which it exercises or is capable of exercising over individuals, and the presence of this power may be recognized in its turn either by the existence of some specific sanction or by the resistance offered against every individual effort that tends to violate it.

Emile Durkheim

IN ORDER TO justify their new discipline, the founders of sociology claimed that the causes of social phenomena were to be found by studying groups rather than individuals.[1] They held that neither social order nor social change could be understood adequately on the basis of individualistic assumptions: the individual was a consequence, not a determinant of social structures. The early sociologists attacked the economists' assumption that freely contracting individuals could establish and sustain institutions like the free market, asserting instead that social institutions rested upon factors like "noncontractual bases of contract" or structures of property rights that were embedded within the society at large.

Sociologists indicted methodological individualism for its inability to explain both social order and social change.[2] For them, order rested upon the existence of groups based on kinship, religion, or some other common interest. As for change, what sociologist would seek to explain revolutions without the concept of class, or nationalism without the concept of the ethnic group? Classes and status groups—not individuals—were considered to be the principal actors in sociology.

Underlying these contentions is a single idea: that in all societies individuals' actions are decisively affected by the groups to which they belong. If Catholics have higher fertility rates than Protestants, this must be because adherents comply with the directive of the Catholic Church forbid-

[1] "If there is such a science as sociology, it can only be the study of a world hitherto unknown, different from those explored by other sciences" (Durkheim [1897] 1951: 310).

[2] Max Weber may be considered to be the major exception to this rule. Although he advocated individualism in his writings on methodology, this position was largely abandoned in the historical analyses upon which his fame principally rests. For Weber, the course of history was decisively affected by conflicts between status groups whose solidarity was taken as given, rather than regarded as problematic (Bendix 1960: 259).

ding the practice of contraception. But groups need not be so well established nor so formally organized as the Catholic Church to influence the behavior of their members. Even participation in a crowd—a large, spontaneous mass—may affect individuals' actions. By joining a crowd individuals cannot be singled out and held responsible for their actions; hence they can act in ways they would otherwise never dare for fear of legal or social reprisal (Le Bon 1960).

In both these examples individual action is to some extent determined by the properties of groups. Were the Catholic Church to revoke its ban against contraception, in time this would eliminate differential fertility between Catholics and Protestants. Were the police to divide a single large and unruly crowd into several smaller ones, the incidence of antisocial behavior would fall dramatically. In each case a change in group-level properties by itself has a determinate effect on individual action. It is often held that the distinctive concern of sociology is to analyze the effects of group-level, or "emergent," properties upon the action of individuals (Parsons 1937: 737–48).

Despite the centrality of the term *group* in their discourse, sociologists seldom define it explicitly. At a minimum, a group is a collection of individuals who are engaged in a specific type of mutually oriented activity (or set of interconnected activities), entry to which occurs according to one or more criteria of membership (Verdon 1981).[3] By this definition, groups may be distinguished from *crowds* (which have no membership criteria); *social categories* (in which criteria are defined for those people who are *not* involved in the activity); and *corporations* (which are defined by ownership rights, rather than by joint participation in activities).

The sociological insistence that groups influence their members' behavior is unexceptionable. Yet, once made, it leads to a problem that cannot be resolved by considering the group as the elementary unit of analysis. Although the sociological significance of the group derives from its capacity to affect the behavior of its members, clearly this capacity varies widely. Why do groups have differential salience for their members? Why, for example, do more members of some Catholic parishes practice birth control than of others?

One possibility is that groups employ variable degrees of coercion. Although sociologists concede coercion has some role in the process of socialization, they go on to assert that the lessons of socialization are main-

---

[3] Thus a number of individuals who are merely engaged in the simultaneous performance of a given act—sandwich eaters sitting around the fountain at noon, for instance—do not qualify as a group by this definition.

tained in the absence of external sanctions. Their preferred explanation of differential group salience rests upon the concept of *solidarity*. According to Durkheim ([1906] 1974), the quintessential theorist of the phenomenon, the members of solidary groups act in ways that are consistent with collective standards of conduct, or norms, because they are obligated to do so. Further, as Durkheim illustrates in the case of religious groups, the extensiveness of such corporate obligations is by no means constant across different groups:

> Now a religious society cannot exist without a collective *credo* and the more extensive the *credo* the more unified and strong is the society. For it does not unite men by an exchange and reciprocity of services, a temporal bond of union which permits and even presupposes differences, but which a religious society cannot form. It socializes men only by attaching them completely to an identical body of doctrine and socializes them in proportion as this body of doctrine is extensive and firm. The more numerous the manners of action and thought of a religious character are, which are accordingly removed from free inquiry, the more the idea of God presents itself in all details of existence, and makes individual wills converge to one identical goal. Inversely, the greater concessions a confessional group makes to individual judgment, the less it dominates lives, the less its cohesion and vitality.
>
> (Durkheim [1897] 1951: 159)

Whereas Durkheim's language is not entirely clear, an example can illustrate his concept. Orthodox Jews face more *extensive* obligations than Reform Jews: the observant Orthodox Jew is required to commit a greater proportion of his private resources (time, attention, and wealth) to collectively mandated ends (saying prayers, studying the Talmud, observing dietary and other laws) than the observant Reform Jew.

This is the meaning of extensiveness, but we must not forget the other term, *obligation*. Obligation implies a contribution without a corresponding recompense or quid pro quo. When people are obligated to contribute some proportion of their private resources by dint of their group membership, presumably they exchange these private resources for access to collective ones.[4] This is to be distinguished from a situation in which individuals

---

[4] "Whensoever a man Transferreth his Right, or Renounceth it; it is either in consideration of some Right reciprocally transferred to himself; or for some other good he hopeth for thereby. For it is a voluntary act; and of the voluntary acts of every man, the object is some *Good to himselfe*" (Hobbes [1651] 1968: 192). It follows that the collective resources that accrue from membership in an Orthodox Jewish community are only available to individuals who observe their religious obligations.

comply with a given group directive only because they are *compensated* for so doing. When this occurs, members effectively exchange one kind of private resource (say, time or labor power) for another (wages).

The less extensive a group's obligations, the greater scope the member has to engage in independent action ("the greater concessions a . . . group makes to individual judgment"). The extensiveness of a group's obligations therefore can be indicated by the proportion of private resources that each member is expected to *contribute* to collectively determined ends.

The mere existence of such obligations, however, has no necessary bearing on the probability that they will be met. This is a fact that sociologists are occasionally loath to admit. No matter how extensive a group's corporate obligations may be, its solidarity will be low if only a small number of its members comply with all of them at all times.

Thus a group's solidarity is a function of two independent factors: first, the extensiveness of its corporate obligations, and, second, the degree to which individual members actually comply with these obligations.[5] Together, these provide the defining elements of solidarity. *The greater the average proportion of each member's private resources contributed to collective ends, the greater the solidarity of the group.*[6]

The strength of this definition lies in its potential operationality. To illustrate, imagine that there are two large sociology departments in universities A and B. Each has suffered the passing of a faculty member in a given year, and each sponsors a memorial service in honor of the departed colleague. Naturally, all members of the department are obliged to attend. It is a simple task to discover what proportion of the members of each group, in fact, do so. Say that 95 percent of the members in department A but only 50 percent of those in department B show up at the appointed time and place. If this were the only available evidence, we would be forced to conclude that department A has much higher solidarity than department B.

Note that this definition implies nothing at all about the means by which solidarity arises—members can comply with their corporate obligations with more or less enthusiasm. And herein lies a source of terminological difficulty. Although this conception of solidarity has the considerable weight of Durkheim behind it, it differs from others that refer not to potentially observable behaviors of group members but to the strength of the

---

[5] More formally, solidarity = $f(ab)$, where a = the extensiveness of a group's obligations and b = the rate of members' compliance to them. It can easily be seen that groups only can attain high levels of solidarity when the values of both a and b are relatively high.

[6] Does a high variance of individual contributions detract from group solidarity? Whether the mean or the median level of contributions is a better measure of solidarity remains a question for future research.

sentiments binding them together—the love that holds between marriage partners or the brotherhood that links strikers.

Evidently, the strength of group sentiments varies widely across time and groups. Yet there is reason to suspect that it has observable behavioral consequences and that a good deal of it is reinforced by individual interest. Thus when a couple is financially interdependent, their relationship is less likely to dissolve (Blumstein and Schwartz 1983), and when strike pay is tied to picketing, attendance on picket lines will increase (D. Friedman 1983a). However appealing an affective conception of solidarity might appear to be, it is no substitute for a more behavioral definition. Since the strength of sentiment that exists between individuals is so difficult to measure apart from actual behaviors—and is likely to be mercurial to boot—it is hard to conduct empirical research about it. One simply cannot explain variations in the solidarity of given groups without using an operational definition of the term.

Even so, it must be readily admitted that variations in solidarity are difficult enough to measure. Those who attempt to do so are usually accused of catching something quite different in their nets. On this account, hard-headed empiricists are apt to sniff, discount the importance of solidarity, and question its ontological status. Indeed, the difficulty of obtaining convincing indicators of solidarity is a leitmotif of this study. Perplexing as it is to measure, sociologists implicitly resort to the concept when they distinguish among different types of groups. Thus, groups that have relatively low solidarity typically are called coalitions.[7] Interest groups and some political parties are familiar examples. In contrast, groups having the greatest levels of solidarity often are referred to as communal.[8] Some ethnic and religious groups seem to fit this description well.

What then accounts for differences in group solidarity?

SOCIOLOGICAL APPROACHES TO GROUP SOLIDARITY

Sociologists have grappled with solidarity as a solution to the problems of social order and change since the beginnings of the discipline. They have traditionally theorized about the causes of solidarity from three different perspectives. For heuristic purposes, these may be labelled nor-

[7] According to Gamson (1964: 85), a coalition involves "the joint use of resources to determine the outcome of a decision in a mixed-motive situation involving more than two units."

[8] Stinchcombe (1965: 186) defines a communal group as "a set of social relations held together by strong ties of solidarity; by a tendency to socialize the young to loyalty to the particular group; by a tendency to intermarry and restrict membership within the group; by a tendency to solve disputes within the group by standards of justice and need rather than those of game theory."

mative, functional, and structural ways of thinking about the problem. Although each type of explanation has distinctive theoretical premises, all emphasize emergent factors as the causes of solidarity. Briefly, what are the merits of these explanations?

The Normativist Perspective

Nearly all normative explanations in sociology derive from the problem of social order. Normativists deny that high levels of order can ever be the outcome of interaction among rational, self-interested individuals. Order requires collective adherence to a set of corporate obligations, or norms, but it is never in the interest of rational egoists to adhere to such norms if they can profit by spurning them. On the contrary, they will disregard any norms that interfere with the pursuit of their self-interest when this can be done with impunity. But were all individuals to act in the unrestrained pursuit of their self-interest, the result would be the antithesis of order—a war of all against all. Consequently, to maintain social order, individual action must somehow be rendered consistent with collective interests. By what means does this occur?

The classical individualist answer is that it happens via sanctioning mechanisms: people will act in a collectively responsible fashion only if they expect to be rewarded for doing so; likewise, they will be deterred from antisocial behavior only if they expect that punishment will be the consequence. But normativists reject this answer. They claim that if sanctioning alone were responsible for order, a very large proportion of group members would have to be employed as police in order to attain it. Further, who would police the police? Why should they enforce norms rather than do what is individually profitable? If police were required to produce order, then it would be very costly to achieve and to maintain[9]—indeed, so costly that it should hardly be in evidence at all.

In contrast, the normative answer to the problem of order rests on solidarity. And solidarity, in turn, is a function of normative internalization. To the degree that members identify with a group's norms—and carry these norms, as it were, within them—they can be expected to engage in the appropriate behaviors without sanctioning. Internalization makes individuals fit for social life, or socializes them, by removing the conflict between the individual's interest and that of the group. Since this makes compliance unproblematic, variations in solidarity can only be due to obligations of differing extensiveness. For normativists, then, the solidarity

---

[9] See Chapter 7 for a discussion of the costs of control. The normative argument amounts to a denial that sanctioning can ever have economies of scale. This position is challenged in Chapter 8.

of groups is a function of the kinds of normative obligations that are inherent in specific social relationships. Some kinds of relationships, or social
roles, generate limited obligations, whereas others generate extensive ones.
Rather than explaining the reasons for these differences, normativists treat
the obligations of particular groups as given.

Perhaps the most influential version of the argument derives from Ferdinand Tönnies ([1887] 1957), who divided all possible social relationships
into two discrete types. Though his distinction between *Gesellschaft* and
Gemeinschaft relationships owed much to works by von Gierke, Maine,
and Fustel de Coulanges, Tönnies's use of the distinction was original and,
subsequently, has exercised a strong appeal in sociology (see Nisbet 1966:
47–106).

The *Gesellschaft* relationship—which occurs between the parties to a
voluntary exchange—produces limited normative obligations. Its proto-
type is an economic transaction, like the employment relation, in which
each person's rights and obligations with respect to the exchange are con-
tractually specified. The contract defines the scope of the relationship and
is sanctified by the force of law. The relationship is motivated by the narrow self-interest of its participants; it is characterized by a high degree of
individualism and impersonality.

On the other hand, the obligations that are incurred in a *Gemeinschaft*
relationship are considerably more extensive. The most common example
is the family relation. Parents are obliged to take all aspects of their children's welfare into account in their relationship; the marriage vow exhorts
each partner to stand by the other in bad times as well as good. Whereas
the actor's motivation to establish a *Gesellschaft* tie is based on a rational
calculation of benefits and costs, the motivation to establish a *Gemeinschaft*
tie is nonrational—it is based on affective, emotional, or traditional considerations. The actor's commitment in a *Gesellschaft* relation is to narrow
self-interest, but in a *Gemeinschaft* it is to the welfare of all parties in the
relationship.

Because the *Gemeinschaft* tie is not limited to a specific range of interests; because it is tinged with affect; because all parties to it subsume their
self-interest to the interest of the collectivity as a whole; and because en-
trance into the relationship is limited (rather than open, as into a market
relation), the resulting obligation is much more extensive than that incurred in any *Gesellschaft* tie. On this account, Tönnies argued that the
obligations between kin are more extensive than those between neighbors,
the obligations between neighbors more extensive than those between acquaintances, and the obligations between acquaintances more extensive
than those between strangers.

Tönnies's distinction was a keystone for Talcott Parsons, who noticed that the obligations between professionals and their clients combined some elements of a *Gesellschaft* relationship (in Parsons's terms, universalism, functional specificity, and affective neutrality) with an important *Gemein-schaft* dimension (the professional's obligation to serve the community apart from pecuniary considerations alone). Given this complexity, how could the behavior of professionals be categorized? Convinced that Tönnies's dual relationship framework was inadequate, Parsons went on to develop further distinctions, resulting in a more complex typology of "pattern variables." Whereas most of the dimensions of the pattern variable typology were extracted from Tönnies's essay (Parsons 1973), in contrast to Tönnies, Parsons felt it necessary to posit that these dimensions could vary independently of one another. While this scheme may have helped Parsons to pigeonhole various types of social roles, it was no substitute for a theory of group solidarity. Parsons ultimately recognized the need for such a theory, but his own tentative explanation—that solidarity is due to the development of affective ties generated during socialization[10]—was never elaborated.

That people are likely to behave differently in the family than in the workplace is not at issue. The question is how this difference in behavior can be explained. Tönnies's and Parsons's argument makes sense only if the normative obligations of social relationships have an immutable effect on behavior. In fact, however, they do not. Affective ties often arise between people engaged in *Gesellschaft* relations: doctors and nurses, managers and secretaries, sales representatives and clients all have been known to initiate romantic liaisons. Likewise, the parties in a divorce can be expected to engage in strictly self-interested action. In other words, *Gesellschaft* relations are always at risk of becoming *Gemeinschaft* relations, and vice versa. This was clearly recognized by Max Weber. Though he too relies on Tönnies for his ideal-typical distinction between "communal" and "associative" social relationships, Weber nevertheless argues that these elements were likely to become conflated in social life:

> But the great majority of social relationships has this [communal] characteristic to some degree, while being at the same time to some degree determined

---

[10] "I should like to suggest that the primary 'cement' which makes such groups solidary is affective ties. My suggestion . . . is that affect may be considered to be a generalized medium of interchange operating at the level of the general system of action parallel to the societal media, like money, power, and influence. Capacity to 'use' it develops through socialization in the family, and the child's first affectively regulated solidarities are with fellow family members, within the framework of the family as a collectivity. With a sufficiently firm internalized capacity to 'love,' as it is very generally put, it can be transferred to objects outside the family, again always in the context of collective solidarities. The social psychology of these problems is highly complex" (Parsons 1973: 157).

by associative factors. No matter how calculating and hard-headed the ruling considerations in such a social relationship—as that of a merchant to his customers—may be, it is quite possible for it to involve emotional values which transcend its utilitarian significance. Every social relationship which goes beyond the pursuit of immediate common ends, which hence lasts for long periods, involves relatively permanent social relationships between the same persons, and these cannot be exclusively confined to the technically necessary activities. Hence in such cases as association in the same military unit, in the same school class, in the same workshop or office, there is always some tendency in this direction, although the degree, to be sure, varies enormously. Conversely, a social relationship which is normally considered primarily communal may involve action on the part of some or even all of the participants which is to an important degree oriented to considerations of expediency. There is, for instance, a wide variation in the extent to which the members of a family group feel a genuine community of interests, or, on the other hand, exploit the relationship for their own ends.

(Weber [1922] 1968: 41–42)

If social relationships of the same type can lead to obligations of differing extensiveness, then roles have no necessary implications for their incumbents' behavior. The root of the problem is that compliance with norms is never automatic. If internalization is so effective, what then accounts for the observed frequency of deviant behavior in society? Of course, normativists can attempt to account for deviance by claiming that it flows from compliance to subcultural norms. But if this were so, then why are sanctioning mechanisms prominent even in tribal societies with no discernable subcultures (Malinowski 1926)? Even the most committed normativists admit that internalization is an insufficient cause of solidarity and that some sanctioning is also required. But how can one ever know whether a given behavior is due to norms or to sanctions? This measurement quandary renders normative explanations virtually untestable. Norms may well be critical for understanding behavior, but what remains unclear is how they are enforced.

Explaining solidarity by norms alone therefore amounts to a tautology. *Gemeinschaft* and *Gesellschaft* may serve as generalized descriptions of different kinds of behavior, but they are also outcomes that themselves need to be explained.

Normative explanations have been subjected to such rampant criticism that the reader may wonder why they have been discussed at such length. The answer is that normativism provides the justification for a widely held theoretical claim. This claim is that *different theories are required in order to understand different types of social relationships:* "utilitarianism" (read economics) may be appropriate for the analysis of *Gesellschaft* relations, but for *Gemeinschaft* relations, sociology comes into its own (Parsons 1937: 691). Although few contemporary sociologists deem themselves normativists, many continue to accept this distinction between economics and sociology as valid without appreciating its normativist roots.

The Functionalist Perspective

If group solidarity is fostered by the existence of certain types of social institutions (say, by the practice of hazing in fraternities), then it can also be accounted for on functionalist grounds. In functional explanations (Stinchcombe 1968; Elster 1979), the consequences of some behavior or institution are essential elements of the causes of that behavior. The most sophisticated class of these explanations holds that the intentions of the individual actor need not matter because survival is accounted for by an "invisible hand" that, in the long run, selects only those behavior patterns and institutions that are beneficial to the group as a whole. These functional patterns are adaptations that are naturally selected under the pressure of competitive conditions.

Typically, functionalists approach the issue by explaining differential group survival. Comparative study might reveal that the longest-lived groups of a given type share a set of common institutions. These institutions tended not to be adopted by the nonsurviving groups, however. Since solidarity undoubtedly promotes group survival, isn't it reasonable to suspect that part of the function of these institutions is to promote solidarity? If solidarity is positively associated with survival rates, then this association permits an estimate of its magnitude.

Selection arguments of this type may be logically appropriate for analyzing the efficiency of economic institutions (Alchian 1950), but not necessarily of group solidarity. This kind of functional explanation can be sustained only to the degree that some analogue to a natural selection process can be asserted to exist. This has not been an obstacle in evolutionary biology, and it may not be one in the analysis of exchange in frictionless markets either. But since there is no reason to believe that most social phenomena are subject to natural selection, functional explanations cannot be justified on logical grounds.

Empirically, functional explanations are especially difficult to falsify. It is always possible to argue that institution X is not functional for reason Y, but this does not rule out the possibility that it is functional in some as yet unanticipated way. The idea that some institutions may be dysfunctional in the short run but will prove functional in the long run seems question-begging in the extreme. Without specifying the actual mechanisms by which functional adaptations develop, the approach is subject to endless elaboration.

The Structuralist Perspective

Unlike normativists and functionalists, who tend to be concerned with solidarity as a cause of social order, most structuralists are interested in it as a cause of social change. There is another difference as well: structuralists usually consider solidarity to be the product of rational individual action (hence, it is explicable in terms of "utilitarian" logic).[11] In the structural perspective, probably the most fashionable one in current macrosociology, patterns of stratification are held to be the basic cause of group solidarity. Individuals are seen to coalesce into solidary groups—such as collectively conscious classes or ethnic groups—by virtue of sharing common material interests.[12] They learn of this commonality of interest as they interact with one another. But, in this view, solidarity does not arise merely from the existence and awareness of common interest. Instead, it must be forged in competition with the antagonistic interests of individuals in groups located elsewhere in the social structure.[13] In this way, proletarian solidarity is seen to arise from struggle with the bourgeoisie over wages and working conditions, and ethnic solidarity is seen to arise from struggle with other ethnic groups, or the state, over jobs (affirmative action), housing, religion, or government language policy. The struggle from this collision of contradictory collective interests somehow produces solidary groups.

The *somehow* in the previous sentence is significant. No one denies that

[11]Structuralism is a label that applies to many different creatures in contemporary social science. One of its most popular forms in current sociology—network analysis—eschews the practice of making individual behavioral assumptions altogether and views social outcomes as the product of given interactional patterns (Berkowitz 1982). While research of this type can offer rich descriptions of complex social structures, it is not apparent how it can account either for the genesis or the transformation of these structures.

[12]For Simmel ([1922] 1955: 172–73), "the solidarity of wage labor exemplified a group-formation based on a pervasive social awareness. This social consciousness is especially interesting because it presupposes a high degree of abstraction over and above the particularities of individuals and of groups. No matter what the job of the individual worker may be, whether he makes cannons or toys, the very fact that he is working for wages makes him join the group of those who are paid in the same way. The workers' identical relation to capital constitutes the decisive factor, i.e., wage labor is in a similar condition in the most diversified activities and all those who find themselves in this condition."

[13]"The separate individuals form a class only insofar as they have to carry on a common battle against another class; otherwise they are on hostile terms with each other as competitors" (Marx [1932] 1972: 179).

similarly situated groups may have different levels of solidarity. The Marxists even have a name for it—the only difference between a *Klasse an sich* and a *Klasse für sich* is that the latter has attained consciousness, or solidarity. Since class consciousness is the key cog in the Marxist engine of social change, the failure to understand the causes of solidarity has been a critical lacuna in Marxist theory. Despite a resurgence of interest in "class analysis" both among liberals (Jackman and Jackman 1983) and Marxists (Wright 1985), little progress has been made on this score.

To find the most salient bases of group solidarity in any society, then, it is necessary to identify the principal fault lines of individual interest. To be sure, disagreement has arisen within this general tradition over precisely where such fault lines are likely to exist. Marx believes that the relevant groups will form according to their relationship to the means of production (see Dahrendorf 1959 for the key arguments), but later commentators have found it useful to broaden his initial focus.[14] Weber ([1922] 1968: 342), for example, sees group solidarity occurring whenever some economic actors unite to curb competition by monopolizing a sphere of activity and excluding others from participation. To do this, the first group seizes upon some identifiable characteristic of the second as a pretext for excluding its members. Clearly, Weber feels it impossible to make any a priori judgments about the kinds of groups that are thereby likely to form, for this would depend on the nature of relevant group differences in each case (Parkin 1979). In a more recent contribution, Dahrendorf (1959) extends the cleavage to include relations of authority in addition to those of property and market position. Though each of these amendments became the subject of lively debate in its time, the evidence of their common paternity is undeniable.

The structuralist explanation of solidarity rests on the ability to account for the sources of interest homogeneity as well as the causes of differential organization. Both factors depend, at least in part, on institutional structures, because these are critical determinants of the allocation of the relevant resources. Thus, by dividing populations into owners and nonowners, capitalist property rights create interest-homogeneous social classes. This need not imply that all nonowners have the same organizational capacities, however, for less-global structural factors may also come into play. Due to the nature of the work setting, factory workers have greater solidarity than isolated peasants (Marx [1852] 1975). Other struc-

---

[14] It is only fair to note that while some (like Cohen 1978 and Elster 1985) interpret Marx's oeuvre as derived from rationalist premises, this claim is controversial. One is inevitably reminded of Pareto's aphorism that Marx's words are like bats, in that it is possible to see both mice and birds in them.

tural arrangements are responsible for solidarity being more likely to occur in haciendas than in plantations (Paige 1975).

Because structural explanations typically specify measurable determinants of solidarity, they tend to be falsifiable. This affords them a great advantage over their normative and functional counterparts. The structural approach has led to many fine studies of social movements, for commonality of interest is usually implicated in collective action. It is hardly a sufficient cause, however, because collective action often fails to occur despite interest homogeneity. In some societies (such as South Africa during the 1970s or the southern United States during the period of slavery) where, according to structuralist theory, severe ethnic oppression should produce a strong collective interest in political change, there is a low incidence of solidarity and collective action (Hechter, Friedman, and Appelbaum 1982: 414). Similarly, structuralist accounts typically overestimate the incidence of group solidarity, for they leave unanswered one very critical question. If the individuals who share common material circumstances are indeed rational egoists, why should they join forces with their fellows to pursue their common ends? What can they gain, as individuals, by participating in the struggle?

Truly rational actors will *not* join a group to pursue common ends when, without participating, they can reap the benefit of other people's activity in obtaining them. If every member of the relevant group can share in the benefits of some new state of the world (be this something exotic like a revolutionary regime or more prosaic like affirmative action legislation), then the rational thing to do is to free ride (Olson 1965) and to behave individualistically when it is expedient, rather than to help attain the corporate interest.[15] But if everyone does likewise, then solidarity is unlikely to occur at all. This same reasoning led Durkheim and Parsons to reject rationalist theories of solidarity in favor of normative ones: Parsons's (1937) famous discussion of the "Hobbesian dilemma" reflects the fact that the social order is a common good constantly at risk of subversion by the action of free riders.[16]

---

[15] A spate of recent experimental studies on the pervasiveness and intensity of the free-rider problem (Bohm 1972; Sweeney 1973; Marwell and Ames 1979, 1980; and Kim and Walker 1984, among others) has produced a morass of inconsistent findings. In some experiments subjects do not appear to free ride at all; in others there is minimal free-riding; still others report considerable free-riding. The best explanation for this diversity of results is that the experiments were far from identical. When care is taken to set up a proper experiment in a pure collective good situation—the kind of situation that most closely approximates social order problems—free-riding emerges in full bloom (see Kim and Walker 1984). The experimental evidence also is vitiated, to some unknown degree, by problems of external validity.

[16] Hobbes was by no means the only major individualistic theorist who was blind to the free-rider dilemma. Adam Smith ([1789] 1961) frequently explained the adoption of specific

What is there in a structural explanation to inhibit actors from free riding?[17] Fireman and Gamson (1979) are two rare structuralists who seek to provide an answer. They argue that under certain kinds of structural conditions individuals are likely to identify with their groups and that this identification encourages them to comply with group obligations. Identification is promoted to the degree that a person has friends or relatives within the group, shares a common "design for living," shares overlapping memberships with other members, shares the same set of subordinate and superordinate relations with outsiders, and is readily identified and often treated as a member of the group. Factors of this kind give a person an individual stake in the group's fate. When the group prospers, so does the individual member, and vice versa. As a result, members are motivated to act on behalf of group interests by the prospect of gaining collective goods, such as an increase in the resources or the prestige of the group as a whole.

Even if it were true that groups with these particular structural commonalities are especially likely to be solidary, how could this solidarity be explained? Clearly, free riding is still the rational egoist's best strategy in the circumstances. Fireman and Gamson recognize this and therefore reject "utilitarian" logic—enjoining sociologists to "beware of economists bearing gifts." Theirs can only be read as a brief against the wholesale dismissal of normative logic. Yet since normative and economic explanations rest on quite different behavioral assumptions, it is difficult to see how the two can be melded into a single, logically consistent explanatory scheme. Granted, logical consistency may not be the sine qua non of sociological theorizing. But it is also true that empirical generalizations are a far cry from explanations. Because Fireman and Gamson fail to present any alternative to "utilitarian" logic, the mechanism by which these structural commonalities affect individual behavior remains obscure in their account.

In general, structural explanations tend to overestimate the actual incidence of solidarity. Groups that are similarly constrained may nevertheless attain different levels of solidarity. And the solidarity of the same group may change without any significant shift in its structural position: presumably this is why Marxists distinguish between *Klasse an sich* and

---

legislation—ranging from primogeniture to protective tariffs—as the outcome of class-based collective action. In his discussions of politics, Smith had a tendency to abandon the selfsame rational choice principles that informed his economic analysis (Stigler 1971).

[17] The Weberian concept of charisma can be seen to address the free-rider problem. Insofar as charisma directs attention to the fact that leaders can provide resources (including information) to their followers, it leads to important insights (Frolich, Oppenheimer, and Young 1971; Popkin 1979). The popularity of concepts like charisma underscores the point that solidarity must be based on something more than the mere existence of common material interest within a given group.

Klasse für sich. Finally, structuralists take social structures to be the ultimate causes of solidarity, but these are themselves unexplained—that is, social structures are usually treated as exogenous—in their models.[18] Hence structuralists have no way to account for the rise and fall of social structures from their own theoretical premises. Invariably, then, structural explanations raise questions about the effects of social structures on the actors who are subject to them.

Although the concept of group solidarity underlies much sociological analysis, neither normative, functional, nor structural explanations provide an adequate account of it. In the first place, none of these approaches seems capable of explaining differences in the extensiveness of group obligations. In the second, none of them explains when members will honor these obligations. True, groups must induce their members to comply with norms to discourage free riding, but normative theory offers little insight into how such compliance is differentially generated. Long-lived groups may happen to share particular institutions, but how these institutions promote solidarity remains a black box in functionalist theory. Likewise, solidarity may tend to occur in interest-homogeneous groups, but structural theory fails to explain why the members of such groups are so rarely solidary and why they do not always free ride.

These problems are unlikely to be resolved without considering the effect of normative and relational structures upon individuals. Isn't it possible that a theory that leaves room for individual action can provide a better explanation of solidarity? The principal task of such a theory would be to account for variation in the solidarity of different groups in terms that are at least potentially falsifiable. The challenge is to show how group obligations evolve and then how members are induced to honor them. To this end, the theory must take the actions of individuals into account. Yet there is no reason why this concern for individual action cannot be combined with an appreciation for the structural constraints that these actors face. While the theory need not abandon the assumptions about rational action underlying the structural perspective on group solidarity, it must nonetheless take into account the free-rider dilemmas inherent in this approach.

---

[18]Unlike most other structuralists, Karl Marx did set out to explain the genesis and dynamics of social structures—in particular, modes of production. In this attempt, he resorted to two different kinds of causal arguments. Sometimes Marx emphasized that structures can change due to exogenous shocks—such as the growth of world trade or the development of new technology—but no explanation was offered for the rise of such factors. Alternatively, structures can change as an outcome of class struggle. Since he had no theory of group solidarity (discussed earlier in the chapter), however, this explanation is likewise unsatisfactory.

Since a theory of solidarity must explain the conditions under which corporate obligations are devised and enforced, emergent approaches to the problem are insufficient. A satisfactory theory should be based on a set of elementary postulates about human behavior—in other words, it must have microfoundations. But what microfoundations should it have? Since the most general and highly elaborated individualistic theory in social science is rational choice, perhaps it makes sense to begin with this.

RATIONAL CHOICE APPROACHES TO GROUP SOLIDARITY

Rational choice theory is a family of research efforts grounded in the rational actor methodology of microeconomics.[19] In contrast to most other approaches in social science, the aim of all rational choice explanations is to link micro and macro levels of analysis. Typically, they involve three separate elements: individuals, institutions, and collective, or social, outcomes.

Individuals are regarded as the bearers of sets of given, discrete, nonambiguous, and transitive preferences. Individuals' goals (the objects of their preferences) cannot all be equally realized because people live in a world of scarcity and therefore must select among alternative courses of action. When faced with a choice among various courses of action, it is assumed that individuals will choose the course of action that, given the information available to them and their ability to process it, they think will produce maximum utility.[20] In other words, this will be that course of action that satisfies the most preferred goal with the greatest efficiency. In most such explanations, rational individuals are assumed to behave in a coherent, purposeful, maximizing, and occasionally farsighted fashion.

Institutions are thought of as rules or sets of rules that effectively constrain individual behavior in a variety of ways.[21] These range in simplicity from voting rules (for example, majority or unanimity) to more complex sets of written and unwritten rules, such as those that govern an individual's fate in organizations, labor markets, or political regimes.

[19]Although rational choice theories may be found in each social science discipline, the approach—which probably owes its parentage to Hobbes—is most fully developed in economics and game theory. The sociological version of rational choice is, of course, exchange theory. For a lucid discussion of this theoretical tradition by a sociologist, see Heath (1976). Downs (1957) and Olson (1965) are among the seminal attempts to apply rational choice theory to groups.

[20]The first operational version of expected utility theory was presented by von Neumann and Morgenstern (1944). Since then its empirical adequacy has been both challenged and defended repeatedly (see footnote 6 in Chapter 9).

[21]Rational choice theorists do not deny that some of these rules can be so well learned in childhood that they are internalized. They insist, however, that compliance to all rules is ultimately due to the force of sanctions; hence any rule can be unlearned as circumstances—that is, sanctions—change (see Chapter 4).

When a number of individuals act separately, subject to the same institutional constraints, the result is some *social outcome*. The outcome of the action of individual legislators on a pending piece of legislation is a collective vote, and the outcome of the joint action of workers and managers in a firm is a certain quantity and quality of product. Specific social outcomes are more or less efficient, reliable, or just, and rational choice theorists often seek to analyze the conditions under which some collectively preferred end can be best attained.

There are at least two reasons to question whether rational choice can provide a satisfactory foundation for the analysis of groups. In the first place, how can the approach ever lead to testable hypotheses? In the second place, how can individualistic assumptions such as these account for the pervasiveness of groups in social life? These issues must be addressed before rational choice—or, for that matter, any individualistic theory—can be used for macrosociological analysis.

The first question ultimately reflects a concern about tautology. Rational choice assumptions may lead to expectations about individual behavior, but how can they be used to draw testable implications about the behavior of groups? The theory treats individual preferences as sovereign, but if it is to yield testable implications about group behavior, these preferences must be specified in advance. Otherwise the theory is empty, for any behavior can be viewed as rational with the advantage of hindsight. Yet if—as rational choice theorists assume—preferences are both subjective and highly variable, then how can they ever be prespecified?

Aggregation provides one answer. Think of a given population of actors with diverse sets of preferences. Whereas some of everyone's preferences will be idiosyncratic, others will be commonly held by many. On the basis of inspection, perhaps we may infer that preferences for masochism, misogyny, or martyrdom are idiosyncratic, while those for wealth and honor are common to all. The existence of these known common preferences provides the analyst with a considerable analytical wedge. If each individual prefers more wealth to less, then this commonly held preference impels everyone who is subject to the same constraints to act similarly. Some of the idiosyncratic preferences may result in singular action, but so long as the nature and hierarchy of common preferences are known, the actions resulting from idiosyncratic ones will tend to cancel one another out and their average often will approach zero.[22] Although predictions of the be-

---

[22] There is nothing in rational choice theory per se that specifies the common preferences (or utilities) in given populations; these preferences are usually inferred from the observation of behavior. Naturally, the theory's openness in this respect has advantages as well as liabilities. The main advantage lies in the generality of the approach; it is capable of being applied in any social context. The main liability is that the preferences—which provide the

havior of any given individual will be wildly inaccurate, predictions for the aggregate will be more adequate; indeed, they will be increasingly precise as the size of the group rises.[23] Hence the same behavioral assumptions that

---

motivation for all behavior—are exogenous to the theory, and therefore unexplained. No rival approach to macrosociology, however, adequately accounts for the development of individual preferences either.

[23] Stinchcombe (1968: 67–68n), drawing on Gauss, demonstrates how this works: "Suppose that we have a causal force, f, which bears on every member of an aggregate. . . . Then also for each individual there is a large number of idiosyncratic causes. . . . The effect in the population would then look like this:

Individual	Causal Force Bearing on Individual
1	$f + i_1$
2	$f + i_2$
3	$f + i_3$
.	.
.	.
.	.
n	$f + i_n$

"Some of the idiosyncratic forces (the i's) will tend in the opposite direction from f, some in the same direction. If we have a good theory of the systematic forces, the average of these idiosyncratic forces will be zero. Let us suppose that the 'average' size of these idiosyncratic forces is σ. . . . Gauss showed that under these conditions, with reasonable restrictions on the distribution of the idiosyncratic forces, the *mean* force bearing on the individual is $f + \frac{\sigma}{\sqrt{n}}$. So the aggregate force bearing on the entire group would be $nf + \sqrt{n}\sigma$.

"Now let us suppose that the idiosyncratic forces that we do not understand are four times as large as the systematic forces that we do understand—that is, $\sigma = 4f$. Consider the aggregate force exerted on populations of different sizes. The entry at the left is the number of people in the population we are studying, n. In column (1) is the systematic force applied to that population, nf. In column (2) is the total effect of the idiosyncratic forces, $\sqrt{n}4f$, since $\sigma = 4f$. In column (3) is the ratio of the idiosyncratic forces we do not understand to the systematic forces which we do understand.

Population of size	(1) Systematic force	(2) Idiosyncratic force	(3) Ratio (2)/(1)
1	f	f	4.0
100	$100f$	$40f$	0.4
10,000	$10,000f$	$400f$	0.04
1,000,000	$1,000,000f$	$4000f$	0.004

"As the size of the population increases from 1 to 100, the influence of the unknown individual idiosyncratic behavior decreases from four times as large as the known part to four-tenths as large as the known part. As we go to an aggregate of a million, even if we understand only the systematic one-fifth of individual behavior as assumed in the table, the part we do not understand of the aggregate behavior decreases to less than 1 percent (0.004).

"Thus a psychologist explaining migration decisions of individuals might regard himself as massively ignorant, knowing only one-fifth of what goes on. A labor economist explaining the migration behavior of an aggregate of a million people can, with exactly the same theory, regard himself as a genius for having explained over 99 percent of the aggregate behavior." It is instructive to compare this reasoning with that of Rousseau concerning the general will in *Le Contrat social* (Gildin 1983: 29–66).

would lead microsociologists seriously astray are likely to serve macro-sociologists in good stead.

The second question derives from the observation that groups are so pervasive in human experience. If so, then what motivates autonomous individuals to establish and join them? Whereas sociological analyses begin by simply assuming the primacy of groups, their existence in rational choice theory must always be regarded as problematic. Some writers (Dex 1985: 528–29) doubt that rational choice theory can adequately account for group formation. Is their doubt justified?

In large part, no. As Tocqueville ([1835] 1951: 106) once suggested, people join groups in order to better pursue a common object.[24] More specifically, they do so to attain *jointly-produced* (hereafter, joint) goods that they desire but cannot provide at all, or as efficiently, for themselves as individuals. If this is the fundamental motive behind all group formation in rational choice theory, then a necessary condition for the spontaneous emergence of groups is the existence of a shared interest in the consumption of some joint good. Minimally, this requires that the actors in question have the ability to communicate. Hence, propinquity (Simmel [1922] 1955: 128–30; Festinger, Schachter, and Back 1950) and a common language are likely to be important for the emergence of groups. Beyond these two factors, however, other characteristics may affect the initial selection of group members.[25]

Producing joint goods always entails problems of choice, coordination, and allocation. On this account their production ultimately rests upon rules, or institutions, that enable members to resolve these problems.[26] These rules are costly to devise and to enforce (cf. Arrow 1971: 224–25). To devise such rules, actors must first decide how to devise them. This is often termed the problem of *constitutional choice* (Buchanan and Tullock

---

[24] For an analysis of Tocqueville's views on the problem of group formation that stresses their consistency with rational choice theory, see Wade (1985: 501–3).

[25] Consider the process of forming competitive teams at recess among school children who are mutual strangers on the first day of school. The school itself provides the necessary conditions (that is, propinquity and communication) that enable groups to form. Yet there are a very large number of distinct groups at risk of being formed. Team members are probably selected on the basis of signals of their ability to play the game; thus, for basketball, height and quickness are likely to be the key signals. Team members are likely to be selected in order of their decreasing ability to contribute toward a winning team, and some children may not be selected at all. Of course, once the first game has been played, the actual performance of the players provides better information about the quality of their prospective contributions than any purely phenotypical signals.

[26] "Since this joint activity takes place outside each one of us (for a plurality of consciousnesses enters into it), its necessary effect is to fix, to institute outside us, certain ways of acting and certain judgments which do not depend on each particular will taken separately. . . . One can, indeed, without distorting the meaning of this expression, designate as 'institutions' all the beliefs and all the modes of conduct instituted by the collectivity. Sociology can then be defined as the science of institutions, of their genesis and of their functioning" (Durkheim [1895] 1938: lvi).

1962).[27] Next, members must overcome *coordination* problems by linking actors with specific activities that are designed to help produce the good. Finally, they must resolve *allocation* problems by determining who gets to consume how much of the good that has been obtained.[28]

When rules of this sort either are not agreed upon or obeyed, joint goods will not be provided on a continuing and predictable basis. Since (in theory) the only reason that rational actors participate in groups is to benefit from the production of such goods, an inability to provide them reliably calls the benefits of group membership—and, ultimately, the very survival of the group—into question. As a result, the only groups likely to endure are those that have resolved the problems of choice, coordination, and allocation. But once rules to resolve these problems are adopted, then another question immediately arises: why should rational members comply with these rules?

Rational choice theorists have shed some indirect light on this question by studying the conditions governing the *production* of different kinds of joint goods. The key distinction relates to the *publicness* of the joint good. All joint goods can be placed somewhere on a continuum that stretches from publicness to privateness (Snidal 1979). Public goods—such as national defense, lighthouses, and radio waves—are characterized by jointness of supply (or nonrivalness) and nonexcludability. Jointness of supply is the condition where, given a level of physical production, consumption by one person does not thereby diminish the supply of the good potentially available for consumption by others. If one ship makes use of a lighthouse for navigational purposes, this does not preclude others from making simultaneous use of the same beacon. The same is true of radio waves. On the other hand, a pure private good has zero jointness of supply: when one child eats a slice of birthday cake, then there is exactly one slice less for the remaining children to eat.

The second characteristic of a public good is nonexcludability. This means that if the good is available to one person, then it is available to all others. Although American taxpayers are responsible for building U.S.

---

[27] How are collective decisions to be made? One decision rule is unanimity, but under this rule the costs of decision-making escalate rapidly with the number of participants. For this reason, unanimity is completely impractical in large groups. Some majoritarian rule is a far more likely outcome.

[28] Allocation is only a problem in the case of excludable goods. Nonexcludable goods cannot be allocated because there is nothing to stop anyone from consuming them. What determines the kinds of rules that are selected? Research on the determinants of allocation rules is preliminary. Historical studies of the emergence of property rights in the absence of a state (Demsetz 1967; Umbeck 1981) suggest that when the initial agents are roughly equal in power, they are likely to select rules giving everyone equal access to joint goods (thus, during the California gold rush, the first person to claim a mine obtained the right to its yield).

lighthouses, these navigational aids also serve visiting foreign ships; public broadcasting programs can be enjoyed by contributors and noncontributors alike; and no one within the borders of a given territory can be excluded from the benefits of its national defense. The situation is quite different with respect to private goods. By depositing our wages in a bank and by locking our cars and houses, we are usually assured that others can be prevented from consuming these goods.

In general, rational choice theorists predict that *the more public a joint good is, the greater the obstacles to its production*. The reason is simple. Since there is no means of excluding anyone from consumption of a pure public good, members have no incentive to contribute to its production. Instead, the rational thing for them to do is to free ride. If everyone free rides, however, none of the good will be produced at all. Hence there will be no basis for group survival.

How then are public goods like lighthouses and national defense produced? One solution is to coerce people into providing them. By compelling citizens to pay taxes, the state can divert some of the resulting revenues toward public ends that rational egoists would never voluntarily provide for themselves. Although there is ample evidence that coercion has been used to provide public goods, just how the state attains its coercive ability in the first place remains unclear in rational choice theory.

A second solution is to reward contributors with what Mancur Olson terms selective incentives. Unlike public goods, selective incentives are excludable: they can be offered to those who contribute and withheld from those who do not. The existence of valued selective incentives should decrease the attractiveness of free riding. Yet, unless the incentive is of greater value than the individual's share of the cost of providing the public good, it remains irrational to contribute (Olson 1965: 51, n. 72).

Selective incentives can either be social or material, positive or negative. Social incentives have an advantage in that they have an endogenous source of supply. Their liability, however, is that they only tend to work in small groups (or in confederations of small groups) where members can engage in recurrent face-to-face interaction. In contrast, material incentives provide actors with various fungible—that is, highly substitutable—resources. On this account, their efficacy is not directly dependent on group size (as it is for social incentives).

Although this argument has met with a barrage of criticism, it has not been displaced. The thrust of much of this criticism (see Hardin 1982) is that selective incentives are so costly to provide that, on this account, few, if any, large public-goods-seeking groups should ever emerge, let alone survive. If selective incentives have to be produced in order to assure production of the joint good, then they are merely another kind of joint good, one whose production must also be regarded as costly and, therefore, problematic. The question then becomes, Under what conditions will sufficiently valuable selective incentives be produced?

There is also an empirical difficulty with the selective incentive argument. If selective incentives are the necessary and sufficient cause of the provision of public goods, then the survival of a group should be entirely independent of the particular good that it seeks to provide. The reason is that the public good is never sufficient to motivate individual contributions: if selective incentives are the only reason that individuals participate, then the longest-lived groups should be those providing the incentives of greatest value. Hence, the determinants of joint good production should accurately reflect the market in selective incentives. But if this were the case, then how could disadvantaged groups, like the early labor unions, initially mobilize in their struggle against their more privileged antagonists, the employers?

Whereas the cost of attaining selective incentives deters groups from producing public goods, it is clear how profit-making groups that produce *private* goods for the consumption of nonmembers can attain the necessary incentives. After all, the reason that automobile workers comply with rules on the assembly line is that they are *paid* to do so. Their pay, in turn, is generated by selling automobiles in the marketplace (or by providing them to some central distribution agency, as might occur in a socialist economy). But, due to their very nature, public goods cannot be sold in the marketplace: since they are nonexcludable, no one has any interest in paying for them. So this basis for the attainment of the necessary selective incentives is not available in public-goods-seeking groups.

There is no satisfactory individualistic account of how large public-goods-seeking groups can attain sufficient selective incentives to assure their survival. This lack of an explanation, however, is less damaging than it might appear to be. In fact there are few, if any, *pure* public goods (Hardin 1982). It is hard to imagine any good that is in unlimited supply: for instance, both clean air and water are capable of being polluted. If the supply of a good is limited, this means that certain people can be excluded from its consumption. And there is no theoretical reason why groups supplying *collective* (or quasi-public) goods cannot survive.

While private goods are fully excludable, collective goods have positive, but varying, amounts of excludability. To the degree that collective goods are excludable, they can be produced for the sole consumption of members. Since noncontributors can be kept from consuming these goods, the threat of expulsion from the group is a selective incentive in and of itself; it may be one that is sufficient to deter free riders. In this way rational choice theory *can* explain how groups seeking to provide collective goods might be able to survive.)RCT

+

The incentives to join groups providing collective goods can arise either from the effects of cost-sharing or from the intrinsic jointness of production of particular goods. Some goods—such as swimming pools, golf courses, and airports—can be produced by single individuals, but many people find these goods too expensive to provide for themselves. Such goods can, however, be afforded if several individuals form a "club" and agree to share the costs of production jointly. Other kinds of goods are intrinsically joint in production; they cannot be provided by individuals alone. Thus people might seek to establish a social group in order to relieve their loneliness, an orchestra to play symphonies, or a motorcycle club to participate in rallies.

Not only does rational choice theory offer a plausible explanation of the individual's motivation to form and participate in groups providing collective goods,[29] but it also provides testable implications about their size. In the theory of clubs (Buchanan 1965), for example, group size is seen as limited by the effects of crowding.[30] As the total number of members grows, each member's share of the collective good is likely to decrease—that is, the good becomes increasingly crowded. Consider the man who loves to play golf but cannot afford to install his own eighteen-hole course. If no one else shares his passion for the sport, he will have to do without playing. If the taste is widely shared, however, others can join him in pooling their resources; the result is a country club. Up to a certain point, it is in everyone's interest to increase the size of membership, for the greater the number of members, the less each individual's share of the costs. Beyond this point, diminishing returns set in. If too many members are admitted, access to the greens will be severely limited: people may have to spend hours in queues before beginning play. Now the value of membership decreases, for crowding has begun to offset the benefits of cost-sharing. Overall group size is likely to be a function of both crowding and cost-sharing arrangements.[31]

In principle, then—if not yet in fact—many of the questions that have been raised about the adequacy of rational choice theory for group-level

[29] Empirical work on the individual's motivation to form and participate in collective-goods-providing groups from a rational choice perspective has begun only recently. For a study that discusses the determinants of membership in American interest groups, see Hansen (1985).

[30] Sandler and Tschirhart (1980) offer an assessment of empirical applications of the theory of clubs, while Lindenberg (1982) provides a variety of sociological applications.

[31] Note that it is also a function of control costs, as discussed in Chapters 7 and 8.

analysis are answerable in the case of large groups that provide collective goods. Insofar as the theory specifies conditions for the production of such goods, it also has implications for the study of group solidarity.

We should not expect to discover much solidarity in groups (like firms) that produce marketable commodities for profit, for instead of being obligated to comply with production rules, members of these groups can be paid for their compliance. The highest levels of solidarity are likely to be found in groups seeking to provide their members with access to (nonmarketed) joint goods. In this case, compliance with production rules must be generated by the force of obligation. Yet, though solidarity would be necessary for the production of *public* goods, it is hard to see how groups seeking to provide them could ever survive in the face of the free-rider problem. Solidarity is, however, both necessary and feasible in groups providing *collective* (quasi-public) goods. Hence, high levels of solidarity are likely to be confined to this kind of group alone. The key to the successful production of these goods lies in their excludability.

If excludability is necessary to resolve the problem of collective-good provision in large groups, what then determines the marginal cost of excluding an individual from consuming a collective good? Rational choice theorists have tended to emphasize the role of the good's inherent physical properties in determining this cost. Hence it is much less costly to exclude people from golf courses than from consuming insubstantial goods like clean air, radio and television signals, or good ideas. Similarly, due to the cost of fencing and existing technologies of surveillance, it is far less expensive to limit access to small country clubs than to vast national parks.

Yet this is an overly static view. There is another and far more important factor that is quite independent of a good's physical properties: namely, the extent to which it is possible for groups to exert social control over the excludability of their collective goods (Snidal 1979). It is easy to find examples of goods that were once considered nonexcludable but subsequently—due to technological or legal changes—became excludable.

The role that technology can play in determining a good's excludability is illustrated by the recent history of cable television. At first, cable television signals were available to anyone with the appropriate satellite dish, but this dissipated the cable company's profits. By encoding these signals, the cable operators found a solution to this problem: only those households with an appropriate signal decoder (naturally, one that can be supplied by the cable company alone) were henceforth able to receive the program. If technology can play a role in determining the excludability of a good, so can legal instruments. Patent laws can create property rights over insubstantial ideas, copyrights can protect the published word, and the registration of screenplays enables screenwriters to establish priority over storylines.

The degree to which groups are able to preclude free riding therefore depends in large part upon the costs of excluding noncontributors from access to the joint good. And these costs, in turn, are affected by specific institutional arrangements that can vary widely. Due to the nature of their institutional arrangements, some groups are more capable of excluding free riders than others that produce the same joint good.

A group is solidary to the degree that its members comply with corporate rules in the absence of compensation (that is, some tangible payment for value received or service rendered, but not mere psychic gratification). Each of the principal sociological approaches to the problem of group solidarity is inadequate. Normativists recognize that the key to solidarity lies in the obligation to comply with group norms, but they fail to explain the conditions under which compliance is likely to occur. Structuralists recognize the importance of common interest in the generation of solidarity, but they fail to explain how rational actors are dissuaded from free riding. An adequate theory of group solidarity must explain the conditions under which obligation develops and free riding is controlled.

Despite longstanding sociological reservations, rational choice theory offers the prospect of a better solution to the solidarity problem. It conceives of groups as the producers of various types of joint goods. As such, their survival depends upon the enactment and enforcement of rules governing the production and allocation of these goods. Solidarity will be rare in groups whose rationale is the production of marketable commodities, for in this case compliance to group rules can be secured via compensation rather than obligation. High levels of solidarity are likely to be confined to groups whose rationale is the production of joint goods that members themselves desire to consume. The approach has a further implication. Due to the free-rider problem, the only groups that can attain lasting solidarity are those that produce excludable goods. Some of the *necessary* conditions for the development of solidarity flow from these premises. A new theory must be devised, however, to specify its *sufficient* conditions.

CHAPTER III

A THEORY OF GROUP SOLIDARITY

> For he that performeth first, has no assurance the other will performe
> after; because the bonds of words are too weak to bridle mens ambition,
> avarice, anger, and other Passions.
>
> Thomas Hobbes

CONSIDER THE following situation. A large number of tent-dwellers live
in an isolated and relatively unpopulated valley. Land is plentiful and
free for the taking. Life is good, save for one recurring problem. The tent-
dwellers are intermittently victimized by a roving band of outlaws who abscond with their crops and stored food. Each incident causes severe losses
to a large number of households. To forestall this threatened loss, a majority of the tent-dwellers decides to form a protective association. The association determines that two measures must be taken to provide for the
members' security. All the members' tents must be concentrated in one
part of the valley. And members must participate in round-the-clock
watches along the perimeter of the new settlement. Under this plan members alone will receive protection; those who choose not to join will remain
unprotected.

Yet the ability to reach agreement on this set of rules does not guarantee
adequate security. The security of these tent-dwellers is very much a joint
good; its production is only assured when each member lives up to the obligation to stand watch. The member who neglects to do so in order to dally
with the neighbor compromises the security of the whole encampment.
Will the members comply with their obligation to stand watch? How solidary will the protective association be?

An adequate theory of group solidarity must be able to explain variation
in the extensiveness of corporate obligations and in a group's capacity to
induce its members to honor these obligations.

THE EXTENSIVENESS OF CORPORATE OBLIGATIONS

All rational choice explanations start with explicit behavioral assumptions; usually actors are considered to be rational egoists. Strangely, a
similar assumption is smuggled into much classical sociological analysis,
albeit implicitly. As the normativists observed, sanctions exist even in the

40

most solidary of groups. Why? Because there is often a conflict of interest between the individual and the group.

True, at those times when groups encourage their members to pursue their private interests to the hilt, no such conflict need arise (Young 1979: 51–66). And not all compliance to norms need be costly to individuals (Coleman 1966; G. S. Becker 1974; Barry 1970: 44–46). Some norms— which are also called conventions (Lewis 1969)—enable individuals to make decisions about a host of matters that defy rational solution (Durkheim [1897] 1951: 254–56). These are rules that designate appropriate standards of conduct in diverse situations ("one should always drive on the right side of the street"), and people may comply with them simply because it is not costly for them to do so (Stigler and Becker 1977: 82; Thibaut and Kelley 1959: 127–200). In the driving example, noncompliance is in fact the more costly choice. Yet even though conventional behavior imposes few costs, the violation of conventions always brings forth sanctions (Goffman 1959). Naturally, conflicts of interest between the individual and the group increase whenever group members seek predictable and consistent levels of normative compliance from one another, not just fitful compliance when it suits the member's fancy.

Whenever people are faced with two divergent courses of action—one in pursuit of some individual end, the other in pursuit of some collective end—I will assume that they will invariably choose the former.[1] Since the obligations imposed by membership in a group generally interfere with and deflect from the members' pursuit of their own goals, they can be likened to a membership tax. Once a group's obligations are considered as if they were a tax, it is possible to predict how extensive, or costly, they will be in different circumstances.

The obligations of some groups can only be satisfied when members part with a rather large proportion of their private resources, whereas the obligations of others can be satisfied by substantially less onerous contributions. For example, the members of intentional communities like the Bruderhof (Zablocki 1971) face far more extensive obligations than the employees of General Motors. What accounts for variations in the extensiveness of obligations among different groups? The first answer has to do with the nature of the joint good that the group produces.

Recall that groups exist in order to supply their members with some desired joint good. This good can be attained only if members comply with various rules that are designed to assure its production. There are two alternative means of obtaining compliance with these production rules: it can be secured either through compensation or through obligation. In

---

[1] The assumption of rational egoism is examined in Chapter 4.

some groups—for instance, firms—members are compensated (in wages) for the time that they spend complying with production rules. In general, members would always prefer to be compensated for complying with production rules, because this does not diminish their own assets. Since the wages that motivate compliance must themselves be produced, however, compensation is feasible only in groups that produce marketable goods (and services) for the consumption of nonmembers.[2] General Motors can largely rely on wages to fill its assembly line because revenue is generated from the sale of vehicles and other products; since the Bruderhof is not primarily interested in marketing some commodity, it cannot rely on wages to motivate compliance among its members.

In contrast to groups whose rationale is the marketing of commodities to nonmembers, those that are principally formed to consume joint goods must rely on obligation to secure compliance with production rules. The greater the extensiveness of obligation, the greater the tax that members must pay to consume the joint good. Yet (according to the law of demand), the greater the price of a given good, the lower the demand for it.[3] Why then do we find groups whose members consent to highly extensive obligations?

Such groups must provide goods of great value to their members. A rational member will seek membership in a group only if the benefit derived from access to the joint good exceeds the cost of the obligations—that is, the member's share of the costs of producing that good. This reasoning has one immediate implication: the benefit derived from membership in obligatory groups must generally exceed that of membership in compensatory groups. Why must this be so? Because the members of obligatory groups are expected to bear a cost (compliance with production rules) without a corresponding compensation. This can be explained if, in contrast to firms and other compensatory groups, obligatory groups produce *immanent goods*—those that directly satisfy their members' utility (by increasing their sense pleasures, happiness, and so forth).[4] General Motors workers

[2] This definition includes all profit-making firms but is not limited to them: non-profit groups, like universities, also market goods, such as education, to given publics.

[3] It is sometimes the case that demand for a good increases with its price. Thus, in a garage sale it may be easier to sell one's jewelry at a higher price than a lower one (Cialdini 1984). Here the higher price signals higher quality to the naive buyer. This example shows that the law of demand only holds in the case of identical goods. To the degree that groups are successful in differentiating their goods—by claiming that their quality is superior to those provided by alternative groups—they can demand greater obligations of their members.

[4] The distinction between immanent and nonimmanent goods recalls that made in classical economics between goods that are produced primarily for use (immanent) and those produced primarily for exchange (nonimmanent). In a similar vein, Weber ([1922] 1968: 339–40) notes that actors have two distinct reasons for forming groups: to directly satisfy their wants and to reap profits by controlling and disposing of scarce goods.

do not join the firm because they like cars, any more than the people who work in Silicon Valley like silicon chips. Most workers join firms because of their interest in wages, not in the commodities that these firms produce. Since workers do not get to consume the goods that they jointly produce (like nonmembers, they must purchase the goods if they want them), they must be compensated for the time spent in complying with the firm's production rules.

The people who join a group that produces some immanent good for the consumption of members (entertainment, sense pleasures, enlightenment, and so forth), however, do have an interest in helping to provide it without compensation, for utility is its own reward. Hence, obligation is likely to play the predominant role only in groups whose rationale is the production of immanent joint goods.

Yet the extensiveness of obligations also varies among groups that supply immanent goods. After all, Orthodox Jews, Mormons, and members of the Communist Party face far more extensive obligations than Reform Jews, Unitarians, or members of the Republican Party. What accounts for systematic differences in the extensiveness of obligations across groups?

It is reasonable to suspect that the extensiveness of a group's obligations has something to do with the cost of producing a given immanent good—that is, with the sum of all the labor, capital, and other necessary inputs.[5] If security is more costly to produce than the entertainment generated by a weekly poker game, then we would expect the obligations of the protective association to be far more extensive than those of the poker group. Thus, the extensiveness of group obligations ought to be determined in part by the cost of producing the good in question. Evidently, there must be some minimal level of obligation that is required to produce a good in groups of a certain size, but how can the members ever know what it is?

Suppose, for the sake of argument, that the good is produced under the frictionless market conditions specified in conventional neoclassical economic models. In this case competition among rival producers of the good enables members to determine the lowest cost of producing it and thereby to arrive at minimally extensive obligations in the long run. To the degree that there are many different sources of similar or comparable goods in the immediate environment; that members have perfect information about the availability, quality, and cost of all close substitutes; that they have complete freedom of mobility and face no barriers of exit or entry into alternative groups (implying zero moving costs between them); that exchanges

[5]This is not to imply that inputs of labor and capital have the same effects on group solidarity. Due to monitoring considerations (discussed in Chapter 7), groups that obligate their members to pay dues are less likely to be solidary than those that require labor inputs.

between members of the group are impersonal; and that enforcement is costless, members will tend to adopt obligations that are just extensive enough, and no more than are necessary, to provide a given quantity of the good.

It is easy to show why this minimal level of obligations will be realized. Imagine the problems that the members of a protective association might have deciding how extensive their corporate obligations should be. Assume that all pastoralist members can receive an adequate amount of security from the protective association by contributing 10 percent of their total assets.[6] This is a new venture, however, and the pastoralists have no idea how much it will ultimately cost to provide themselves with adequate security. Perhaps most are willing to contribute as much as 20 percent of their assets to attain it. Even if they initially agree to a 20 percent contribution, the rate will not remain at this high level for long. If they could obtain adequate security at less cost (say at 15 percent) by joining (or forming) a different protective association, then it would be rational for members to desert the first group and "vote with their feet."[7] (Note that in this case the availability of free grazing land and portability of their tents mean that the nomads' moving costs are negligible.)

This out-migration will stop only when the initial group lowers its rate to that of its competition, namely 15 percent. Then suppose that another group offers security on the basis of a 10 percent contribution. (We happen to know that this is the lowest possible rate, but this information is unavailable to the pastoralists.) This leads either to wholesale migration or to a downward readjustment of the initial group's rate. What will stop the process? Suppose another protective association lowers its rate to 5 percent. A host of new members will join. But soon they will discover that the association is unable to live up to its promises, for a 5 percent contribution is too low to provide adequate security. In the wake of this group's failure, everyone will rush back to join the 10 percent group. In time, then, the competition between rival protective associations (or rate experimentation within one group caused by the threat from potential new producers)[8] will induce all groups to offer the same quantity of security (for a membership

---

[6] Although 10 percent is an arbitrary proportion, it is interesting to note that when Brigham Young led the Mormons to Salt Lake City, he levied a 10 percent tithe on each (Arrington 1958).

[7] There is an entire class of economic models known (following Tiebout 1956) as voting-with-the-feet. For a brief introduction to these models, see Mueller (1979: 125–29); Cebula (1980) assesses the adequacy of Tiebout models for evidence about human migration.

[8] A competitive equilibrium can exist in a market with only one producer if this market is highly contestable and new competitors can freely enter and exit it in the event of monopolistic rents (Baumol, Panzer, and Willig 1982).

of a given size) at roughly the same, or equilibrium, rate of contribution.[9] Whatever the immanent good may be, in this world of frictionless markets groups will provide it to their members at minimal cost—that is, with minimally extensive obligations (Brennan and Buchanan 1980: 172).

Since rational egoists always seek to minimize their costs, why can't minimally extensive obligations be arrived at in the absence of fully competitive markets? After all, members have an incentive to find ways either to reduce costs (if their initial estimate of the production cost was too high) or to increase costs (if their estimate was too low). Even though they seek to minimize their obligations, there are at least three reasons why members are unable to do so in the absence of frictionless market conditions. In the first place, each collective consideration of the level of obligations entails time and other costs of decision-making (Buchanan and Tullock 1962; Buchanan 1975), and these costs rise geometrically with the size of the membership. Rather than incurring such costs, members will settle for greater than minimal obligations. In the second place, to the degree that members place a high value on continued access to the immanent good, they may be reluctant to risk suboptimal provision of it (this may account for the sanctity of the defense budget in the eyes of American voters). Finally, if there are no alternative sources of the same good, then initial members may levy higher obligations on all subsequent ones and consume the resulting surplus themselves. This will create a two- (or multi-) tiered tax structure within the membership and raise the average extensiveness of obligations for the group as a whole.

The problem is that the assumption of frictionless markets is extremely stringent and unrealistic, and to the degree that it does not hold, the minimal production cost cannot be inferred. Hence, it is more reasonable to regard the dependence of members rather than the cost of production as the key determinant of the extensiveness of group obligations.

Rational egoists choose to belong to a group because they are *dependent* (Thibaut and Kelley 1959; Emerson 1962; and Blau 1964) on other members for access to some desired joint good. If they could attain this good without incurring the obligations of membership, they would always prefer to do so. Yet their degree of dependence varies widely. Our nomads may have only one source of security—their local protective association. But similar individuals living on the populated plain may have a multitude of security options; on this account they are likely to be less dependent on

---

[9] I ignore the fact that the nomads' productivity will increase under secure conditions, so that the cost of protection will in future consume a smaller proportion of their total resources. This might, of course, be offset by increased population.

any one protective association. *The more dependent people are, the more tax they must pay for access to the same quantity of a given good.* This variable degree of dependence is indicated by the opportunity cost of leaving the group, or what may be termed (after Hirschman 1970) the members' cost of exit. This is the difference between the value received from membership in the group and the value that is gained from the member's best alternative, taking into account any costs incidental to the transfer.

To the degree that members face a high cost of exit, they are dependent on that group. As exit costs approach prohibitive levels, dependence on the group increases; ultimately, members may become beholden to it for their very survival. In this extreme situation (analogous to a monopoly) members will accept the most extensive obligations to gain access to a given immanent good.[10] Correlatively, when the cost of exit decreases, members' dependence on the group diminishes. When the average dependence of members declines significantly, the extensiveness of obligations begins to approach the minimum as specified in the neoclassical analysis.[11]

Ultimately, dependence is affected by environmental shifts, many of which are beyond the control of group members themselves. It is increased by limits on the supply of close substitutes available outside group boundaries, a lack of information about these alternatives, moving costs, and the existence of strong personal ties among members. Let us consider each of these factors separately.

1. *The supply of close substitutes.* If the number of distinct sources of substitutable goods in the environment is not large, the chance of finding a better alternative generally decreases. Groups may collude and levy the same tax for providing a given joint good to their members. If there are only a small number of groups, this collusion may be easy to organize and enforce. As the number of alternative sources increases, however, the costs of organizing and enforcing collusive agreements grow disproportionately.[12]

2. *Lack of information about alternatives.* On the one hand, since groups are more or less exclusive, knowledge of their internal workings may be relatively difficult to obtain (Goffman 1959: 77–105). Uncertainty about the relative advantages of alternative groups breeds inertia. On the other

---

[10] The reasons that rational members are willing to subject themselves to these obligations in the first place are explored more fully in Chapter 6.

[11] Even in many real market situations involving private goods, dependence is unlikely to be zero. This is what makes supermarkets such profitable ventures. Shoppers save moving costs by remaining in the same store to purchase goods rather than travelling from shop to shop to capture "loss leaders."

[12] Partly for this reason Brennan and Buchanan (1980: 168–86) conclude that federalism is a system of government that minimizes the state's taxing ability.

hand, many groups are able to restrict information about available alternatives. To the degree that members are unaware of the existence of alternative sources of joint goods outside group boundaries, they will be willing
to bear the cost of more extensive rules. If people are unaware of the existence of a better alternative, they can hardly choose to take advantage of it.
And information is always costly to gather.

3. *Costs of moving.*   Transfer costs, which must be taken into account in
any decision to join or leave a group, are seldom zero. Since moving costs
among the nomads are minimal, they can be very responsive to marginal
differences in the cost of protection. It is not very costly to pack everything
on your camels and move to another part of the valley where security is a
better bargain. Were the nomads to opt for a sedentary lifestyle, however,
then their moving costs would rise, thereby increasing their dependence
on the initial protective association. It is far more costly to move a house
than a tent. Beyond this, however, groups sometimes impose entry and
exit costs. Entry to the most rudimentary rotating credit association requires character references, which are developed over a lifetime and thus
are costly to obtain. Many intentional communities demand that exiting
members leave some part of their personal assets with the group. Finally,
groups vary widely in their exclusiveness; for example, younger groups are
more likely to be open than older ones.[13] To the degree that there are barriers to entry/exit (and to the degree that moving between groups entails
costs), this increases the dependence of members.

4. *The strength of personal ties.*   Sociability is one of the most important
immanent goods that groups provide. Since personal ties tend to arise with
repeated interaction—and thus only in the course of time—they are akin
to an irredeemable investment (or sunk cost) in the group. The probability
of repeated interaction increases with limitations of supply and with costly
information and mobility, lowering the chance that close substitutes can be
found outside group boundaries.

a Hectian transcend's rationality

If these are some of the factors that create dependence, constitutional
and legal arrangements have decisive implications for generating them. For

---

[13] "In the case of many relationships, both communal and associative, there is a tendency
to shift from a phase of expansion to one of exclusiveness. . . . Both the extent and the methods of regulation and exclusion in relation to outsiders may vary widely, so that the transition
from a state of openness to one of regulation and closure is gradual. . . . The principal motives for closure of a relationship are: (a) The maintenance of quality, which is often combined
with the interest in prestige and the consequent opportunities to enjoy honor, and even profit
. . .; (b) the contraction of advantages in relation to consumption needs . . . ; (c) the growing
scarcity of opportunities for acquisition" (Weber [1922] 1968: 45–46).

most of human history the number and composition of voluntary associations has been regulated by political authorities. As Adam Smith ([1789] 1961) was at pains to emphasize, without effective constitutional guarantees of individual private property rights and the freedoms of mobility and association, dependence flourishes. It is also strengthened whenever rights are granted to groups, rather than to individuals. This occurs in western feudalism, but the Indian caste system provides perhaps the classic example (Weber [1916–17] 1946a; Bouglé 1971; Leach 1962; Dumont 1970; Barth 1962; Berreman 1972).

While there has been much disagreement about the precise definition of caste, nevertheless it is usually held that caste implies three things: hereditary occupational specialization, a hierarchical ranking of groups, and great social distance between them. Interaction between the members of different castes is governed by canons of purity and impurity. If an untouchable so much as gazes at the dinner of a Brahman, it will be considered impure. Exogamy is prohibited, and imbalanced sex ratios among the members of higher castes lead to hypergamy as well as female infanticide. The caste system restricts intergroup mobility and thereby limits the availability of benefits outside group boundaries. Less extreme instances follow from the distinctive legal status of groups such as Jews and Greeks under the Ottoman *millet* system, Indians in North America, or blacks in South African Bantustans. In each case the state makes individuals dependent on corporate membership by allocating resources to groups qua groups (Van Dyke 1977).

Just as laws that limit the individual's alternatives outside group boundaries promote dependence, those that provide new alternatives lessen it. Here the development of the welfare state takes pride of place. The welfare state provides citizens with a wide range of benefits, or entitlements, that were customarily supplied by mutual benefit associations, churches, trade unions, political parties, and other kinds of voluntary associations. Once these benefits are offered to all as public goods, the incentives to belong to these other kinds of organizations erode. In this way, the growth of government welfare is implicated in many significant social changes, from the decline of the American urban political boss to the rise of divorce and family instability.

Due to constitutional and legal arrangements, among other factors, the competition among providers of joint goods is often restricted. The less competitive the market for the joint good is, the greater the dependence of group members. This means that the obligations (taxes) that the members of different groups adopt for the production of the same joint good are likely to vary. As the cost of leaving a group rises, so does the net benefit of remaining in it. And the greater this benefit is, the greater the willingness to tolerate extensive obligations. Although the average dependence of group members may vary, it never disappears altogether, for the members of groups always depend upon the efforts of others for the production of joint goods. The solitary consumer of private goods, however, need not incur dependence.

Since it permits the initial members of a group to demand higher obligations of new members, dependence also has implications for the evolution of group hierarchy.[14] The older members' ability to extract what in effect are rents from newer ones is, however, limited by the dependence of these new members. The less their dependence, the less extensive the obligations they will incur.

In summary, then, the greater the dependence of members, the greater the extensiveness of group obligations. The extensiveness of a group's obligations alone, however, has no necessary implications for group solidarity. What also matters is the probability that members will comply with these obligations. It is to this problem that I now turn.

THE PROBABILITY OF COMPLIANCE

Rational egoists may desire the benefits derived from group membership, but they hope to receive these unconditionally. If members value the joint good, they are willing to commit themselves (or to be obliged) to help produce it; yet they will still have an incentive to free ride. Even though all the members of the protective association place a high value on security, still they would prefer to receive it without honoring their full obligations (say, by understating their assets or—better yet—by refraining from making any contribution at all).[15] This is precisely the difficulty encountered with the provision of public goods: since they can be consumed by anyone, then rational egoists will not help to produce them. Even though members may place a high value on some joint good, free riding can be curtailed only if there is some means of assuring compliance with corporate obligations. A group's ability to do this is a function of its control capacity. While extensive obligations arise only in groups that provide immanent

[14] The extensiveness of obligations in hierarchical groups is likely to vary directly with each individual's level of dependence. This explains why assistant professors often face larger teaching loads and committee responsibilities than senior luminaries.

[15] Even the pious Mormon settlers in Utah attempted to evade their tithing obligations. This was the source of Brigham Young's complaint that "at times it seems as though all hell and earth are combined to keep money out of my hands. A great many people would give me millions if they had it; but most of the those who have it will not part with it" (Arrington 1958: 136–37).

joint goods, control is an issue in *all* groups—even in those producing marketable commodities.[16]

The relationship between control and compliance is intricate for two reasons. In the first place, the group must have sufficient resources at its disposal to effectively reward or punish its members contingent on their level of contribution or performance. This ability to provide what are essentially selective incentives can be called the group's *sanctioning* capacity.

By virtue of the fact that members are more or less dependent (by definition), all groups have at least one potential sanction—namely, exclusion from the group. Exclusion is the ultimate sanction in that it denies individuals access to the jointly produced good that they value. Yet some groups use this sanction more readily than others. For example, intentional communities are more likely to expel deviant members than are families. Though the effectiveness of the threat of expulsion varies with the member's dependence on the group, the group's willingness to employ it as a sanction is analytically distinct from the dependence of its members.

In any case, many groups employ additional sanctions that fall short of expulsion to motivate compliance with corporate obligations. Although these sanctions are collectively produced, *they are quite different from the benefits that lead people to join the group initially.* Like exclusion, many of these sanctions are negative and therefore cannot count as benefits at all: if members do not live up to their obligations, they will suffer the consequences. In further contrast to the good that motivates membership, the provision of sanctions need not be regular or guaranteed but can be intermittent and provisional. A union's strike pay, for example, can be an incentive for picketing, but it only comes into play during a strike.

In order to be effective, these sanctions must be distributed to members selectively. Whether these sanctions are material or nonmaterial, their supply is never unlimited. Thus, to attain maximum compliance, groups must not only devise means of producing or procuring stores of adequate sanctions, but they must also convince all members that they will receive the particular sanction that is appropriate to their past behavior. If compliant members are consistently punished while noncompliant ones are consistently rewarded, then the overall level of compliance will be at its nadir. And if there is too long a delay between behavior and subsequent sanctioning, the efficacy of a sanction declines.

---

[16] If control is required in all groups, then what is the difference between compensation and obligation as means of assuring production? Compensation is based upon a strict quid pro quo, and the agent is paid for each compliant act. In obligatory groups, however, there is no quid pro quo: compliance is expected of members and, as such, merits no special attention or reward.

The second reason for the intricacy of the relationship between control and compliance is that the group must be able to detect whether individuals comply with their obligations or not. This is its *monitoring* capacity. Monitoring is problematic because individual behavior is often difficult to observe, much less to measure. Some acts—those conducted in utter privacy—are intrinsically harder to monitor than others—those carried out in the full view of other members. When a group tries to attain attitudinal as against visible behavioral compliance, its monitoring task is all the more demanding.

True, not all members have an interest in concealing their behavior. Deviants alone have this incentive, but the compliant can usually be relied upon to publicize their virtue. Yet this does not mean that groups composed of the relatively virtuous can do without monitoring. Monitoring is required not only to ferret out the noncompliant but also to check on the allegedly compliant, for claims of virtuous behavior can never be taken at face value. In the absence of monitoring, deviants or shirkers are also likely to describe their past behavior as virtuous. Hence, all self-reports of compliance must be sifted to separate the wheat from the chaff, and this, in turn, requires monitoring.

Altogether, then, noncompliance with obligations (and with rules of any sort) can have at least two separate roots: it can be due to inadequate sanctioning or to impaired monitoring. Since each of these activities is costly, the total costs of control constitute a severe constraint on any group's ability to attain compliance.

What determines a group's control capacity? Many considerations come into play (see Chapters 7 and 8), and for illustrative purposes I shall only mention two of them here. The first determinant is the measurability of the individual's contribution. Whenever an individual's contribution to the production of a joint good cannot be reliably indicated by an output—as is the case, for example, in teamwork—control is problematic. Since acts carried out in privacy are more difficult to monitor than public acts, another factor is the group's ability to limit the privacy of its members. It is in the interest of members to extend their privacy, just as it is in the interest of the collective to limit it.

A group's survival depends upon the adoption of effective techniques to control its members. Yet insofar as control enables group members to produce joint goods, it must be considered a second-order collective good (Laver 1981: 62–71). As such, the provision of control is itself subject to the free-rider dilemma. While each member may gain from the overall solidarity of the group (because solidarity is an enabling condition for the supply of the joint good), free riding remains each rational agent's best strategy. Members will not voluntarily assume the burden of control without sufficient compensation. It follows that all long-lived groups must include some individuals—sometimes called *agents*—who are compensated for providing control and are motivated to do it on this account. Without such agents groups cannot secure routine compliance. But agents come in varying sizes and shapes. In informal groups everyone is simultaneously an agent and a member; in more complex structures agents and members are differentiated and perform mutually exclusive roles. In some groups (American academic departments) members rotate into and out of the agency role; in others (capitalist firms) access to this role is more restricted. Different institutional arrangements—particularly those that affect the distribution of the joint good—determine the relations between agents and members in all groups.

Whereas dependence characterizes all voluntary groups, it is insufficient to solve the free-rider problem.[17] Without control, group solidarity is, at best, a chimera. Large groups with relatively great control capacity are fundamentally different from those lacking this capacity. They are likely to have clear and consistent corporate goals, for these are necessary to precisely define the members' obligations. Control promotes the stability and exclusivity of groups.

To recapitulate, solidarity varies with the extensiveness of corporate obligation together with the probability that members fully comply with these obligations. The theory suggests three conclusions. (1) Since groups that produce goods for the marketplace can compensate their members with wages, solidarity will be confined to groups concerned with the production of joint, immanent goods for internal consumption. (2) Variations in the extensiveness of corporate obligations are due to the cost of producing the joint good (which sets the lower bound of extensiveness) and the dependence of its members (which sets the upper bound). Since the market for immanent joint goods is never the pure, frictionless market of the economists, dependence is crucial in determining the extensiveness of these obligations. Finally, (3) variations in compliance with corporate obligations are due to the control capacity of groups.

Thus the solidarity of any group increases to the degree that members are dependent on the group and their behavior is capable of being con-

---

[17] This is not to say that dependence has no effect on control. It is reasonable to suspect that before members honor a corporate obligation, they calculate whether the benefit of noncompliance will exceed that of the severity and probability of punishment (Gibbs 1981). If so, then the obligation will go unmet. The point, however, is that the severity of punishment (ultimately, expulsion) varies directly with each member's dependence on the group. Thus dependence is likely to partially affect each member's decision about compliance quite apart from the group's control capacity (see page 126).

trolled by the group's agents. If agents have the means to fully control members' behavior, solidarity will be a function of their dependence on the group: the less the dependence, the less the solidarity, and vice versa. If agents do not have the means to control members' behavior, a group is unlikely to attain solidarity regardless of its members' level of dependence. More formally, dependence and the group's control capacity are both determinants of solidarity, but each is by itself insufficient. Solidarity can be achieved only by the combined effects of dependence and control.

Whereas members themselves tend to determine variations in control capacity, variations in dependence are often due to environmental factors that are beyond their control. For example, once a state enacts policies that limit its citizens' rights—to geographic mobility, education, information, association, suffrage, and the like—this raises the dependence of the affected members. Democratization therefore plays a vital role in making group boundaries permeable. In societies where persons have the right to join any group, individualism flourishes and people can become as distinctive as snowflakes. This very distinctiveness, in turn, tends to liberate them from having extensive obligations to any particular group (Simmel [1922] 1955: 140). In this way an analysis of group solidarity that begins by considering the action of individuals inexorably leads to a conclusion emphasizing the primacy of institutional factors.

The theory holds that individuals comply with corporate obligations when they desire some good that is provided by membership in a given group. In practice, however, the situation is seldom this clear-cut. People can, and often do, belong to the same group for different kinds of reasons. And groups often produce more than one joint good.[18] These points become critical when the analyst must specify the best existing alternative in an individual's environment. This alternative is identified by the fact that it provides access to the same joint good. But there is always some ambiguity here. If the individual's interest in joining a group is merely the attainment of fellowship, then this can be fulfilled by membership in nearly any kind of group. For such people the purpose and type of the group is irrelevant: to them a church group and a political party are viable alternatives.

---

[18]This is especially the case with primordial ones like the extended family or village community. Yet even groups whose ostensible rationale is the production of a single joint good, like the capitalist firm, are likely to provide their members more than one type of benefit. On this account, it is difficult to sort out the reasons for the existence of any given group. For instance, there is no a priori reason to believe that the goods produced by different churches are in any way equivalent. Some churches may provide insurance benefits, while others may not. And the goods that a group produces can also change over time. That groups may be so protean has evident implications for empirical social research. The analysis of groups defined by standardized survey or governmental statistical measures has obvious hazards, for adequate comparative studies of groups must carefully attend to the types of goods that each provides.

Individuals who participate in a group to gain access to a highly specific good (the pleasure to be gained by playing chamber music) usually have fewer alternatives than people with more diffuse interests. In general, the more specific an individual's interest in a particular group, the greater that person's dependence. The specificity of goals is likely to vary across individuals, however, and, worse, it is not directly measurable.[19] Thus there is a subjective element involved in specifying the individual's dependence.[20]

Despite these qualifications, the theory proposes that the prospects for solidarity will be maximal in situations where individuals face limited sources of benefit, where their opportunities for multiple group affiliation are minimal, and where their social isolation is extreme. But even in these most favorable of circumstances, solidarity can be achieved only when groups have the capacity to monitor members' behavior so that sanctions can be dispensed to promote compliance.

The theory of group solidarity melds elements from earlier accounts of the evolution of group solidarity and integrates them into a more comprehensive whole. Whereas normativist discussions insist upon the importance of norms (here termed corporate obligations) for the creation of solidarity, they offer little insight into their origin or enforcement. The group solidarity theory retains this emphasis on norms but argues that they are not given. Rather, it looks to shifts in the dependence of members to explain variations in their extensiveness. Further, it addresses the issue of enforcement by introducing the concept of group control capacity.

Structuralist discussions, based as they are on rational egoistic behavioral assumptions, stress the role of common interests in the generation of solidarity—an emphasis that is retained in the present theory's claim that group members share a common interest in consuming a joint good. Yet structural explanations fail to address the free-rider problem. Using the same behavioral assumptions, the theory insists that group solidarity will occur only in the presence of controls that dissuade members from free riding.

Whereas the rational choice literature does not attempt to explain group solidarity, it has much to say about one of the key aspects of the problem,

---

[19] It is, however, indirectly indicated by the size of different types of groups. In general, the more specific the goals, the smaller the size and number of groups.

[20] The theory can also be applied to multiple group affiliations. Assume that a person is a member of multiple groups, and that compliance with the obligations of one (working on a weekend) entails noncompliance with those of another (spending the weekend with the family). With which of these sets of obligations (if any) will the person comply? The theory predicts that compliance will be determined by the individual's relative dependence and the relative control capacities of each group. When all groups have equivalent control capacities, individuals will comply with the group they are most dependent on. If they are more dependent on X than Y, but Y has great control capacity and X does not, they will comply with Y (since this choice yields the maximum net benefit).

namely, the conditions underlying the production of collective goods. The present theory distinguishes between two kinds of collective goods—immanent and nonimmanent ones—which have quite different implications for solidarity. Solidarity is to be found only in groups producing immanent collective goods, for these alone are unable to compensate members for compliance. The production of collective goods requires selective incentives. Given an ample supply of these incentives, rational choice theorists have tended to regard the production of such goods as unproblematic. In contrast, the group solidarity theory suggests that a collective good still may not be adequately produced even if a group has sufficient stores of selective incentives at its disposal. The production of collective goods may be inadequate because the control capacities of groups are crucial in determining the efficacy of given selective incentives.

If monitoring and sanctioning are costly—so costly that few large groups can have sufficient resources to attain even a modicum of solidarity—how then does the present theory account for solidarity in large groups? That control is costly goes without saying. Yet it is only by recognizing these costs that means of economizing on them become clear. The group solidarity theory helps show how large groups can attain relatively high levels of solidarity by adopting institutional arrangements that, in effect, lead to monitoring and sanctioning economies. These complexities of social control have received too little sustained theoretical attention.[21]

There are basically two reasons to propose a new theory. The first is to explain a particular set of findings for which no really adequate explanation seems to exist. If it offers a superior explanation of these data, then the theory is likely to be met with relatively rapid acceptance. The other reason—the one that motivates this book—is to resolve a theoretical problem. Here, too, the new theory must offer the promise of yielding better empirical results, but there is a crucial difference. Often the data required to test this kind of theory do not exist. Perhaps if enough researchers become intrigued with the theory, systematic attempts to collect the relevant evidence may be made. But the lack of suitable ready-made data hinders the appeal of any new theory.

Basically, this is my dilemma. The theory of group solidarity is constructed from elements that have a long academic pedigree. It has a host of potential applications, for solidarity is problematic in every kind of group. Yet independent measures of the theory's three essential components—de-

---

[21] Sociologists have long regarded social control as the primary defense against antisocial behavior (E. A. Ross 1901; for a recent example, see Janowitz 1978). Yet the concept is often utilized so vaguely that it is virtually without any explanatory power at all (Gibbs 1981).

pendence, control, and solidarity itself—are extremely difficult to find. Any theory that comes out of the blue is suspect—why should it be taken seriously without some demonstration of superior explanatory power?

In the remainder of the book, I try to assess the merits of various parts of the theory in light of some existing evidence. But before turning to this, it may be helpful to illustrate in the broadest of brush strokes how the theory can be applied to some familiar macrosociological questions.

If dependence plays a key role in the extensiveness of corporate obligations, then the threat posed by outsiders can provide a motive for increased solidarity among members of any group. This was illustrated at the beginning of the chapter. In essence, the case of the tent-dwellers is a little parable that has a few implications for understanding the rise of the western European state. When the nobility in the feudal regions of western Europe perceived that the growing wealth of the free cities beckoned to their dependent serfs, thereby threatening to erode their social position, these nobles were willing to cede more of their individual resources to a state apparatus representing their interests (Hechter and Brustein 1980: 1082–87). Their counterparts in other western European regions, however, faced no comparable challenge to their livelihoods. As a result, the landowners in nonfeudal regions were much less willing to cede their personal resources to a central state apparatus. The threat posed by the growing wealth of the towns in the feudal regions heightened the demands of the nobles there for a state apparatus, for previous to their perception of this threat, they likewise had been unwilling to combine for the purpose of mutual defense. Since there was a relatively small number of significant nobles, this group could easily organize and obtain relatively high control capacity as well. As the size and spatial dispersion of a group increases, its control costs rise; in consequence, solidarity becomes more difficult to attain. Hence, a similar perception of threat among the peasantry would not have yielded an equivalent amount of pan-local solidarity.[22]

The theory also helps explain a central puzzle of Durkheim's *Suicide:* namely, why the Catholics of his day generally were subject to more extensive obligations than the Protestants. Durkheim ([1897] 1951: 374) ascribed the cause of their differential obligations to the nature of each group's credos, but he never explained what accounts for variations in group credos. That the Catholic Church demands more extensive obligations of its adherents than Protestants sects do can be explained by the

---

[22] Hanagan (1980) uses this kind of explanation, however, to argue that when artisans became threatened by the advance of manufacturing technology, their solidarity increased and they helped to organize the industrial workers' movement in three French towns. High levels of residential segregation may have contributed to the artisans' control capacity.

different ages of the respective churches. Catholicism existed for centuries in medieval western Europe as the universal church; there were no legal alternatives to it until the Reformation. Being a religious monopolist, the Church could require much of its followers—both in the financial and spiritual realms. Protestant sects, however, initially had to challenge the established Catholic Church for adherents. In order to succeed, Protestants had to lure away religious Catholics by offering a more attractive product: salvation, the same benefit, but with a lower tax. One part of this lower tax was the elimination of the sale of papal indulgences; the other was the granting of more individual freedom of worship. (When a Protestant church had a political monopoly in a given territory, it often demanded extensive obligations—witness Calvin's Geneva.) A similar story can be told about the transition from Orthodox to Reform Judaism. When the bulk of eastern European Jews were confined to the shtetl, they subscribed to a religion with extensive obligations. Once individual Jews were granted full citizenship and became less dependent upon their coreligionists for their life chances, Reform Judaism began to supplant the Orthodox variety.[23]

Finally, the theory allows us to interpret some of the massive changes in family structure that have occurred in the course of industrialization. One way to read the history of the family in western societies is as the story of the erosion of family members' dependence on the head of the household (Coleman 1982: 119–52; cf. G. S. Becker 1981: Ch. 11). The preindustrial family was the sole source not only of shelter, sustenance, and emotional support for most wives and children, but also of education, occupational training, employment and, most generally, welfare. Women and children were extremely dependent on the heads of households, the men whose powers were described so vividly by Sir Henry Maine in *Ancient Law*. Since the members of such households worked at home, these families had a high control capacity. As a result, the solidarity of families was at a peak. Today, much has changed. In the first place, many of these functions have been taken over by the welfare state, making women and children much less dependent on men. In the second place, the separation of workplace and residence, coupled with high levels of female labor force participation, have sharply reduced the family's control capacity. In consequence, family solidarity has reached a nadir: high rates of divorce are one outcome of these changes (for American evidence, see Bane 1975; Hannan, Tuma, and Groeneveld 1977; Moles 1976; and Ross and Sawhill 1975),

---

[23] This does not imply that voluntary groups that demand extensive obligations cannot persist in advanced capitalist society (see Chapter 8).

runaway children another. Evidently, the theory can offer a plausible account of a variety of familiar macrosociological findings.

Sociologists often divide their field into subareas on the basis of differences between formal organizations and informal ones, such as religious groups, racial and ethnic groups, and social movements. To the degree that these types of groups differ systematically from one another, this kind of substantive classification has its advantages. Yet the practice also obscures the underlying similarities that these different groups often share. The theory of group solidarity has implications for groups of all kinds: it provides a disciplined means of attacking a key problem in sociological analysis.

CHAPTER IV

THE NECESSITY OF FORMAL CONTROLS

The sociological mind reels at the cost of social controls which would have to cope with the unrestrained exercise of amoral human intelligence.

John Finley Scott

THE GROUP solidarity theory suggests that the survival of any group hinges on members' routine and consistent compliance with the rules and obligations governing the production of joint goods. Yet rational members will comply only if they expect that their noncompliance might result in a loss of access to the good. This expectation, in turn, is significantly affected by the group's control capacity. The theory claims that the production of joint goods requires formal controls to promote coordination and to deter free riding. By *formal controls* I refer to rules and enforcement procedures that are the outcome of conscious planning. These are to be distinguished from informal rules that arise spontaneously, in the absence of forethought or collective agreement, and that are enforced through the self-sustaining mechanism of reciprocal exchange. By providing the requisite sanctions, formal controls promote coordination by assigning each member to a specific productive task, discourage free riders, and reassure the compliant that they are not being exploited by the unscrupulous few who would break the rules with impunity.

Any control system must have monitoring and sanctioning capacities. A group's *monitoring* capacity depends on the degree to which it possesses information about individual compliance with corporate rules or obligations, and its *sanctioning* capacity on its ability to generate and dispense resources that discourage noncompliance. Hence compliance can be problematic for at least two reasons: a group may not be able to detect all instances of noncompliance, or it may not possess sufficient sanctions to dissuade its members from free riding or shirking.

Since there are so many possible sources of noncompliance, the attainment of adequate control capacity would appear to be difficult and costly. To the degree that a group makes expenditures on control, it is left with fewer remaining productive resources. If too many resources are drained from production, the group as a whole might begin to unravel. Due to the costliness of control, therefore, it might seem surprising that many groups (or for that matter, relatively high degrees of social order) can persist at all.[1]

Despite this, however, many groups are long-lived; there is even a fair amount of social order as well. Are these facts sufficient to cast doubt on the group solidarity theory? While there is nothing controversial about the role of dependence in social life, the same cannot be said about controls. That controls are likely to yield compliance is nowhere disputed. Yet are controls necessary for group survival? And, if so, how formal need they be?

Two quite different kinds of arguments bear on these questions. The first is that both formal and informal controls are unnecessary for group survival because—contrary to the theory's assumption of rational egoism—individuals are liable to act in a prosocial, or altruistic, fashion. In one version of this argument, people engage in prosocial behavior because they have been socialized to do so. In another version, prosocial behavior is seen to emanate not from socialization, but from selection processes that emerge in particular kinds of environments.

The second argument does not rest its optimistic conclusion on claims about altruistic motivations. On the contrary, it suggests that even rational egoists will sometimes behave prosocially in the absence of formal control systems. According to this view, individuals who are engaged in repeated interactions are likely to establish informal self-sustaining controls that are sufficient to deter free riding. As a result, costly formal control systems are superfluous for the production of joint goods. Since these arguments challenge the group solidarity theory by questioning the necessity of formal controls for group survival, each must be considered in turn.

PROSOCIAL MOTIVATIONS

If the free-rider problem is not as severe as has been assumed in the group solidarity theory, then people might comply with corporate rules and obligations in the absence of elaborate control mechanisms. True, small amounts of sanctioning might still be required to attain compliance—perhaps to strengthen members' normative commitments, as Durkheim (1901) argued—but control would cease to play a preponderant role. This would drastically reduce control expenditures, providing more compliance and social order as a result.

The theory's assumption of rational egoism is certainly controversial.

---

[1] Hence, classical sociologists doubted the ability of individualistic (or "utilitarian") theories to account for social order.

Not only do many social scientists question it, but research on the extensiveness of free riding has yielded ambiguous results. Many experimental studies designed to investigate the severity of the free-rider problem show that people often fail to behave in a purely self-interested fashion (Sweeney 1973; V. Smith 1979; Marwell and Ames 1980). Such findings are not merely confined to the laboratory. There is an ample literature on helping behavior (or altruism) that demonstrates that the incidence of prosocial behavior is far from negligible in the most impersonal urban environments. Many New Yorkers will mail back an apparently lost wallet to its owner (Hornstein, Fisch, and Holmes 1968); subway riders will sometimes extend aid to someone who suffers a staged knee injury (Latané and Darley 1970) and to someone who appears drunk (Piliavin, Rodin, and Piliavin 1969). While not typical, activities such as the voluntary anonymous donation of blood (Titmuss 1971) and of organs before death (Rushton 1980: 2–7) are not unknown.[2]

So, now and then people try to help others. They do not always free ride, shirk, or act opportunistically. Nearly every country has its handful of martyrs who gave their lives not out of the belief that salvation awaited them after death, but rather out of the conviction that their nation was worth dying for. Even some economists, who tend to be skeptical about the importance of morality in human behavior, have become convinced that employees follow instructions and citizens obey the law to a much greater extent than can be explained on the basis of formal controls alone (Arrow 1970; North 1981).[3] Does this evidence of prosocial behavior con-

---

[2] Hobbes ([1651] 1968: 186–87) forcefully reminds us of the other side of the coin: "It may seem strange to some man, that has not well weighed these things; that Nature should thus dissociate, and render men apt to invade, and destroy one another; and he may therefore, not trusting to this Inference, made from the Passions, desire perhaps to have the same confirmed by Experience. Let him therefore consider with himselfe, when taking a journey, he armes himselfe, and seeks to go well accompanied; when going to sleep, he locks his dores; when even in his house he locks his chests; and this when he knows there bee Lawes, and publike Officers, armed, to revenge all injuries shall bee done him; what opinion he has of his fellow subjects, when he rides armed; of his fellow Citizens, when he locks his dores; and of his children, and servents, when he locks his chests. Does he not there as much accuse mankind by his actions, as I do by my words?"

[3] Kenneth Arrow makes this point amusingly in the context of his critique of the neoclassical theory of discrimination. Commenting that this theory fails to explain why entrepreneurs who could make profits cheaply by hiring labor from groups who are subject to discrimination fail to do so, Arrow notes that "Sherlock Holmes, a man much concerned with the formulation of hypotheses for the explanation of empirical behavior, once asked about the barking of a dog at night. The local police inspector, mystified as usual, noted that the dog had not barked at night. Holmes dryly noted that the silence was precisely the problem. Have we some dog whose silence should be remarked? Yes; those vast forces of greed and aggressiveness that we are assured and assure students are the mainsprings of economic activity in a private enterprise economy; not the best, but the strongest motives of humanity, as Marshall has said." (Arrow 1972: 90). Similarly, how can widespread evidence of prosocial behavior be reconciled with rational egoism?

trovert the assumption of rational egoism made in the group solidarity theory?

Socialization Theories

Sociologists often portray humans not as rationally calculating individualists but as social beings. In their view, orientations to prosocial behavior arise in the course of socialization. By doing away with the need for costly controls, prosocial behavior seems to make compliance with corporate rules and obligations easy to achieve. In his critique of the Hobbesian theory of social order, Parsons (1937) contended that there is more compliance and order in social life than can be attributed to sanctioning mechanisms alone. Like Durkheim ([1925] 1961b: 157) before him, Parsons accounted for this ostensible surfeit of social order by postulating that, in addition to (external) sanctions, internalized norms have salience for individual action.

Norms are rules for conduct that provide standards by which behavior is approved or disapproved. There are a bewildering variety of them, and the problem is to explain when and why they are observed. For this purpose it is critical to distinguish between two quite different kinds of norms. People routinely observe some norms—like driving on the right side of the street or behaving according to the dictates of etiquette—because compliance with them is relatively costless and breaching them brings forth sanctions.[4] Compliance with norms of these varieties poses no theoretical dilemmas, but neither does it resolve any.

But there is a second kind of norm, the observance of which causes individuals to bear some cost, yet for which sanctioning is problematic. Observant Muslims celebrate Ramadan, Orthodox Jews keep kosher, and pious Catholics forswear birth control even when noncompliance is hardly visible. Why would anyone ever comply with such norms in the absence

---

[4] Of course, this argument about self-interested normative compliance can be pushed too far. Durkheim ([1925] 1961b: 44–45) is guilty of this error in the following passage: "Imagine a being liberated from all external restraint, a despot still more absolute than those of which history tells us, a despot that no external power can restrain or influence. By definition, the desires of such a being are irresistible. Shall we say, then, that he is all-powerful? Certainly not, since he himself cannot resist his desires. They are masters of him, as of everything else. He submits to them; he does not dominate them. In a word, when the inclinations are totally liberated, when nothing sets bounds to them, they themselves become tyrannical, and their first slave is precisely the person who experiences them. What a sad picture this presents. Following one upon the other, the most contradictory inclinations, the most antithetical whims, involve the so-called absolute sovereign in the most incompatible feelings, until finally this apparent onmipotence dissolves into genuine impotence. A despot is like a child; he has a child's weaknesses because he is not master of himself." By this reckoning nearly all observance of norms can be justified in terms of subtle self-interest.

of external controls? The sociologist's traditional answer is that these norms are

> 'internalized' so as to become part of the conscience or self-ideal of the individuals in question; if so, there will be much conformity even if there is no external surveillance of conduct or punishment for deviant behavior. Norms not thus internalized can be enforced only through external rewards and penalties.
>
> (R. M. Williams 1968: 206)

Far from being weathervanes responding to each capricious change in the winds of sanctioning, actors who have internalized norms observe them at a spatial and temporal remove from sanctions. In consequence, they are capable of following organized and long-range courses of action for which there are no external sanctions.

I have already commented on the problems often raised by this kind of normativist analysis. Ultimately, the salience of normative commitment can be determined only by observing behavior. But since behavior can arise from a multitude of quite different sources, it is difficult to gauge the independent significance of norms. There is no justification in assuming that behavior is always due to norms; there is always the possibility that it can be explained on the basis of pure self-interest (Wrong 1961; Homans 1964; Gibbs 1981). As Durkheim, Weber, Pareto, and Parsons were all at pains to emphasize, much ritual and religious behavior, however, cannot be regarded as the outcome of benefit/cost calculation in any meaningful sense of the term. Whatever the importance of this behavior, it must be caused either by the internalization of norms or by some analogous mechanism. The issue is important because people who internalize prosocial norms presumably monitor and sanction themselves.

Do humans have an inherent proclivity to engage in prosocial behavior? Few social scientists consider it to be intrinsically rewarding—no one thinks children value it as they do, say, eating sweets. Infants are generally considered to be hedonistically motivated; as a result, they engage in quintessentially selfish action (cf. Durkheim [1925] 1961b: 174–222). When it does occur, the acquisition of prosocial orientations to action takes time and energy. Jean Piaget (1932) and Lawrence Kohlberg (1969) have argued that moral reasoning is to some degree limited by stages of cognitive development. But even if this is true, deviance is evidently a commonplace among adults.

It is plausible to assume that the acquisition of prosocial values results, at least in part, from learning experiences. If so, then how are these values learned? In general, learning can occur through direct reinforcement and through relatively indirect processes, such as modelling.[5]

Direct Reinforcement.   Reinforcement provides rewards and punishments apart from those resulting from the performance of a specific act. As the relative value of these rewards and punishments increases, so does their influence on a person's subsequent action. The more positive reinforcement an individual receives for the performance of some act, the greater the probability that it will be repeated subsequently.

On the basis of learning theory, John Finley Scott (1971) deduces that higher levels of moral behavior will be found in settings where such behavior is positively reinforced (where heroism is rewarded, for example) than in those where it is not reinforced at all or where it is reinforced negatively. How does direct reinforcement have this effect? In part, it conveys information to actors about the types of behavior that are appropriate. Selective reinforcement directs their attention to stimuli that signify probable consequences; previous reinforcements create expectations that motivate actions designed to secure desired rewards and to avoid injurious outcomes; and punishing experiences can endow persons, places, and things with fear-arousing properties that inhibit responsiveness.

Whereas the concept has long been associated with rather crude versions of behaviorist psychology, reinforcement can be provided in subtler ways than is often appreciated. In the most familiar scenario—one in which rational choice theorists use the term *incentive*—reinforcement enables the powerful to exert their will on the powerless. Reinforcers are the trusty arrows that nestle in the quivers of parents, teachers, and bosses, ready to be launched in struggles with their respective charges.

Direct reinforcement is the most familiar type of reinforcement, if not necessarily the most effective. Here is how it works. People are often confronted with situations that compel them to respond in one way or another. Some of their responses to these situations produce consequences that they find undesirable, whereas others produce more desirable consequences. As a result of prior experiences, individuals come to expect that certain actions will gain them valued outcomes, whereas others will not. This expectation depends on their ability to recognize and make the appropriate inferences from the covariation between disparate events. In this way actions are regulated to a large extent by anticipated consequences. Differential

[5] The following discussion is confined only to those explanations of socialization that lend themselves to empirical falsification. The perspectives of Mead and Freud, among others, are therefore given short shrift.

reinforcement eventually induces people to engage in those actions that provide them with desirable rather than undesirable consequences.[6]

To change the behavior of any individual in a predictable direction, it is necessary to establish some kind of consistent reinforcement schedule. If the preference for reinforcers remains constant, then as long as the act in question is always positively reinforced, the person will tend to engage in it because it produces desirable results. Likewise, acts that consistently produce undesirable results will be shunned. In the absence of a consistent reinforcement schedule, people will not behave in a predictable fashion. Anyone who is rewarded for performing some act at one time but punished for repeating it later can have no clear expectation about the future consequences of engaging in such action.

While the logic is straightforward, applying this logic is by no means a simple task. It is difficult to establish consistent reinforcement schedules in the absence of a high degree of control. Even in the nuclear family they do not spring into place spontaneously. Unquestionably, psychologists have an easier time providing consistent reinforcement schedules in their laboratories than in their own homes. Consider how tricky it is for a mother and father to arrive at similar sanctions in response to unforeseen instances of a child's disobedience. Can they agree about whether the offense should be sanctioned at all, or ignored? When the child is caught repeating the offense, will the parents remember their earlier response? What happens if the father is unaware of the mother's previous sanctioning decision and unwittingly responds differently to the same egregious act? No family has a *Code Napoléon* to aid parents in child-rearing.[7]

Although the difficulties of maintaining consistent reinforcement constrain a group's ability to influence its members' behavior, the extent of these difficulties should not be exaggerated. Learning does not require perfect reinforcement. Whereas reinforcements must be consistent in valence, they need not be administered constantly. Indeed, reinforcement is more effective when it is provided on an intermittent basis:

[6] This effect need not depend on the subject's conscious awareness of the link between act and reward. Hefferline and his associates (Hefferline and Keenan 1963; Hefferline, Keenan, and Harford 1959) and Sasmore (1966) successfully modified the behavior of adults through reinforcement even though the latter were unable to observe their rewarded responses. In these studies visibly imperceptible muscular responses, detected by the experimenter through electronic amplification, are reinforced either by monetary reward or by termination of unpleasant stimulation. Unseen responses increase substantially during reinforcement and decline abruptly after reinforcement is withdrawn. None of the subjects could identify the response that produced the reinforcing consequences.

[7] For a summary of evidence that ineffective familial control systems are responsible for the development of juvenile delinquency, see J. Q. Wilson (1983). Wilson and the authors he relies upon, however, do not sufficiently appreciate the difficulty of establishing effective control systems in the nuclear family.

To produce good results, perhaps the subject should know explicitly that surveillance is not constant, but at the same time not know when he is under surveillance. If the subject continues to perform the behavior, and he knows that he is not consistently under surveillance, then his behavior appears to him to be more "self-emitted." If we then arrange for his new behavior to be occasionally reinforced (perhaps not from the group members), then we may have the conditions for a more permanent behavioral change and a consequent private acceptance of the group norm. This sounds very mechanistic and Orwellian—but we are convinced that, to some extent at least, this is what parents unwittingly do to teach their children certain rules of society. Parents seem to tune children in and out, even in close physical proximity. A transgression missed at one time might be attended to if repeated later. From the child's point of view, it is inconsistent surveillance. The pressure for compliance with social or family rules also varies, depending largely on the parent's mood or the frequency of previous transgressions.

(Kiesler and Kiesler 1969: 95–96)

The less visible the behavior, the less subject it is to subsequent modification: everyone knows that it is easier to toilet train children than to teach them not to lie. Finally, direct reinforcement is only suitable for those people who are already dependent on groups; independent souls have no incentive to submit themselves repeatedly to such discipline.

Direct reinforcement can evidently modify behavior, but how lasting are its effects? If individuals only responded to direct reinforcement, then every time they became subject to changing reinforcement schedules, their behavior would shift correspondingly, much as weathervanes in a light breeze. But human behavior is much more stable than this image would suggest.[8]

Since direct reinforcement is effective only in the presence of control, visibility and dependence, it is an unlikely cause of a generalized tendency toward prosocial behavior.[9] Whereas it may be a powerful method for regulating behaviors that have already been learned, it turns out to be a relatively inefficient way of creating new behaviors (Bandura 1971: 5). Ques-

---

[8] One well-known analysis of the effects of brainwashing among Chinese political prisoners (Lifton 1961) suggests that adult preferences are difficult to permanently modify even under the most extreme reinforcement schedules. For a discussion of more effective measures of persuasion, see Cialdini (1984).

[9] This conclusion must, however, be tempered by the privileged status of early childhood learning, whose effects tend to persist throughout a person's life. Kohlberg (1969) makes a strong case for the privileged nature of childhood learning, and—in the pragmatic realm— this principle has always been at the cornerstone of Jesuit pedagogy. On the other side, Freud argued that the effects of early childhood reinforcement can be undone, but only at the high cost of psychoanalysis.

tions of efficacy aside, it is obvious that direct reinforcement offers no alternative to formal controls, for *a reinforcement schedule is actually a control system parading under a different name.*[10]

Learning by reinforcement, however, is by no means limited to power imbalanced relationships. Individuals can also serve as indirect reinforcers through modelling. That reinforcement can take on such different forms is significant. Although direct reinforcement is nothing other than intensive control, indirect forms of reinforcement can induce learning using substantially reduced levels of control.

Modelling.   Most of the behaviors that people engage in are learned, either deliberately or inadvertently, through the influence of example rather than through direct reinforcement (Bandura 1971: 6–7). People are often affected by witnessing the fate of others. Observation of others conveys information about the types of actions that are likely to be approved or disapproved. Learning the ropes is an important survival skill in any social setting, and one of the commonest ways to do it is by taking note of the fate of colleagues and friends in prospective situations.

Seeing others reinforced can arouse expectations that observers will be likewise rewarded for similar performances. Hence variations in the generosity with which other people are reinforced can determine the speed, the vigor, and the persistence with which others behave. Models can exhibit emotional reactions while undergoing rewarding or punishing experiences, and observers can be easily aroused by the emotional expressions of others. None of these effects, however, is of the stimulus-response type, for the observer is not the one who is subject to direct reinforcement.

What accounts for the selection of models that people tend to imitate? The most important determinant is differential association, for it is diffi-

---

[10]Freud's solution to the solidarity problem lies in his concept of the superego: "Civilization, therefore, obtains mastery over the individual's dangerous desires for aggression by weakening and disarming it and by setting up an agency within him to watch over it, like a garrison in a conquered city" (Freud [1930] 1961: 79). Strictly speaking, Freud's is not a learning theory, because it places considerable stress on the importance of unconscious drives. Yet in doing so it incorporates elements from both reinforcement and modelling mechanisms (Parsons 1958; Schafer 1968, 1976.) Freud posits that infants seek pleasure in the form of the gratification of basic desires for material and emotional sustenance. The absence of the mother leads to the painful discovery that the satisfaction of these desires is not entirely in the infant's control. The infant is overwhelmed by the realization of his dependence. In order to minimize the pain of not knowing when these pleasurable stimuli will be taken away—sometimes as a result of the infant's "misbehavior"—the child sets up his own internal control device, the superego. He would rather determine his own punishment than be subject to the vicissitudes of external sanctioning. The superego enforces normative compliance, but note that its development hinges on the initial existence of control mechanisms. If the child could not predict which of his potential actions would be punished, he could not develop a superego at all.

cult to model oneself after someone one is unable to observe. For this reason models tend to be selected from the ranks of parents, peers, and teachers (although books, television, and movies have widened these possibilities somewhat).

Whereas the pool of potential models is largely determined by differential association, this still leaves considerable latitude for the choice of particular persons as models. Among these, people often select models who appear to have succeeded in attaining the goals that they share: powerful people will be imitated more often than powerless ones, more prestigious rather than less prestigious ones, and similar rather than dissimilar ones (Rushton 1980). To take an admittedly trivial example, pedestrians are more likely to jaywalk when they see someone dressed like an executive do it than when the same model dressed shabbily jaywalks (Lefkowitz, Blake, and Mouton 1955). Evidently, observers tend to assume that models with high status are more likely to be generally successful than those without it. In this example the model's clothes serve as a tangible indicator of past successes (Bandura 1971: 19).

Instead of relying on sanctions, then, subjects learn on the basis of the experience of others. If these others are closely controlled, then subjects will assume (unless there is evidence to the contrary) that their own behavior will also be subject to control. Modelling therefore offers a way to multiply the effects of given control expenditures, making compliance and social order easier to attain than they would otherwise be. It is likely that parental practice is a more forceful determinant of the acquisition and development of moral commitment in children than parental reinforcement (Rushton 1980: 114–22).

Yet, although socialization may be a boon to the production of collective goods, it is not a panacea. Like all tools, socialization can be put to many different uses. In certain conditions socializing agents may try to produce generalized altruists, but in others they may try to produce free riders. If the family is an autarkic productive unit (or *oikos* economy), rational parents seek to raise children who are "amoral familists" (Banfield 1958). Such children act altruistically within the family by being obedient, working hard at their jobs, and supporting their parents once they are unable to earn their own keep, but they are opportunistic in their dealings with outsiders (Weber [1924] 1981: 358–61). This is precisely the kind of behavior that is demanded by the Deuteronomic Code.

But it is not always rational for parents to raise amoral familists. To the degree that the family is not economically autarkic, the parents' socialization goals will also include maximizing the children's prospects for obtaining income *outside* the family. Raising children as amoral familists inhibits the attainment of this end. Hence it will often be narrowly rational for the parents in nonautarkic families to teach their children to at least *simulate* altruism. Why? Because opportunistic behavior is discouraged (if not actually punished) in those institutions—like schools, the church, armies, factories, offices, and even the marketplace—to which the children must turn in order to support themselves. So rational parents will tend to stress the virtues of good citizenship.[11]

Finally, even when socialization is directed toward the establishment of prosocial behavior, attaining that goal can be a lifelong process. As Confucius wryly noted of himself: "At fifteen I thought only of study; at thirty I began playing my role; at forty I was sure of myself; at fifty I was conscious of my position in the universe; at sixty I was no longer argumentative; and now at seventy I can follow my heart's desire without violating custom" (quoted in Ware 1955: 25).

To conclude. The very prevalence of socialization mechanisms in society attests to the severity of the problem of rational egoism. Groups whose members are not rational egoists—bees and other social insects—have no need to socialize them. *Far from being an alternative to formal controls, socialization is itself a product of these controls.* Take these away, and the internalization of norms withers. Finally, under certain conditions, socialization can foster generalized prosocial behavior that will reduce free riding and thereby lower expenditures on control.

There are, of course, other kinds of arguments for the existence of prosocial behavior. Some theorists explain its genesis on the basis of selection mechanisms. They argue that engaging in prosocial behavior is really in the individuals' self-interest, even though they may be unaware of it.

Selection Theories

Population geneticists have devoted rigorous and sustained attention to the explanation of prosocial, or altruistic, behavior in nonhuman species. They see the enduring traits of human and animal nature as a consequence of natural selection. The organisms that are most likely to be selected are those that maximize their reproductive fitness, or the ratio of offspring numbers to parent numbers at corresponding points in the generational life

---

[11]The same logic holds for the "ideological" content of the agencies of secondary socialization—schools, the military, and the church. In rare cases when such agencies are relatively autarkic (perhaps in the German SS), little premium will be placed on the establishment of socialization that promotes generalized altruism. Otherwise, when these agencies depend on the good will of actors and institutions beyond their control (who serve, for example, as employers of their students, soldiers, and clerics), it is rational to invest in the moral socialization of their charges.

cycle. Self-interested behaviors are easy to understand from this perspective because they can easily contribute to an organism's reproductive fitness.

The altruistic behaviors, however, that are sometimes observed among animals as well as among humans appear to pose a puzzle. Indeed, E. O. Wilson (1975: 3) considers their existence to be the central theoretical problem in sociobiology. Altruism would appear to reduce fitness, but, if so, how can the individual possibly survive by natural selection? The answer is that where altruism is observed, there must also exist some offsetting mechanism that makes this unselfish behavior profitable in some sense. That which is ostensibly altruistic turns out, in the final analysis, to be selfish.

Population geneticists have identified two principal mechanisms by which altruistic behavior can be reconciled with selection. The first mechanism (one that is also favored by game theorists) is reciprocal altruism (Trivers 1971). In effect, one individual does something for another in the expectation of a quid pro quo. As we shall soon see, this solution to the puzzle of prosocial behavior is limited by stringent informational requirements.

The second mechanism, kin selection (Hamilton 1964), does not appear to share this liability. Here altruistic behavior is selected because, despite initial appearances and as fuller analysis reveals, it yields a net selfish benefit. Selection favors the organism that maximizes not its own fitness but instead the reproductive survival of its genes. Since each parent shares half of its offspring's genetic endowment, the principle of inclusive fitness predicts that it is more likely to endure sacrifice for the sake of its own offspring than for more distantly related offspring whose genetic endowment is not shared to this extent. The theory of inclusive fitness not only explains how altruism can be selected but also predicts its specific beneficiaries with a good deal of precision. The boundaries of altruistic behavior are determined by genetic relatedness, and nepotism is the word of the day.

This approach may do wonders for the study of prosocial behavior within nuclear and extended families, but can it explain the genesis of altruism in large non-kin-related groups? Apparently, population genetics holds out little hope for the evolution of this kind of generalized altruism. There is one slim exception to this dictum (as noted by G. C. Williams 1966). Kin selection could produce behavior that benefits everyone within helping distance if it is likely that there is a disproportionate number of relatives in the actor's environment, and if it is too costly (or otherwise impossible) to reserve help for relatives alone. Except for this remote possibility, the biological models depend upon the organism's ability to detect kin. In order to exhibit the appropriate altruistic behavior, the actor must be able to assess the genetic endowment of potential beneficiaries. While possible in small kin-related networks, this kind of detection becomes prohibitively expensive as the number of strangers increases.

The adequacy of biological reasoning for the explanation of prosocial behavior in humans is undoubtedly limited. Whereas some human behavior is consistent with the expectations of inclusive fitness theory, some is not. As the evidence summarized above attests, human prosocial behavior is far from wholly determined by patterns of genetic similarity. Population geneticists themselves concede that cultural patterns play a large and independent role in human behavior (E. O. Wilson and Lumsden 1981).

In any case, more general results can be obtained without resorting to genetic arguments but merely by appealing to standard neoclassical economics. Gary Becker's (1976) "Rotten Kid" Theorem provides a good example (see also Becker 1981).[12] In this theorem—so called because it leads even rotten kids to act as if they were good ones—altruism is assumed to be randomly distributed in a population.[13] In Becker's hypothetical family, the man (the benefactor) often behaves altruistically toward his dependent wife and children (the beneficiaries); as a result, he spends some of his own income on these dependents rather than on his own consumption. The amount that the benefactor is willing to contribute is partially determined by the beneficiaries' alternative sources of income. The greater they are, the less his resulting contribution.

Since this would appear to leave benefactors vulnerable to the depredations of selfish beneficiaries (children demanding an unlimited allowance), the persistence of altruism in the family is problematic: why don't these benefactors end up alone and in the poorhouse? It turns out that even selfish beneficiaries come to recognize that their own welfare depends on that of their benefactor. As a result, these beneficiaries are willing to—indeed are even anxious to—act altruistically toward their benefactors. Thus is social interdependence born. Further, this result does not hinge on the benefactor's ability to monitor the behavior of his beneficiaries: "Since a selfish beneficiary wants to maximize [joint] income, she is led by the invisible hand of self-interest to act as if she is altruistic toward her benefactor" (G. S. Becker 1981: 179).

This is an intriguing conclusion. Ultimately, the theorem explains the survival of prosocial behavior through a selection mechanism, for the altruists are made better off by their altruism despite an utter lack of concern for their own welfare. Yet the explanation it offers for the genesis of altruism is quite different from those employed by population geneticists.

---

[12] For other economic treatments of altruism, see Collard (1978), Margolis (1982), and Kolm (1983).

[13] It should be pointed out that Becker offers no justification for this assumption.

Can the Rotten Kid Theorem account for prosocial behavior in large and impersonal groups? On this score Becker is dubious. His expectation is that the same person who acts altruistically in the family will act selfishly in the marketplace. Why should altruism be found in some settings but not in others? Because it is more efficacious in the family than it is in the marketplace. The advantage of the family over the marketplace is partly a function of its small size. As the number of beneficiaries increases, the benefactor's average contribution to each declines. In addition, selfish beneficiaries take less account of their benefactors' interests when their contributions are small. Hence the "friends of humanity" are likely to end up being ministered to by the Salvation Army.

The theorem has other limitations as well. It assumes that benefactors know the utility functions and consumption of their beneficiaries (G. S. Becker 1981: 183), but such knowledge is not likely to exist among strangers. Benefactors must be in a position to have the last move in the interaction, for if beneficiaries do, they may ruthlessly destroy their benefactors (Hirshleifer 1977: 28).[14] Finally, beneficiaries must know both the identity of their benefactors and the nature of their altruistic interest. But this entails monitoring costs. In the family and other intimate groups social relations are often sufficiently transparent to render these monitoring costs inexpensive, but this can rarely, if ever, be the case in large, anonymous groups.[15]

As an explanation of prosocial behavior that is based on selection processes, the Rotten Kid Theorem has an important advantage over its biological alternative. By eschewing genetics, it can more easily explain how altruism can arise outside the family among groups of nonrelated individuals who have the opportunity to closely observe one another's behavior. As an account of the development of prosocial behavior in general, however, the Rotten Kid Theorem has little to offer.

Yet even in the absence of altruism it may still be possible to have compliance without costly formal control mechanisms. Some groups are likely to evolve spontaneous self-sustaining controls that, in effect, provide order within anarchy. Such controls are then *self-reinforced*—that is, each mem-

---

[14] In this context George Orwell (1959: 134) observed that "A man receiving charity practically always hates his benefactor—it is a fixed characteristic of human nature." Hobbes ([1651] 1968: 162–63) offers a clear explanation of the phenomenon: "To have received from one, to whom we think our selves equall, greater benefits than there is hope to Requite, disposeth to counterfeit love; but really secret hatred; and puts a man into the estate of a desperate debtor, that in declining the sight of his creditor, tacitly wishes him there, where he might never see him more. For benefits oblige; and obligation is thraldome; and unrequitable obligation, perpetuall thraldome; which is to ones equall, hatefull."

[15] There is also merit to Elster's (1979: 144) objection that genuine altruists would cease being altruists if and when they realized that the false altruists really are egoists.

ber is motivated to assume a share of the monitoring and sanctioning burden—by virtue of reciprocity.

GAMING STRATEGIES AMONG RATIONAL EGOISTS

If rational choice theorists have a Holy Grail, surely it is the concept
of the invisible hand, which provides for the establishment of a self-
sustaining and—in some sense—ethically justifiable social equilibrium
(Nozick 1974: 18–22). By transforming private vices into public virtues (as
Mandeville's famous phrase has it), this kind of equilibrium allows for the
possibility of order among rational egoists without the necessity of formal
controls. To what extent can an invisible-hand explanation account for
compliance in large groups or for social order?

In his sophisticated defense of anarchism, Michael Taylor (1976: 29–62)
claims that under certain conditions, prosocial behavior can result from
rational self-interested action in the absence of formal controls (cf. Williamson 1975, on peer groups). His argument is drawn from analyses of
the Prisoner's Dilemma game, but it also has implications for many other
kinds of exchanges as well (Hardin 1982). In the Prisoner's Dilemma both
players have the choice of acting cooperatively (and not confessing to some
joint criminal action) or defecting (that is, confessing). Each individual's
payoff depends on the other's choice, but each player's choice is not known
to the other. My best outcome occurs when I defect while you cooperate,
but if you decide to defect, I receive my second-worst outcome. We stand
to jointly gain most (and individually receive our second-best outcome) if
we both cooperate, but by doing so I risk receiving my worst outcome
(which occurs if you defect). Since the players are not in a position to make
enforceable contracts, neither can be certain how the other actually will
behave. It is easy to show that in single plays of this game each player's best
strategy is to defect. And most do just this.

Yet in situations where two players engage in repeated games with each
other, the optimal strategy may change. Now it may shift toward one of
contingent cooperation, or tit for tat. On the one hand, if I am convinced
that you will choose to cooperate in our next game—and if I know that we
will continue to play together indefinitely—then I am more likely to cooperate, in which case both of us will be better off. On the other hand, if I am
convinced that you will not cooperate, my best strategy is to defect. But
how can I ever be certain of your future intentions? The answer to this is
simple. If you cooperated in the past, it is reasonable to expect that you
will continue to do so under the same circumstances in the future.

Why should anyone rationally choose to cooperate in the *first* instance and thereby risk being a sucker who receives the least favorable outcome? Robert Axelrod (1984) has shown that the strategy of initial cooperation in tit for tat yields the best outcome against a large number of various alternative strategies (see also Axelrod and Hamilton 1981). Hence, this strategy will be selected in competition with alternatives. The people who stick to it will prosper more than those who resort to alternative strategies. If the others wish to improve their outcomes, they will have to convert to this most successful one. Does this provide an explanation of prosocial behavior that does not rely on formal, or third-party, controls?

Axelrod applies this theory to an arresting case, the live-and-let-live system of trench warfare during World War I. British and German troops who faced each other across the trenches routinely failed to engage in the constant battle demanded by their superiors. One British officer who had toured the trenches was

> astonished to observe German soldiers walking about within rifle range behind their own line. Our men appeared to take no notice. I privately made up my mind to do away with that sort of thing when we took over; such things should not be allowed. These people evidently did not know there was a war on. Both sides apparently believed in the policy of "live and let live."
>
> (Dugdale 1932: 94, cited in Axelrod 1984: 73–74)

The development of this system is taken as evidence that even among enemies a stable pattern of mutual cooperation can evolve on the basis of reciprocity. Both sides (note that this is really only a two-person game, where each army is a player) adopted the strategy of nondefection except in the case of the other's defection. This cooperative equilibrium rested, however, on each side's ability to monitor the enemy's behavior. Each side's monitoring capacity was extremely well developed, for defection (that is, aiming the artillery to kill the opposing troops) would have been readily apparent.

Monitoring is obviously important in this story; perhaps it is so obvious that Axelrod pays it little heed. This neglect is all the more curious because Axelrod is quite aware that monitoring difficulties are responsible for the *failure* of cooperation to emerge between officers and their own troops. The high commands of both armies desired to end these tacit truces. Yet, except in large battles, during which men were ordered to leave their trenches and risk their lives in charging enemy positions, the commanding officers' monitoring problems were acute:

After all, it was hard for a senior officer to determine who was shooting to kill and who was shooting with an eye to avoiding retaliation. The soldiers became expert at defeating the monitoring system, as when a unit kept a coil of enemy wire and sent a piece to headquarters whenever asked to prove that they had conducted a patrol of no-man's-land. What finally destroyed the live-and-let-live system was the institution of a type of incessant aggression that the headquarters could monitor. This was the raid, a carefully prepared attack on enemy trenches which involved from ten to two hundred men. Raiders were ordered to kill or capture the enemy in his own trenches. If the raid was successful, prisoners would be taken; and if the raid was a failure, casualties would be proof of the attempt. There was no effective way to pretend that a raid had been undertaken when it had not. And there was no effective way to cooperate with the enemy in a raid because neither live soldiers nor dead bodies could be exchanged.

(Axelrod 1984: 82)

Appearances can be deceptive. Although the logic of tit for tat may be superior in these two-person noncooperative games, it breaks down when there are more than two independent actors. The trench warfare example only works because each army acts as if it were an individual player. To engage rationally in tit for tat, one must be confident in one's estimate of the other party's future intentions. Past behavior is as good an indication as any, but this information can only come from previous monitoring activity. The larger the number of players, the more costly this monitoring will be.[16] It is one thing to argue that A can trust B only if A knows that there will be an opportunity to punish B when B does not cooperate. For this kind of logic to account for cooperation in large groups, every member of the group must know whether every other member will cooperate. But except in the smallest of groups, it is impossible for each member to have direct knowledge about the past behavior of every other member or even about a group of players who might be capable of forming a conditionally cooperative coalition (Schofield 1985).

All told, then, none of these game theoretic analyses can easily account for the emergence or maintenance of compliance in large groups without the leavening of substantial doses of formal control. Control may indeed

---

[16] Thus Michael Taylor (1976: 93) stresses that informal controls are most likely to arise in small and stable communities where the strong information requirements of his theory are likely to be satisfied. In a later work (Taylor 1982), however, he retreats from this moderate position by arguing that formal controls are required to prevent free riding even in (small) tribal societies and intentional communities.

be produced by an invisible hand, but its effects are limited to small groups alone.

Social theorists have always held out the hope that normative compliance and social order could arise in complex societies having extensive divisions of labor. Once the costliness of control is appreciated, attention naturally turns to the possibility that joint goods can be produced without recourse to costly formal sanctions. A variety of explanations of such prosocial behavior have been advanced. By and large, sociologists have gravitated towards arguments about socialization, whereas rational choice theorists have been attracted to selection and invisible-hand explanations. Do any of these explanations permit us to conclude that formal control mechanisms are unnecessary for group survival?

All but one of these theories themselves presuppose the existence of some control mechanisms—though not necessarily formal ones. The one exception—the biological theory—fails from the start, for it cannot account for the evolution of prosocial behavior in non-kin-related groups. The other selection explanation, the Rotten Kid Theorem, requires such fine-grained information (that is, monitoring capacity) that its efficacy in accounting for prosocial behavior is confined to the most intimate of groups. The game theorists' invisible-hand solution (tit for tat) also rests upon stringent informational requirements.[17]

Socialization theories fare somewhat better. Whereas direct reinforcement is merely another way of describing sanctioning—and sanctioning of the most costly variety at that—modelling does provide significant sanctioning economies. Yet if the members of some large group had been perfectly socialized so that each was a generalized altruist, formal controls would *still* be necessary to resolve coordination problems. And the larger the group, the greater the difficulty of coordinating members' behavior. Even Karl Marx, who usually railed against the necessity of control in social life, recognized that

> all combined labour on a large scale requires . . . a directing authority, in order to secure the harmonious working of the individual activities, and to

[17] That control is a requirement of rational choice models should be no surprise, for the concept of quid pro quo is fundamental to the economic theory of exchange. Not coincidentally, all of the preference-revealing techniques that public choice economists have proposed for the efficient allocation of collective goods—such as insurance purchase (Thompson 1966), demand-revealing (Vickrey 1961; Groves and Ledyard 1977), or voting by veto (Mueller 1978)—rely upon control mechanisms to achieve this outcome. In effect, each provides individuals with incentives to reveal their true preference for a collective good (Mueller 1979: 68–89). Once this preference is known, they can be assessed or taxed appropriately for its provision.

perform general functions that have their origin in the action of the combined organism, as distinguished from the action of its separate organs. A single violin player is his own conductor, an orchestra requires a separate one.

(Marx [1867] 1965, I: 330–31)

Although altruists may always be willing to act in the corporate interest, they have to know what action this requires of them. It may be a sad fact that too many cooks spoil the broth, but it is a fact nonetheless. One is thus forced to conclude that while it is possible for *small* groups to survive on the basis of informal controls, it is not possible for *large* ones to do so.

CHAPTER V

DEPENDENCE AND PARTY SOLIDARITY

Lawyers, businessmen, teachers, doctors, all face difficult personal decisions involving their integrity—but few, if any, face them in the glare of the spotlight as do those in public office. Few, if any, face the same dread finality of decision that confronts a Senator facing an important call of the roll. He may want more time for his decision—he may believe there is something to be said for both sides—he may feel that a slight amendment could remove all difficulties—but when that roll is called he cannot hide, he cannot equivocate, he cannot delay—and he senses that his constituency, like the Raven in Poe's poem, is perched there on his Senate desk, croaking "Nevermore" as he casts the vote that stakes his political future.

John F. Kennedy

ACCORDING TO THE theory, the extent of solidarity in any group is limited by its members' dependence. Since control is also a cause of solidarity in the theory, how can the separate role of dependence ever be assessed empirically? One solution is to examine measurable instances of solidarity that occur in the relative absence of variations in control capacity. Given that so much of social life resembles a seamless web, evidence of this sort is usually difficult to obtain. Yet one particular setting—the legislature—offers it in abundance.

Legislatures are an important site for the analysis of group solidarity on several accounts. First, both members (legislators) and their respective groups (parties) can be identified unequivocally because legislatures are closed systems with a limited number of parties and each legislator can be a member of only one party at a time. Composed solely of elected representatives, the legislative party is quite distinct from the extra-parliamentary organization that forms the party's base.

Second, it is relatively easy to specify the goals of individual members in advance of any analysis. The most parsimonious assumption is that they desire reelection and career advancement in the government and that their actions are generally consistent with, if not wholly determined by, their pursuit of these immanent goals (Downs 1957: 28). In order to realize these goals, legislators usually must join a political party. Reelection and career advancement in the legislature are, however, somewhat distinct goals. When legislators are compelled to choose between them, reelection is the more fundamental, for the ability to advance through the legislative ranks is a privilege only of those who are elected. This points to an unusual feature of the legislative party: *membership in its ranks is ultimately determined by nonmembers*—that is, by voters. These parties arose in the first place to represent constituents' interests; the origin of that unusual institution, the roll call, results from this aspect of the legislative party's mission.

The joint good that legislative parties seek is control of the government apparatus (cf. Downs 1957: 24–25). Government control gives the party a store of valued positions in the legislative and executive branches and great influence over the formation of state policy as well. In order to produce this good—to win control of the government or, once in power, to maintain it—the party counts on the allegiance of its members; in effect, they must act as a team.[1]

Because legislators are primarily interested in their individual fortunes, the party faces a potential free-rider problem. As a result, legislators' allegiance to the party (that is, their compliance with rules for producing the joint good) cannot be assumed. Thus the United States Congress has seen many mavericks in its day. How then does the party manage to obtain the loyalty of its members? It cannot *compensate* legislators for their loyalty because it does not employ them (the constituents do). Instead, when they join the party, legislators accept an *obligation* to support it. The degree to which they live up to this obligation is, of course, variable.

Third, it is possible to find indicators of all the theoretically relevant concepts—party solidarity, dependence, and control capacity. *Party solidarity*, the explicandum, is least difficult to measure. Much of what the legislator, like persons in most other kinds of groups, actually does as a party member is hidden from public scrutiny. Yet, unlike the members of most other groups, legislators are periodically obliged to make personal declarations on controversial questions in full public view and for the historical record. Each time they face a roll-call vote, legislators must decide (among other things) whether to vote with their party or not. Thus the roll call compels legislators to make decisions that test their compliance to party

[1]In parliamentary systems a party in opposition requires the loyalty of all its members, but this is not necessarily true of a governing party with a large electoral margin. Such a party can maintain its control even if some members are disloyal (the precise number depends, of course, on the party's margin of seats in the legislature). Despite this, however, party members are always urged to be loyal.

obligations. As a result, data on roll-call voting can serve as a relatively error-free and quantitative measure of the party loyalty of legislators and of the solidarity of their parties.[2]

Whereas the roll-call vote may have developed to enable constituents to monitor the behavior of their representatives, it also has the unintended consequence of providing each party with an equivalent monitoring capacity. What of their sanctioning capacities? Another mark of the legislative party's distinctiveness is that sanctioning is principally carried out not by other group members, but by nonmembers. If the voters disapprove of their legislators' performance, they can sanction them by preventing their reelection. Legislative parties themselves have no comparable sanction with which to discipline their disloyal members.[3] As a consequence, differences in party *control capacity* are liable to be relatively unimportant. Thus, if the theory is correct, most of the observed variation in solidarity should not be due to the different control capacities of the parties, but rather to differences in members' *dependence*.

The greater the value of party-derived benefits that aid legislators in their quest for reelection and career advancement, the greater their dependence on the party. Conversely, the greater the value of benefits available to them from alternative sources, the less their dependence on the party. Since legislative parties offer their members well-defined benefits, these can be used to indicate members' relative dependence. Parties offer one critical benefit: nomination. Gaining the party's nomination not only gives every candidate a place on the ballot—often in a position that reflects the overall popularity of the party—but the nomination, on average, is also worth a certain percentage of a constituency's votes. In some constituencies ("safe" seats) this percentage is large enough to guarantee electoral victory; in others ("marginal" seats) it is not. A party's ability to select candidates for particular constituencies is therefore an added benefit. Beyond this, some parties offer other kinds of resources that can benefit members. Thus, legislators in parties that play a large role in determining either reelection (say, by providing campaign funds) or career advancement (say, by offering important committee assignments or cabinet posts) are more dependent than those in parties that have fewer such resources.

The final advantage provided by the legislative party case is evidentiary. Not only are roll-call voting data extensive, but they exist in a variety of

---

[2] This is not to claim that roll-call data are entirely unproblematic. See Crane (1960) and Greenstein and Jackson (1963) for discussions of the validity of roll-call voting analysis.

[3] True, some of the most solidary parties on occasion expel dissident members (MacRae 1967: 103) or limit their access to campaign funds, but this discipline does not necessarily prevent candidates from being reelected under a different party's banner.

distinct institutional settings as well. Ever since A. L. Lowell's (1902) pioneering comparison of party voting in Britain and the United States, political scientists have been assembling and analyzing roll-call voting data in quantity. With the dawn of the computer age in social science, contributions to the study of legislative voting have increased at an exponential rate.[4] Though the rationale behind this research is different from mine, the findings emerging from this voluminous literature have clear implications for understanding the general causes of group solidarity.

For all of these reasons, then, legislative voting records provide a virtual laboratory for naturally occurring trials in group solidarity. The data indicate that both the loyalty of individual legislators and the solidarity of their parties vary considerably. To wit:

1. There are dramatic cross-national variations in the solidarity of major political parties. (The average level of solidarity for the major parties of Britain is high; for those in France and West Germany, moderate; and for those in the United States, relatively low.)

2. In parties having relatively low solidarity, individual delegates systematically differ in their party loyalty. (Republican congressmen from large cities with a significant foreign-stock population are less likely to be loyal than colleagues elected from rural Midwestern districts.)

3. In parties having relatively low solidarity, party voting occurs more frequently on some types of roll calls than on others. (Party solidarity is higher on procedural than on substantive votes.)

4. Some parties are more solidary than others in the same legislative system. (French and West German Communist and Socialist parties are more solidary than their bourgeois counterparts.)

5. Levels of party solidarity can vary over the long run within the same country. (In the United States, Democratic and Republican solidarity was considerably greater in the 1890s than it has been at any subsequent time.)

What accounts for these variations in the loyalty of individual legislators and in the solidarity of their parties? The theory suggests that legislators will comply with their obligation to vote with their party on roll calls to the degree that they are dependent upon it, rather than upon other sources,

---

[4]A very select group of important contributions includes Rice (1928); Turner (1951); MacRae (1958); Truman (1959); Shannon (1968); Fiorina (1974); Mayhew (1974); and Kingdon (1977).

for valued benefits. Differences in members' dependence, in turn, can result from a variety of factors—including the legislator's individual attributes, constituency characteristics, the party's extra-parliamentary organization, and certain features of legislative institutions and regime types.

LEGISLATORS' DEPENDENCE ON THE PARTY FOR REELECTION

Since reelection is ultimately in the hands of constituents, it is to be expected that legislators will curry their constituents' favor before complying with party obligations. Now when the interests of constituents converge with the party's policies, legislators should vote consistently with these two. But when party policy is at variance with the constituents' interests, then party voting should decrease. Legislators may woo organized single-purpose interest groups to aid in their reelection efforts, but this should have no determinate effects on their overall patterns of party voting.

To the degree that the party can extend significant benefits to legislators, however, they should become increasingly Janus-faced. Because all parties offer at least some benefits to legislators (else why do they belong?), they should try to comply with party obligations whenever possible so as to gain maximum benefit. Where votes on party matters do not directly affect constituents (as is the case on procedural roll calls), legislators should therefore cast loyal party votes.

One can no doubt see exceptions to these simple propositions. When nomination carries with it the prospect of certain reelection, legislators will depend on whoever determines the party nomination. If party leaders have the power to arbitrarily assign candidates to particular constituencies out of the public eye, this will increase legislators' dependence on them, for assignment to a safe seat provides a virtual guarantee of reelection. All else equal, parties having this power should have higher party solidarity. If, however, candidate selection occurs through direct primaries, party voting should diminish.

Does the differential dependence of legislators on their parties affect voting solidarity in the expected ways?

Constituency Characteristics

In general, party voting should decline when the interests of the constituency and party diverge. Political parties derive support from a variety of constituencies. Some, known in the literature as "typical" constituencies, contain the safe seats that are the base of the party's strength. Naturally, the party tends to advocate policies that reflect the interests of its core support-ers. Invariably, however, the party also wins some marginal seats in "atypi-cal" constituencies. By definition, the interests of the voters in these dis-tricts tend to be at variance with the party's stated policies. It follows that legislators who represent typical constituencies should be greater party loy-alists than those who represent atypical districts (Mayhew 1966: 23; Fio-rina 1974: Ch. 1).

American congressional elections provide considerable supportive evi-dence, at least when constituency interest is assumed to be indicated by the crude socio-demographic characteristics of the voting district. One study of the 1964 Congress provides evidence for both Democrats and Republi-cans (Turner and Schneier 1970: 223–25). During this period, the Demo-cratic party had quite different bases of support in the North and South. Then, as now, the core of the party lay in the Northern industrial cities with large immigrant and black populations. Constituencies composed of these kinds of voters are the most typical Democratic districts. However, the Southern party was dominated by urban white Dixiecrats of native stock; they constituted an atypical group having a different political stripe. In reaction to the influence of the Dixiecrats, Southern blacks tended to support the Republicans. Therefore, constituencies with large rural black populations were the most atypical from the perspective of the Democratic leadership. As anticipated, the average party loyalty scores of Democratic representatives varied from a low of 39, for those representing the least typical districts (southern rural black), to a high of 85, for those from the most typical constituencies (Northern metropolitan districts with a large immigrant population) (Table 1).

The Republican results are also consistent with these expectations (Table 2). At this time the party's strongest support came from Midwestern farmers and from the native-born more generally. Consequently, its most loyal representatives were from rural native Midwestern districts (with an average score of 84), whereas its least loyal members represented coastal metropolitan districts with a large proportion of immigrants (44).

Further, the loci of power in the two parties had shifted in 1932, when urban Northern Democrats usurped power from rural Southerners and the social base of the Republicans correspondingly shifted from Northern cities to the rural Midwest, and previously loyal representatives had be-come insurgents while the former insurgents had been transformed into loy-alists (Turner and Schneier 1970: 4). All told, these data indicate that Re-publicans from solidly Republican districts vote Republican, while those from marginally Republican districts do so less frequently—and similarly for Democrats.

TABLE I.   Effect of Conflicting Pressures on Democratic Loyalty:
Average Indices of Loyalty of Democrats with Different Attributes in
Constituencies, 1964

Attributes of Districts	Number of Members of Congress	Average Indices of Loyalty
Least Typical		
▲ Southern Rural Native Black[a]	9	39
Southern Rural Native Mixed[b]	32	50
Southern Rural Native White	18	58
Southern Metropolitan Native Mixed[b]	12	63
Southern Metropolitan Native White	11	69
Northern Rural Native	31	73
Northern Rural Mixed[c]	7	85
Northern Metropolitan Native	27	79
Northern Metropolitan Mixed[c]	58	84
▼ Northern Metropolitan Foreign[d]	27	85
Most Typical		

SOURCE: Turner and Schneier (1970: 223).

NOTE: Includes all Democrats except those representing one Southern metropolitan black district and one Southern rural foreign district. The index of party loyalty of each Democratic member of Congress is the percentage of votes cast with the majority of Democrats on a roll call when that majority is opposed by the majority of Republicans.

[a] More than 40 percent black.
[b] Between 20.0 and 39.9 percent black.
[c] Between 20.0 and 39.9 percent foreign stock.
[d] More than 40 percent foreign stock.

Studies of this type presume that constituency characteristics have a constant weight in influencing the legislator's vote. However, Fiorina (1974) challenges this assumption. Fiorina argues that constituencies whose populations have relatively homogeneous interests are more capable of exerting determinate, concerted pressure on their delegates than are constituencies characterized by relatively heterogeneous interests. In the latter districts, the legislator's vote should merely correspond with the interests of one particular subgroup within the district; therefore it will not be representative of the preference of the district as a whole. In practice, this means that the votes of legislators from heterogeneous districts will not be a function of the socio-demographic characteristics of the districts themselves.

TABLE 2. Effect of Conflicting Pressures on Republican Loyalty: Average Indices of Loyalty of Republicans with Different Attributes in Constituencies, 1964

Attributes of Districts	Number of Members of Congress	Average Indices of Loyalty
Most Typical		
⬆ Rural Native Interior	34	84
Metropolitan Native Interior	29	77
Rural Mixed[a] Interior	8	76
Metropolitan Mixed Interior	13	76
Rural Native Coastal	13	76
Metropolitan Native Coastal	14	75
Rural Mixed Coastal	15	68
Metropolitan Mixed Coastal	38	59
⬇ Metropolitan Foreign[b] Coastal	8	44
Least Typical		

SOURCE: Turner and Schneier (1970: 225).

NOTE: The index of party loyalty of each Republican member of Congress is the percentage of votes cast with the majority of Republicans on a roll call when that majority is opposed by the majority of Democrats.

[a] Between 20.0 and 39.9 percent foreign stock.

[b] More than 40 percent foreign stock.

Party voting evidently depends on both the concurrence of the homogeneity and the typicality of the district. The representative from a homogeneous district with interests similar to those of the party should be a party loyalist, while the representative from a homogeneous district with interests frequently at odds with the party should be a renegade. Similarly with heterogeneous districts. If it is simplistically assumed that there are two factions of equal weight within a district, on any given vote at least one of these factions should take the party line. If the party itself exercises any influence, the representative should vote with the party frequently. That is, the anticipation of receiving benefit from the party should tip the balance in favor of the party line. The situation is obviously more complex in districts with more than two factions, and when these factions are not equally weighted.

Recent research presents new evidence on other aspects of legislators' behavior that is consistent with this analysis. While some amount of every candidate's electoral support is due to factors beyond personal control—relatively fixed constituency characteristics such as class, religion, and ethnicity; reactions to macroeconomic fluctuations; or evaluations of the party head's performance—each legislator has an incentive to build a personal base of support within the district that is independent of popular reactions to national conditions. The most common means of doing this is to engage in a variety of service activities—by helping constituents in their dealings with the state bureaucracy and by advancing the particularistic interests of the locality (Cain, Ferejohn, and Fiorina 1984). Naturally, some legislators spend more time servicing their districts than others, and the best predictor of the amount of their constituency service is the marginality of their seat, both in the United States and in the United Kingdom (Cain, Ferejohn, and Fiorina 1983). Presumably, the occupants of marginal seats feel more insecure about their reelection prospects and therefore have a greater need to do what they can in order to further these prospects than those in safe seats.

Procedural versus Substantive Votes

One way to interpret the relationship between constituency characteristics and party voting is to say that it is due to the relative costliness of party votes to legislators in atypical districts. If this is so, then in one context the cost of a party vote is sharply reduced. When votes on party matters do not directly affect constituents, most legislators—even those from the most atypical constituencies—will tend to be party loyalists, for loyalty in this situation allows them to live up to their party obligations costlessly.

This contention is supported by evidence that the most solidary roll calls in the American House of Representatives are on procedural rather than substantive issues. The highest levels of party voting in the House occur on votes selecting the Speaker of the House and other congressional officers (Table 3). Procedural votes—appeals from the ruling of the chair, motions to adjourn, and other challenges to the authority of the Speaker—also produce high levels of solidarity. Finally, motions to recommit bills tend to produce more party solidarity than the roll calls on final passage. These findings are usually explained by procedural questions having low public visibility and thus being unlikely to offend constituents: "Roll calls on most recommittal motions are somewhat less visible because the electorate, at least, is likely to have difficulty in understanding what is involved in such a vote" (Froman and Ripley 1965: 59). Since most legislators want to go along with party leaders whenever possible, procedural votes "provide an opportunity for Congressmen who face strong pressures from their

TABLE 3.   Party Cohesion on All Contested House Roll Calls by Category, 1961–1963

Category	1961 (%)	Rank	1962 (%)	Rank	1963 (%)	Rank	Average (%)	Rank
Democrats								
Election of Speaker	100.0	1	100.0	1	100.0	1	100.0	1
Rules	83.7	4	90.2	2	94.0	2	90.6	2
Miscellaneous Procedure	81.2	5	83.3	5	89.2	3	84.5	4
Final Passage	84.3	3	85.9	3	85.6	5	85.2	3
Recommittal Motions	86.9	2	85.6	4	80.9	6	84.1	5
Conference Reports	77.2	7	82.2	6	89.2	4	82.6	6
Amendments	77.4	6	73.6	7	79.8	7	76.6	7
Republicans								
Election of Speaker	100.0	1	100.0	1	100.0	1	100.0	1
Rules	80.0	4	75.7	7	79.0	6	77.9	6
Miscellaneous Procedure	91.8	2	87.2	2	97.6	2	91.9	2
Final Passage	77.9	5	77.1	4	78.8	7	78.0	5
Recommittal Motions	87.7	3	85.4	3	89.9	3	87.8	3
Conference Reports	76.1	6	77.0	5	81.8	5	78.1	4
Amendments	72.5	7	75.9	6	89.0	4	77.7	7

SOURCE: Froman and Ripley (1965: 57).

NOTE: "Contested roll calls" are those with more than ten dissenting votes. The figures in this table represent the percentage of Democrats and the percentage of Republicans voting alike on the roll calls analyzed.

constituencies to go at least part of the way with the leadership" (Turner and Schneier 1970: 44).[5]

[5] Note that the existence of the roll call makes it feasible for party members to expend resources influencing one another. If there were no means of accountability in voting, logrolling and other exchanges (Coleman 1973) would not exist, for any such agreements could not be enforceable.

Candidate Selection

To the degree that parties—rather than constituents or interest groups—select candidates, their influence on reelection is much extended. By assigning safe seats to some candidates and marginal ones to others, the party can almost surely determine which of their members will be reelected. In this circumstance, prudent legislators are more likely to vote the party line, even when this leads them to vote against the interests of their constituents.

Party control over candidate selection is one of the factors that has been held to contribute to the higher voting solidarity of British than of American parties (Schattschneider 1942: 99–100; Finer 1949: 243; for a cautionary note, however, see Ranney 1968). In Britain, the final local party selections are made by procedures that are drawn up and enforced entirely by the parties themselves. Candidates are selected

> in secret by small bodies of local dues-paying party activists; local party officers count the ballots and report the results; and deviations from the prescribed procedures are appealed to national party officials, not to the courts or other public authorities. The British system rests upon the prevailing belief that political parties are purely private associations, like garden clubs or societies to end cruel sports; hence their internal affairs, such as the way they select their parliamentary candidates, are no concern of the law or general public.
>
> (Ranney 1968: 145)

In contrast, most final local party selections in the United States are determined by direct primaries under procedures that are almost identical with those used in general elections. The rules are enforced by the state, not by the parties themselves; candidates' campaigns are conducted openly; all eligible voters, no matter how little committed to the party, can participate in the selection of its candidates; and public officials count the ballots and enforce the procedures.

These differences have led many observers to believe that the American primary system, which gives nominating power to party voters at large rather than to party leaders, contributes to its greater party disloyalty (Sorauf 1964: 98–204; Key 1964: 454; Schattschneider 1942: 99–100). This logic explains why the American electoral reforms of the 1970s, which decreased the party's influence in presidential nomination by more than doubling the number of states holding direct primaries, have contributed to lower party solidarity (Fiorina 1980).

Campaign Finances

Election is always a costly process, and in societies where there are no ceilings on expenditures these costs have tended to rise dramatically. Legislators therefore must acquire financial support to defray their campaign expenses. There are several possible sources of financial support. As a last resort, wealthy legislators have the ability to fund their own campaigns, although they would always prefer not to do so. Of course, those who are unable to subsidize their own campaigns must turn elsewhere for funds— to constituents, to interest groups (in the United States, political action committees [Jacobson 1983: 49–59]), or to their own political party. The party, therefore, is only one of four potential sources of campaign funding to which legislators have recourse. Legislators' dependence on the party increases to the degree that it is their *predominant* source of campaign funds.

But some parties have greater campaign funds than others. Robert Michels once noted that

> a party which has a well-fitted treasury is in a position, not only to dispense with the material aid of its comparatively affluent members, and thus to prevent the acquirement by these of a preponderant influence in the party, but also to provide itself with a body of officials who are loyal and devoted because they are entirely dependent on the party for their subsistence. Before the year 1906, when the payment of members was conceded by the German state, the German Socialist Party had provided the salaries of its deputies. In this way the party leaders, poor men for the most part, were enabled to enter parliament without being in a position to emancipate themselves from the party, or to detach themselves from the majority of the parliamentary group of socialists—as has happened in France with the formation of the group of "independent Socialists."

> ([1911] 1962: 142)

The relatively large treasuries of socialist and communist parties help explain why these parties have higher solidarity than their bourgeois counterparts in France and West Germany (see Tables 4 and 5).

What accounts for the comparative financial strength of the left-wing parties? In good part it is their extra-parliamentary party organizations. Parties with large treasuries are often based on mass membership organizations, whereas those with small treasuries are often based on a cadre-type organization (Duverger 1963).

Cadre parties are often made up of legislators with independent means, for their candidates must themselves raise a considerable portion of their

TABLE 4. Average Cohesion of French Parties in the Lower House of *Parlement* during Four Selected Periods, 1910–1953

Party or *Groupe*	Period			
	1910	*1930*	*1946–1951*	*1951–1953*
Communiste	——	100	100	100
Socialiste	96.2	98	97	98
Radical Socialiste	76.8	91	——	——
Radical	——	——	60	69
Républicain Socialiste	75.0	37	——	——
Gauche Radical	82.0	53	——	——
Démocratique et Social	——	94	——	——
Gauche Démocratique	77.8	——	——	——
UDSR (Union Démocratique et Socialiste de la Résistance)	——	——	72.3	74.3
Démocratique Populaire	——	91	——	——
MRP (Mouvement Républicain Populaire)	——	——	94.0	72.0
Républicain Progressiste	92.2	——	——	——
Gauche Républicain	——	92	——	——
Républicain Indépendant	——	——	50.6	81.8
Action Libérale Populaire	87.4	——	——	——
RPF (Rassemblement du Peuple Français)	——	——	91.3	72.2
Indépendant	75.6	77	——	——
Droite	92.4	——	——	——

SOURCE: Turner and Schneier (1970: 23).
NOTE: Measured by the index of party cohesion. This is obtained by subtracting the percentage of party members voting in a minority on the roll call from the percentage whose votes constitute a majority of the party's representatives.

costs of nomination and election. Before the days of heavy political involvement by interest groups, independent means were virtually a precondition for all the party's candidates, regardless of their political predilections. Thus, the late nineteenth-century British Liberal party (which was based upon a cadre-type organization) always nominated bourgeois candidates to represent working-class constituencies. The growing working-class movement decried this practice but was powerless to elect representatives from its own ranks until the creation of a new kind of party organization— one, like the Labour Party's, that was based on dues generated by mass membership.

TABLE 5. Average Cohesion of Political Parties in the West German *Bundestag* during Three Selected Periods, 1949–1961

Party	Period		
	1949–1953 (*130 roll calls*)	*1953–1957* (*155 roll calls*)	*1957–1961* (*46 roll calls*)
SPD (Social Democratic Party)	99.8	99.4	99.6
CDU/CSU (Christian Democratic Union/Christian Social Union)	87.2	90.0	94.0
FDP (Free Democratic Party)	82.6	79.0	92.6
DP (German Party)	79.6	80.4	88.0

SOURCE: Loewenberg (1967: 357) as computed by Ozbudun (1970: 318).

By spreading the costs of election equally among adherents, parties based on mass membership organizations make possible the nomination and election of representatives having no independent means of support. This gives the leaders of mass membership parties a powerful tool with which to achieve solidary voting. Particularly before the advent of universal free education, but even today as well, the mass membership party provides an important channel of mobility for workers and the members of disadvantaged minority groups. Mass membership parties do, in fact, tend to select fewer candidates with independent means than the candidates of cadre parties. During the Fourth French Republic—a period for which particularly good evidence exists—the French Communist Party put up disproportionate numbers of working-class candidates; the Socialists did likewise for public school teachers. The cadre parties of the center and right, however, recruited the bulk of their candidates from the liberal professions and from owners and managers (MacRae 1967: 51–53). Clearly, manual workers who escape their role in production—or public school teachers who leave the tedium of their classrooms—by entering the political arena are much more dependent on their party than legislators whose extra-parliamentary options are more favorable (Kriegel 1972: 198–200).

Not only are the legislators in cadre-type parties likely to have independent means, but they are also more likely to have bases of political support that are independent of their party. Thus in France, where legislators are permitted to hold national and local offices simultaneously (the practice is known as the *cumul*), cadre parties consistently had more members with multiple offices than any of the mass membership parties during the Fourth Republic (MacRae 1967: 54). Such differences in candidate selection have direct effects on party solidarity, for parties whose candidates have independent bases of support will have greater difficulty in maintaining solidarity.

If sizeable party treasuries contribute to party voting, legal restrictions on the party's role in campaign financing serve to erode it. A recent example is provided by the American electoral reforms of the 1970s, which limited the ability of parties to finance the campaigns of presidential candidates. Previous to these reforms, national parties played a significant role in financing presidential campaigns. But during the 1970s the rules changed. Serious presidential candidates were subsequently financed publicly, and the law currently obliges the candidate to set up a finance committee separate from the national party. Other limits on contributions and expenditures have extended the role of political action committees in the financing of congressional campaigns (Jacobson 1983) at the expense of party organizations. Although American parties have traditionally been among the least solidary of any democratic parties, these reforms have led to even lower levels of solidarity by severely limiting the party's benefits. And this has occurred at a time when candidates have become more reliant on public opinion polling, the media, and the use of modern marketing methods—services that increasingly can be provided by consultants who are independent of the formal party apparatus.

Legislative rules also affect the party's control over reelection resources. For example, "British governments have rigorously suppressed everything likely to enable the individual members to build up independent support—residence requirements, private bills, services to constituents, personal expertise" (Huitt 1969: 141). Even legislative salary levels can have an effect: to the degree that they are high, some party-derived benefits invariably lose their lustre; low salaries have the opposite effect (Michels [1911] 1962: 138).

LEGISLATORS' DEPENDENCE ON THE PARTY FOR PATRONAGE

To this point, the analysis has focussed exclusively on the party's relative capacity to facilitate reelection. But legislators have another goal as well— career advancement. If the theory holds, parties that can offer their members plum committee assignments, cabinet portfolios, and other valued offices should be more solidary than those that have no such patronage to dispense. Variations in legislative systems and structures crucially affect the capacities of parties to supply patronage to their members.

Legislative Divisions of Labor

Though a large treasury is an important resource available to legislators in their quest for reelection, patronage has direct implications for the course of their legislative careers. Party voting should vary directly with the party's ability to dispense patronage. But the same question arises once more in this realm—namely, to what extent do legislators depend on the party—as against other sources—as a supplier of patronage?

One factor that affects the party's control over patronage is the legislative division of labor. Legislatures have varying divisions of labor, or degrees of centralization. The American House of Representatives has a wide division: it is constituted by numerous legislative committees that exercise control over the fate of bills falling under their purview. Membership on some of these committees, such as Ways and Means, is sufficient to bestow power and influence on a legislator. To chair a powerful House committee is a career in itself. The committee structure, therefore, represents a basis of power and influence that is orthogonal to that of the party. On the other hand, the role of legislative committees in relatively undifferentiated (centralized) systems like the British House of Commons is minimal (Huitt 1969: 141).

In a system with considerable legislative differentiation and strong committees, the procedures by which legislators are assigned to these committees evidently take on great importance. To the degree that party leaders control committee and chair assignments, legislators' dependence on them grows. In these circumstances, high levels of voting solidarity should be found. But, in a system where committee assignments are determined according to a seniority rule, the dependence of legislators on the party is substantially reduced. Since seniority effectively reduces the legislators' dependence on the party, it should decrease party solidarity.

The point is well illustrated by the history of American political parties. During some periods in the nineteenth century, American parties had greater solidarity than their British counterparts (Lowell 1902: 538–41). Subsequently, however, American party solidarity suffered a long secular decline. The adoption of a seniority rule that governed committee assignments in 1910 helps explain this decline. Previous to 1910, committee assignments were under the unilateral control of the Speaker of the House, who, as leader of the majority party delegation, was endowed with formidable powers. The Speaker had the formal power to name committees

TABLE 6. The Growth of Seniority, 1881–1963:
Violations of Seniority in the Appointment of Committee Chairmen in the
U.S. House of Representatives

Congress	Year	Party	Senior-ity Fol-lowed	Senior-ity Not Followed	Total[a] Commit-tees	Percentage of Party Votes in Selected Years[b]
47	1881	R	2	37	39	
48	1883	D	8	30	38	
49	1885		21	19	40	
50	1887		20	21	41 ⎫	13.6 (1887–89)
51	1889	R	20	27	47 ⎬	
52	1891	D	12	35	47	
53	1893		25	24	49	
54	1895	R	13	39	52	
55	1897		36	16	52 ⎫	50.9 (1897–99)
56	1899	R	42	15	57 ⎬⎫	
57	1901		49	8	57 ⎭	49.3 (1899–1901)
58	1903	R	43	11	54	
59	1905		51	8	59	
60	1907		45	13	58	
61	1909		42	18	60	
62	1911	D	25	27	52	
63	1913		33	20	53	
64	1915		50	6	56	
65	1917		45	10	55	
66	1919	R	35	22	57	
67	1921		44	15	59	28.6 (1921)
68	1923		40	17	57	
69	1925	R	37	22	59	
70	1927		43	1	44	7.1 (1928)
71	1929		38	7	45	
72	1931	D	27	18	45	31.0 (1930–31)
73	1933	D	38	7	45	22.5 (1933)
74	1935	D	32	13	45	
75	1937		42	4	46	11.8 (1937)
76	1939	D	37	9	46	
77	1941		39	7	46	
78	1943		34	11	45	10.7 (1944)
79	1945		37	9	46	17.5 (1945)
80	1947	R	9	4	13	15.1 (1947)
81	1949	D	19	0	19	16.4 (1948)
82	1951		18	0	18	
83	1953	R	17	1	18	
84	1955	D	19	0	19	
85	1957		19	0	19	
86	1959		19	0	19	
87	1961	D	20	0	20	
88	1963	D	20	0	20	

SOURCES: Polsby, Gallaher, and Rundquist (1971: Table 1); Shannon (1968: 42).
[a] Total equals the number of committees in the Congress minus the number of new committees in which the three top members in the previous Congress are absent in the present Congress. The latter are excluded because there are no data on members below the number-three position in the previous Congress.
[b] A party vote is one on which 90 percent or more of the members of one party opposed 90 percent or more of the members of the other.

from top to bottom, majority and minority. He was expected to use this power to enhance his ability to lead his party to legislative success. His allies expected to be favored, his rivals to be placated (Polsby, Gallaher, and Rundquist 1971: 182). In addition to this, the Speaker had the power to determine the schedule of business, recognize members on the floor, appoint members to conference committees, and dispense favors of various kinds (Jones 1968). For reasons that need not detain us at this time (but see Polsby, Gallaher, and Rundquist 1971), the powers of the Speaker came under attack in the House in 1910. Thereafter, a rapidly declining proportion of committee chairmanships violated the seniority rule until, in 1947, a full-fledged seniority system was adopted in the House. Levels of party voting declined in consequence (Table 6).

Another oft-cited cause of the decreasing solidarity of American parties is the decline of competition in congressional elections (Turner and Schneier 1970: 37–39; Jones 1964; Ferejohn 1977). This has resulted in an increase in the number of safe seats and therefore of incumbents. Most of the advantages of incumbency are well appreciated and need not be mentioned here. But one advantage that is not so apparent is that in the American system, in which seniority plays such an important role in the legislator's career, the incumbent legislator is less dependent on the party than the first-termer, who is more subject to the whims of party leaders, as in the process of committee assignment (Shepsle 1978: Ch. 9).

Legislative Regimes

One of the fundamental institutional factors that affects legislators' party dependence is the extent of separation of executive and legislative powers in the regime (Lowell 1902; Ranney 1968; Ozbudun 1970: 380; Epstein 1967: 35; for a qualifying view, see Turner and Schneier 1970: 17–18). Most parliamentary systems have little separation of powers: when the government loses its legislative majority, the executive is compelled to resign. Most presidential systems, on the other hand, have a considerable separation of powers: presidents are elected to set terms and maintain their tenure in office regardless of shifts in legislative margins. Legislators in these different types of regimes have quite different incentives to be party voters. When legislators' access to patronage hinges entirely on the party's maintenance of a legislative majority (as it does in most parliamentary regimes), then their dependence on the party is high; they have a strong incentive to vote with the party and to encourage other party members to do likewise.[6] If access to patronage does not hinge on any given legislative

---

[6] Differences in voting procedures and even in the architecture of the legislative body can also affect the legislator's vote (Miller 1971: 138; Turner and Schneier 1970: 33, n. 31).

vote (as occurs in most presidential regimes), however, then party dependence, and, correspondingly, the incentive for party voting, is considerably weakened.

This factor explains why, despite its cadre form of organization, the British Conservative party is nevertheless highly solidary. Tory legislators have much greater dependence on their party than the representatives of the American cadre-type parties. When the Conservatives are in power, they directly control the executive branch of government, giving them dispensation over a large number of important government offices, ministerial posts, knighthoods, and other honors (Jackson 1968). Access to patronage therefore depends to a great extent upon party solidarity. The prospect of receiving party patronage is even a viable inducement to loyalty among opposition party members. Opposition party legislators have a personal interest in the parliamentary fate of their party, since only a victorious party is in a position to dispense patronage.

In the United States, where executive and legislative powers are divided, the situation is quite different. The president, senators, and representatives all continue in office until their constitutional terms expire, regardless of what happens to the administration's legislative program. The only direct and immediate consequences of congressional votes are programmatic, not electoral. Further, the presidential party can rule without maintaining a congressional majority.

> The individual legislators of a governing (or potentially governing) party have an entirely rational motivation for cohesion in a parliamentary system that they do not have under the separation of powers. Each parliamentary vote on an important policy involves the question of whether the MP wants a cabinet of his party or of the opposition. Thus each vote becomes a party vote in a sense politically meaningful to the individual MP. . . . No such incentive operates with sufficient force to impel American Congressmen, under the separation of powers, to be so cohesive.
>
> (Epstein 1964: 56)

Since American legislators are less dependent on the party's fortunes than their British colleagues, the group solidarity theory suggests that their parties should demand *less extensive obligations* of them. And this is precisely what seems to occur. Party dissidents are treated quite differently in the two systems. Party dissidence has occurred so often in the history of the United States Senate that the role of maverick has been institutionalized. Senators like LaFollette, Sr., Borah, Langer, Byrd, Morse, Douglas, and Proxmire, among others, established themselves as mavericks and were accepted by their colleagues as playing a legitimate role (Huitt 1961).

The contrast with Britain—at least until the 1970s[7]—could hardly be more marked. Despite the fact that the Labour Party has long been split into left- and right-wing factions, when the left-wing faction was in opposition, it took care never to threaten the party's majority.

> Despite their disenchantment with some of the policies of the [Parliamentary Labour Party] and the lower probability they have had of achieving governmental rewards, it is likely that even most left-wing members have stood to gain more in light of their overall policy objectives and feelings of party identification by working to maintain or achieve a Labour government in preference to the Conservative alternative. To do this required that members of the left wing limit the extent and perhaps also the number of their rebellions, for the price of defeating their party might have been to enable the Conservatives either to gain or to sustain power. All of this appears to be well recognized by the left wing itself. When Labour was in power, Michael Foot, one of the leaders of the left wing, said that none of the left wing rebellions "has threatened to destroy the Government. [The left wing] knows how damaging that could be to the whole future of the Labour Party and the broader Labour movement."
>
> (Schwarz and Shaw 1976: 146)

In a parliamentary system, then, the prospect of receiving official and honorific rewards is thus contingent, to some degree, on the team play of legislators in a way that does not hold in presidential regimes (Ranney 1968: 154–55). Differences in the legislative separation of powers therefore help account for the fact that the highest level of party solidarity occurs in Britain and the lowest in the United States, while France and West Germany (which have somewhat mixed systems in this respect; see Schwarz and Shaw 1976) have intermediate levels (Table 7).

If party voting is motivated by the prospect of access to party-derived patronage, presumably this inducement should be weaker among the members of minority parties within parliamentary regimes—those having

---

[7]In the 1970s the United Kingdom House of Commons began witnessing a significant increase in backbencher disloyalty. One study (Schwarz 1980: 20–37) comparing rival explanations of this phenomenon concludes that the decline in party loyalty in this decade was due to the weakening of the parliamentary rule that obliged a government to resign if it lost a roll-call vote. In the 1970s British governments ceased to resign automatically in the face of roll-call defeats. This change in the rules of the game altered the benefit/cost calculations of legislative actors: party disloyalty suddenly became less onerous. The causes of this apparent shift in the institutional arrangements of the House of Commons are not fully understood.

TABLE 7. Voting Cohesion of Twelve Legislative and Parliamentary Parties from the United States, Great Britain, France, and West Germany

Party	Percent of Voting Cohesion[a]	Periods
Communist (Fr)	99	1946–1951
	99	1951–1955
	99	1955–1958
	99	1963
	99	1966–1968
Conservative (Br)	99	1951–1955
	99	1955–1959
	99	1959–1964
	99	1964–1966
	99	1966–1968
Gaullist (Fr)	86	1951–1953
	99	1963
	97	1966–1968
Labour (Br)	98	1946–1950
	99	1959–1964
	99	1964–1966
	95	1966–1968
Socialist (Fr)	97	1946–1951
	97	1951–1955
	96	1955–1959
	99	1963
	99	1966–1968
SPD(WG)	99	1953–1957
	97	1957–1961
	99	1961–1965
Catholic (Fr)	90	1946–1951
	79	1951–1955
	91	1955–1959
	50	1963
	47	1963–1968
CDU/CSU/(WG)	85	1953–1957
	93	1957–1961
	78	1961–1965
FDP(WG)	72	1953–1957
	96	1957–1961
	78	1961–1965
Radical (Fr)	56	1946–1951
	61	1951–1955
	43	1955–1959
	85	1963
	90	1966–1968
Democrat (USA House/Senate)	below 67	1949–1970, yearly
Republican (USA House/Senate)	below 67	1949–1970, yearly

SOURCE: Schwarz and Shaw (1976: 153).
[a] Percentage of roll-call votes upon which 90 percent or more of the legislative party voted with the party. The number 99 means at least 99 percent and up to and including 100 percent.

little chance of organizing a government (or participating in a ruling coalition). Since the members of minority parties cannot realistically expect to profit from gaining control of the government apparatus, the prospect of receiving patronage cannot induce high levels of party voting. As expected, some minority parties, including the French Catholic Party, do not have high levels of solidarity (Table 7). Yet there are some unanticipated results in this table, as well. The French Communist and Socialist parties have higher-than-expected solidarity, whereas the French Radical Party has lower-than-expected solidarity.

How can the high solidarity of Communist and Socialist parties in France be explained for the years 1946–1963? If the high solidarity of these parties is not due to the hope of gaining control of the state apparatus, perhaps it has something to do with their extra-parliamentary organizations. Since the legislators in mass membership parties often are financially dependent on these organizations, this factor alone could account for their high levels of party solidarity. Another conceivable factor (though one for which quantitative evidence is scarce) is that such parties may have a significant capacity to sanction their members. This is probably true of the French Communist party (PCF), whose members are embedded in social as well as merely political networks. This probably subjects them to greater sanctions than those facing the members of most other legislative parties (Ross [1982] examines postwar centralization in the PCF). Even so, the role of social sanctions in the French Socialist party is probably not comparable.

If minority mass membership parties can have high solidarity, why did the French Radicals, who were often partners in government coalitions during the Third and Fourth Republics, have such low solidarity between 1946 and 1963? Perhaps the answer lies in the tenuous nature of coalition governments (Turner and Schneier 1970: 32). Legislators who have ministerial portfolios or who otherwise participate in the executive may vote against their party's policies when these threaten the governing coalition. But those who do not participate in the government have no comparable incentive for party disloyalty. Indeed, since cabinets in the Fourth Republic were generally drawn from among members of a relatively narrow range of centrist parties, the individual backbencher could sometimes view the overthrow of a party colleague as a means of career advancement by being included in a subsequent government. All told, a party's inclusion in a coalition government may diminish its solidarity voting by creating opposing incentives for its members: those whose basic interest is in the maintenance of the coalition are likely to vote differently from the rest. This explanation is only plausible, however, if a large proportion of the members of the party are participants in the government. Otherwise, the defecting legislators will be too few to significantly depress the overall rates of party voting. A test of this explanation must await further research.

Although the existing evidence on legislative party voting is far from ideal (Fiorina 1974), it is generally consistent with the claims about the role of member dependence made in the theory of group solidarity.[8] In fact, this is roughly the same kind of reasoning that has been used implicitly by students of political parties since the early works of Ostrogorski ([1902] 1964: Appendix) and Michels. The rapid increase of research on roll-call voting in the past seventy years has only strengthened the enthusiasm of most political analysts for explanations of this sort.[9]

Not only does the group solidarity theory anticipate these associations between individual characteristics, structural factors, and party solidarity, but the theory helps us to understand *why* these kinds of variables have the consequences for party solidarity that they do. The separation of legislative and executive powers, the typicality of constituencies, procedural and substantive votes, extra-parliamentary party organizations, seniority rules, and, finally, direct primaries all affect party solidarity through the same simple mechanism. In each instance, they do so by altering the legislator's dependence on the party for reelection and career advancement (Figure 1). Further, the factors that most directly impinge upon the legislator's dependence should have the strongest effects on party solidarity. But without a more rigorous multivariate analysis, it is impossible to gauge the *relative* importance of these different kinds of party resources and institutional structures.

The theory not only offers the prospect of explaining the factors now known to be associated with party solidarity, but it can be predictive as well. That is, any new factors that can be shown to affect the legislator's dependence must, as a consequence, be associated with party solidarity. In the United States, for example, downgrading the importance of primary

[8] Of course, this does not rule out the possibility that these findings might also be consistent with some other kind of theory.

[9] A great deal of work needs to be done to extend the logic of this kind of theory even to the example of legislative voting. At present no one has successfully attacked the problem of intersessional variation in party voting, for instance. There are also some peculiar findings that appear to show that mechanisms of party solidarity differ across parties (see, for example, Table 3; Mayhew 1966: 158; but also Fiorina 1974: 10). While some of the contributors to this field have thrown up their hands in the face of data that seem to be inconsistent with the most popular explanations of party solidarity, it should be clear that any such judgment is premature. As the number of determinants of party solidarity increases, so the methodological complexity of further analysis grows apace. Few, if any, studies of voting solidarity have been conducted with a proper respect for the inherent complexity of the problem.

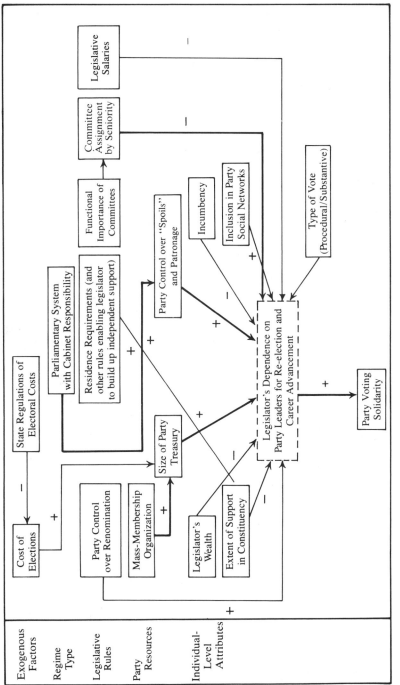

FIGURE 1   Some Factors Affecting Legislative Party Solidarity

Source: Michael Hechter, ed., *The Microfoundations of Macrosociology* (Philadelphia: Temple University Press, 1983).

elections, lifting limits on party campaign contributions, and stripping power from legislative committees each should result in increased levels of party solidarity.

Despite these promising signs, sociologists may remain unconvinced that evidence on party voting has any significance for the development of solidarity—or related phenomena, like collective action—in society at large.[10] It cannot be denied that legislators make up a peculiar sort of population. In most democracies they have decidedly bourgeois origins (Matthews 1961; Brady 1973: 14–19; of course, this is less true in mass membership parties, where working men and women penetrate into these positions) and cannot on this account be regarded as representative of their constituents. Further, politicians are popularly held to be notoriously opportunistic, if not wholly untrustworthy; they are considered to be the veritable incarnation of *Homo Œconomicus*. Why then should it be a surprise if a theory built on rational choice principles can account for the behavior of such obviously self-interested actors? But how useful is it in predicting the behavior of the average person? Perhaps the average person is willing to comply with group norms without the payoffs that are ostensibly required in order to curtail free-riding among legislators.[11]

Finally, the solidarity-building processes of most concern to sociologists occur in workplaces, neighborhoods, and voluntary associations—or in combinations of these—not in closed and highly structured settings such as legislative bodies. Are distinctive mechanisms of group solidarity likely to emerge in these different settings? There is no reason to think so, if only because recent students of social movements and collective action have also recognized the key role played by dependence mechanisms in their own research (Oberschall 1973; McCarthy and Zald 1977; Tilly 1978). Revolutionary and nationalist movements are likely to prosper only when they are able to make greater numbers of people dependent on them, rather than on

---

[10]As used here, the concept of group solidarity is different from that of collective action. When the members of a solidary group engage in some concerted activity (a strike, protest march, or revolution, for example), this is collective action. However, it is possible to conceive of a solidary group that for whatever reasons does not choose to act collectively in a given historical situation: it may collectively decide on a strategy of inaction, or wait-and-see. But this decision not to engage in collective action in no way implies the absence of solidarity (that is, compliance to group directives in the absence of compensation) in the group as a whole. Thus solidarity is conceived to be a necessary condition for all planned collective action, but it is by no means a sufficient one. For a formal theory of collective action, see Coleman (1973); see also D. Friedman (1983b).

[11]The extent to which legislators' voting behavior is a direct result of their self-interest has been the subject of a lively debate. Several economists (Kau and Rubin 1979; Kalt and Zupan 1984) have come to the conclusion that "ideology" is a better predictor of congressional voting behavior than narrow self-interest. For a study that disputes these claims, see Peltzman (1984).

traditional authorities. Successful revolutionary parties can win adherents by distributing land to poor peasants and by supplying them with better services than those provided by the existing regime (Popkin 1979).

Yet there is one feature of the legislative voting case that is distinctive and therefore bears reemphasis. The reason that dependence does so well in explaining legislators' voting behavior is not that politicians are particularly self-interested actors. Rather it is that the institution of the roll call itself provides constituents, party colleagues, and all other interested observers with a readily available means of monitoring their representatives' voting behavior. Presumably, voting outcomes would differ if the roll call were replaced by the secret ballot, for rational egoists will not routinely comply with the wishes of any group if their behavior cannot be monitored. Similarly, voice votes should enable legislators to express their own preferences much more readily than roll calls. Needless to say, this extraordinarily great monitoring capacity is unique to legislative parties. In fact, the evidence needed to assess the group solidarity theory must always be a by-product of some monitoring system. Since legislatures are the only natural social setting for which evidence of this quality exists, formal tests of the theory in other kinds of social groups must await new data collection efforts.

Imperfect monitoring is not a problem for social scientists alone, however; more fundamentally, it is a problem facing group members themselves. Because most groups have nowhere near the monitoring capacity of legislative parties, they must employ alternative mechanisms of control.

CHAPTER VI

THE PRODUCTION OF
FORMAL CONTROLS

Man, by the construction of his body, and the disposition of his mind, is
a creature formed for society. The body, being subject to infirmity and
disease, is exposed to difficulties that would involve him in despair and
death, but for the friendly aid of his fellow-mortal, whose sympathetic
nature prompts him to cheer and alleviate the anguish of an afflicted
brother. — The mind, a much more exalted and active principle, would
suffer much in its energy, and more in its enjoyments, was it denied the
mutual comforts and advantages of society. . . . The vicissitudes to which
mankind are liable, are as numerous as they are various, and happen to
the wise and good, as well as to the inconsiderate; it is a duty, therefore,
everyone owes to the community at large, to encourage every attempt cal-
culated to soften and relieve the wants of others, whilst it holds out the
same prospect to themselves, should the Providence of Almighty God
reduce them to circumstances requiring it.

from the *Rules and Regulations* of The Good Intent Society,
instituted at Newcastle upon Tyne, July 12, 1813

R ATIONAL CHOICE theorists have never had any difficulty understanding
why formal controls are instituted in hierarchical groups where members are differentially powerful. They know that formal controls exist because it is often in the interests of the powerful to extract rents from those
who are dependent upon them. As Hobbes ([1651] 1968: 228) notes, one
route to the establishment of controls is "by Naturall force; as when a man
maketh his children, to submit themselves, and their children to his government, as being able to destroy them if they refuse; or by Warre sub-
dueth his enemies to his will, giving them their lives on that condition." In
a similar vein, Adam Smith ([1789] 1961: I, 74) argues that the fact that
masters tend to have more power than workers keeps wage rates low.[1]

It seems far more difficult, starting from rational choice premises, to explain how formal controls can ever arise among individuals who, at least
initially, are endowed with relatively *equal* amounts of power. That rational

[1]Using a similar concept, the shifting power differentials between rulers and their subjects,
Levi (1987) attempts to explain variations in state tax policies.

104

choice theory could account for the development of formal controls among equals was explicitly denied by Talcott Parsons in his famous discussion of the Hobbesian dilemma. Hobbes's fundamental problem was to explain how social order could emerge from a state of nature in which men were equal and, on this account, engaged in a perpetual war of all against all. The Hobbesian solution—that men would freely relinquish some of their individual liberty and establish a state once they realized that this was the only means of providing social order—was roundly criticized by Parsons for

> stretching, at a critical point, the conception of rationality beyond its scope in the rest of the theory, to a point where the actors come to realize the situation as a whole instead of pursuing their own ends in terms of their immediate situation, and then take the action necessary to eliminate force and fraud, [and purchase] security at the sacrifice of the advantages to be gained by their future employment.
>
> (Parsons 1937: 93)

Although this statement is not without ambiguity, its key lies in the distinction between individuals who pursue their own ends "in terms of their immediate situation" and those who "come to realize the situation as a whole instead of pursuing their own ends in terms of the immediate situation." Whereas the former kinds of individuals will pursue pure private goods, the latter may contribute to the production of collective goods—in this instance, a coercive state—if this is what is required for the development of social order. Yet Parsons can see nothing in Hobbesian rationality that would lead rational egoists to produce such a collective good.[2]

Formal controls may be required for the survival of large groups, but they are a second-order collective good whose provision is threatened by free riders. Why then would rational egoists agree to establish such institutions in the first place (Coleman 1986)? Understanding why formal controls are adopted in groups composed of relative equals is the first step in a theory of institutionalization.

Since Parsons cannot imagine how it could be narrowly rational to contribute to the production of a collective good, he concludes that these two kinds of individuals must be motivated by fundamentally different types of rationality. This is the basis for his condemnation of "utilitarianism"

---

[2] Durkheim ([1895] 1938: 122) thought it curious that Hobbes never seemed "to have realized how contradictory it is to admit that the individual is himself the author of a machine which has for its essential role his domination and constraint."

(read rational choice theory) for its inability to provide an internally consistent explanation of the production of collective goods, including that of institutions like the state. By now several generations of sociologists have accepted the validity of Parsons's critique.

But Parsons and his followers err in conflating collective and public goods. Whereas rational choice theorists have struggled (for the most part unsuccessfully, in my view) to explain the production of pure public goods, in principle they have no difficulty accounting for the production of collective goods, because these are potentially excludable (see Chapter 2). If collective goods are excludable, then at least some kinds of formal controls might be expected to arise from the interaction of rational individuals.

If the establishment of formal controls is necessary for the production of some joint good, then individuals will be led by their very interest in consuming the good to help produce these controls. This kind of logic should also be able to account for variations in controls across groups, since it is reasonable to suppose that the production of different joint goods requires the institution of different kinds of formal controls. Many of the controls adopted by a group of chamber musicians evidently will differ from those adopted by a group of yachting enthusiasts.

This logic will be illustrated by considering the production of formal controls in rotating credit associations and insurance groups. Among the least hierarchical of all types of groups, these form spontaneously all over the world. Although insurance groups have more complex controls than rotating credit associations, the goods afforded by membership in both of these groups flow from the existence of a common fund that is generated by the contributions of each participant. Members agree to establish formal controls so as to preserve the security of their investment, thus guaranteeing the integrity of this fund. Hence, the same reason that individuals join groups in the first place—namely, to gain access to joint goods—is also sufficient to account for their adoption of formal controls when no better sources of these goods are available.

This analysis leads to a surprising twist. Once the problem of producing formal controls in nonhierarchical groups is resolved, it offers a foundation for the development of many other kinds of groups—among them those, like trade unions, that are concerned with the provision of public, as against collective, goods. There is some evidence that trade unions emerged as a by-product of successful insurance groups. The emergence of public-goods-seeking groups has been difficult to account for previously on rational choice grounds. The chapter therefore underlines what may appear to be the ironic conclusion that the desire to consume private goods can lead individuals to produce collective goods (like formal controls)—and sometimes even public goods—in the absence of any ideological or altruistic motivations.

ROTATING CREDIT ASSOCIATIONS

Rotating credit associations are made up of individuals who agree to make regular contributions to a fund that is given, in whole or in part, to each contributor in rotation (Ardener 1962: 201). They are among the most elementary—and short lived—of all groups; many come into being for a period of as little as ten weeks. As such, they can be distinguished from longer-lived (and more institutionalized) insurance groups, in which all contributions are held by an official or banked, and therefore not distributed on a rotary principle.

Although rotating credit associations can vary widely in their degree of institutionalization, they all share a common structure:

> if there are ten members of the association, if the association meets weekly, and if the weekly contribution from each member is one dollar, then each week over a ten-week period a different member will receive ten dollars (i.e., counting his own contribution). If interest payments are calculated, by one mechanism or another, as part of the system, the numerical simplicity is destroyed, but the essential principle of rotating access to a continually reconstituted fund remains intact. Whether the fund is in kind or in cash; whether the order the members receive the fund is fixed by lot, by agreement, or by bidding; whether the time period over which the society runs is many years or a few weeks; whether the sums involved are minute or rather large; whether the members are few or many; and whether the association is composed of urban traders or rural peasants, of men or women, the general structure of the institution is constant.
>
> (Geertz [1962] 1966: 422)

Evidently, the requirements of starting a rotating credit association are minimal. Any small number of acquaintances who have even the slightest amount of disposable income are capable of establishing one. Since these groups continuously rise and fall, and since they often exist without the sanction of political authorities, little evidence of them survives in written records. What is known about these groups comes largely from ethnographic research, and their existence has been documented all over the world (for a recent bibliography, see Vélez-Ibáñez 1983).

Goods Produced in Rotating Credit Associations

Rotating credit associations provide members with several distinct kinds of goods (Ardener 1962). One is a secure place to deposit savings (Kurtz and Showman 1978; Vélez-Ibáñez 1983: 63). In societies where the risk of embezzlement is high (or the security of banks is in question), the advantage afforded by rotating credit associations is that each fund (or part thereof) is immediately possessed by one of the contributors and therefore cannot be embezzled. Yet since rotating credit associations are found in many countries where savings deposits are highly secure, they must provide other benefits as well.

Membership can also motivate savings behavior among participants. As their name implies, these groups supply credit—credit that may otherwise be more expensive or not available to participants at all. The credit provided by rotating credit associations is often less expensive than that provided by banks. Further, these groups offer the kind of small-scale credit in which banks are not normally interested. Rotating credit associations can also provide members with larger amounts of capital: some groups in central Mexico, for instance, distribute Volkswagen Beetles as the share, whereas others distribute Datsuns and deposits to be used in the purchase of homes (Vélez-Ibáñez 1983: 22). Finally, membership in a rotating credit association may enhance the social status of its participants. In South Africa, for instance, "a recognized motive in joining these associations is prestige," because membership is taken to be a signal of an individual's personal reliability (Kuper and Kaplan 1944: 184).

Controls in Rotating Credit Associations

Why do the members of this most elementary kind of group agree to adopt formal controls? If the benefit afforded by participation in such groups is the guarantee of access to the rotating fund, then anything that threatens the fund's integrity vitiates the value of membership. It is irrational to join a rotating credit association unless the risk of default is considered to be acceptably slight. Members agree to the institution of controls in order to protect their investment and to recruit new members into the group, thereby increasing its collective assets.

There are two potential threats to the integrity of the common fund. The first, noncontribution, turns out to be trivial. It stands to reason that if members fail to make their regular contributions, the fund will not be replenished. Yet since access to these assets can easily be denied to any noncontributing member, nothing is to be gained by this course of action, and noncontribution is unlikely to constitute a problem.

This is not the case, however, with regard to the second kind of threat, default. The member who has received the fund (because of position in a fixed rotation or submission of the highest bid for it) somehow must be kept from absconding with it. The gain from default varies with the size of the group's assets, but it is always substantial. The risk of default is generally reduced by the enforcement of sanctions and the adoption of selection rules.

Sanctions.   If members are apprised that default will be met with sufficiently severe sanctions, then there will be no reason to abscond—the act will yield net negative benefits. The first source of sanctions comes from the group's members themselves. Since all of them place their money into the central fund, all have an incentive to seek out and sanction any defaulter in order to recapture their investment.[3] But in addition to the power of members to sanction defaulters, many rotating credit associations can call on sanctioning by third parties.

In many societies the state will prosecute defaulters and make them subject to imprisonment (Geertz [1962] 1966; Cope and Kurtz 1980; Bonnett 1981). But the literature on rotating credit associations suggests that other types of sanctions are more likely to come into play. Geertz ([1962] 1966: 426), for instance, claims that the incidence of default in rotating credit associations is rare because the members are frequently fairly close acquaintances and so would be deeply ashamed to evade their obligations. Members are said to go to great lengths, such as stealing or selling a daughter into prostitution, in order to fulfill their obligations to the association (Embree 1939: 147). But who is motivated to sanction a defaulter? The ethnographic literature often speaks of these community sanctions as a public good, but if this were the case, then none but the members of the injured group would have a motive to sanction defaulters.

Fortunately, a much simpler way of explaining community sanctioning is at hand. A person who is known to have defaulted in one rotating credit association is not likely to be accepted as a member of any similar group. By keeping their own investments out of the hands of a known defaulter, the members of other rotating credit associations thereby also inadvertently contribute to the production of community sanctions. Defaulting in one rotating credit association leads to exclusion from all others in the same locality. To the degree that rotating credit associations are central to

---

[3] In rotating credit associations like the *cundina*, which has been found among Mexican-Americans in San Ysidro, California (Kurtz 1973), the responsibility to control default lies in the hands of an organizer, who is expected to make up the loss from a default to the membership. In this kind of group the motive for sanctioning then becomes the organizer's alone.

economic and social exchange in a given community, this constitutes a most serious deprivation (Ardener 1962: 216).[4]

Third-party sanctions of this sort—which the literature portrays as the predominant deterrent to default—can be effective only in small communities where monitoring is inexpensive. Even then, their efficacy is limited to those members who are likely to remain in the community (and thereby be subject to these sanctions). This limitation probably helps explain why rates of default are greater in urban than in rural areas (Kurtz 1973).

Selection Rules.   A second means of reducing the risk of default, alluded to earlier, is the adoption of selection rules that narrow the field of potential participants to those who are sincere, solvent, and likely to remain in the community. Four such rules are employed most commonly. A first rule is to *admit only kin.* This rule held, for example, among the Chinese immigrants to the United States who participated in a rotating credit association known as the *hui* (Bonnett 1981). In the *hui* a member's kin are obligated to pay off debts in the case of death or default. The family, then, guarantees the credit of the member, and admission to the group is limited to those whose families have a good reputation (Light 1972). Where membership extends beyond the kin group, other kinds of rules are frequently adopted.

One such rule is to *admit only those who are unlikely to leave the community.* The careful selection of participants who are tied to the local community, creating what is in effect a situation of repeated interaction, reduces the risk of default, for it is impossible to sanction a defaulter whose whereabouts are unknown. This selection rule is probably the reason that a significant number of members of Mexican *tandas* share characteristics like low educational attainment, marital stability, and the holding of more than one job: these all contribute to residential stability. Only those "individuals who show a commitment to remaining in the community or the immediate area are acceptable for the *tanda.* Individuals who are likely to move to other areas apparently are eliminated systematically from participation" (Cope and Kurtz 1980: 229).

A third rule is to *admit only those of proven creditworthiness.* Persons with

---

[4] "He therefore that breaketh his Covenant, and consequently declareth that he thinks he may with reason do so, cannot be received into any Society . . . but by the errour of them that receive him; nor when he is received, be retayned in it, without seeing the danger of their errour; which errours a man cannot reasonably reckon upon as the means of his security: and therefore if he be left, or cast out of Society, he perisheth; and if he live in Society, it is by the errours of other men, which he could not foresee, nor reckon upon; and consequently against the reason of his preservation; and so, as all men that contribute not to his destruction, forbear him onely out of ignorance of what is good for themselves" (Hobbes [1651] 1968: 205).

substantial means and property are principally selected in rotating credit associations in China (Gamble 1944; Wu 1973). And Light (1972: 58–60) reports that candidates to admission to the associations established in the Japanese and Chinese communities of the United States were subject to intense moral scrutiny. A final rule is to *take no chances with new members*. If new members are placed last in the rotation, the money they might be tempted to abscond with is their own.

Rotating credit associations operate in such a way that the only threat to the member's investment is the possibility that another member will default or abscond with the common fund. The controls adopted in such groups are designed to minimize these particular risks. Since these groups have no bankers who take responsibility for the common fund, for example, they do not adopt controls specifically against embezzling. But in groups where loss can come about in a greater number of ways, it follows that more extensive controls are required to reduce the risk to acceptable levels. This expectation is borne out in the case of insurance groups.

INSURANCE GROUPS

In the most general sense, insurance refers to the spreading of risk in the face of future uncertainty. Although not always calling it insurance, writers like Emile Durkheim, Max Weber, Sigmund Freud, and Karl Polanyi have traditionally emphasized its importance as a motive for group formation. Their more or less implicit assumption is that rather than being mere wealth- (or utility-) maximizers, actors must relentlessly pursue control over their environment in order to attain any valued goal. The desire for insurance, or security, also figures strongly in the individualistic theoretical tradition.[5]

Insurance can be supplied either individually or collectively. The fundamental individual strategy is portfolio diversification, which accounts for the popularity of mutual funds in capitalist societies, and perhaps for the medieval English peasant's preference for cultivation in scattered strips rather than in consolidated holdings as well (McCloskey 1976). When

[5] For Hobbes ([1651] 1968: 160–61), the desire for security was ultimately responsible for the development of the state. In a somewhat different vein, Adam Smith ([1789] 1961: 426) regarded security as a precondition for all investment: when people "are secure of enjoying the fruits of their industry, they naturally exert it to better their condition and to acquire not only the necessaries, but the conveniences and elegancies of life." Frank Knight (1921: 232–63) later argued that rational action is possible only in the face of (measurable) risk, but not in the face of (unmeasurable) uncertainty. Insurance offers one of the principal means of eliminating uncertainty. It does so by consolidating individual cases into groups of cases whose central tendencies can be established statistically. By reducing situations of uncertainty to those of mere risk, all social institutions in effect perform an insurance function.

people spread risk by diversifying their assets, they engage in a form of self-insurance. Since they control their own resources, problems of non-compliance simply do not arise. This strategy works best, however, when people have substantial, and readily divisible, assets. To the degree that their assets are limited or have substantial sunk costs, self-insurance provides less risk-spreading than may be desirable. This need for greater risk-spreading creates a demand for additional insurance.

Risk can also be spread among the individual members of an insurance group. These members are analogous to the policyholders in commercial insurance contracts. Although their forms can vary, insurance groups all operate according to similar principles. Members agree to put some amount of money (akin to a premium) on a regular basis into a common fund in return for protection against specific losses. Optimally, these contributions are determined on the basis of sound estimates of the probability that a member will suffer a given loss.

Most primordial groups—such as the extended family, the clan, and the corporate village community (J. C. Scott 1976)—offer protection against a wide variety of losses (flooding, drought, poor harvests) as one among many of their benefits (Kropotkin 1902). Specialized groups that are formed primarily to provide insurance against highly specific kinds of losses, however, tend to be of recent origin.[6] The demand for specialized insurance groups arises only in special circumstances. War, rapid technological change, or political transformation can disrupt customary social arrangements or encourage migration to environments where insurance is unavailable.[7]

British friendly societies and American fraternal ethnic associations are two examples of insurance groups for which considerable documentary evidence exists. The friendly societies were both first to develop and more amply documented. As early as the mid-eighteenth century, a number of pamphlets were published devoted to them, but the first comprehensive treatment of friendly societies dates from Eden's (1801) report on the characteristics of 7,200 local groups.

By the early nineteenth century, the British government had come to regard friendly societies as useful organizations for lowering the poor rate, but

---

[6] Walford (1871–80), however, claims to trace their evolution all the way back to ancient Greece.

[7] Of course, the formation of insurance groups may be affected by many other factors, such as the asymmetric sex ratios of immigrant flows. For example, when Asians migrated to the United States in the prewar years, most were men, and they developed a series of institutions to take over "family functions." Recent Asian immigrants to this country have had a more balanced sex ratio and consequently have had less of a propensity to establish these kinds of groups (Lyman 1977: 119–30).

their potential for extra-parliamentary collective action was also feared (Gosden 1961: 6). For these reasons the government took an interest both in fostering these groups and in keeping track of them by registration.[8] The government enacted legislation aimed to make the societies more reliable as insurers and to encourage members to efficiently manage their own financial affairs. The establishment of the Office of the Registrar of Friendly Societies served to centralize information about these groups (Gosden 1961: 185).

According to a knowledgeable nineteenth-century observer, the motives behind the founding of friendly societies were evident: "The sense of the insufficiency of mere *individual* effort, forethought, or prudence, in warding off many of the afflictions to which humanity is liable, in every age, civilized or barbarous, has unquestionably been the prolific parent of these combinations for mutual protection" (Hardwick 1879: 11). The first recorded society was founded in Bethnal Green in 1687. Thereafter these groups began to spread, most rapidly in industrializing counties, from the late seventeenth century on. By 1801 the average society was estimated to have 90 members (Eden 1801); this number had increased to 132 by 1875. Members were recruited from no distinct social class. In general, offices were held by rotation (Gosden 1961: 89).

Goods Produced in Insurance Groups

The principal goods afforded by membership were payments in the event of sickness, disability, and death.[9] The Amicable Society of Patrington in the East Riding was a typical local friendly society. It was founded in

---

[8] The government elicited the cooperation of friendly societies with its registration policy by offering members certain benefits in return. Thus, members of a society who could produce a certificate of membership were not removable under the laws for the settlement of the poor unless they actually became chargeable to the poor rate (Gosden 1961: 174). In addition, registration enabled members to protect themselves against dishonest officers by allowing them to be sued in the courts. Registration also gave societies priority of claim on the estate of a deceased or bankrupt officer for any of the monies of the society and exemption from certain stamp duties. Finally, registered societies were given the right to deposit their funds in savings banks at a favorable rate of interest from 1817 on. The rules adopted by friendly societies from this time on therefore cannot be wholly ascribed to the spontaneous action of their members. The state too played a role—often a preponderant one—in determining the controls that were adopted in friendly societies. This illustrates the dilemma that the existence of evidence about the workings of groups presupposes some agency's interest in monitoring the activities of its members. The availability of systematic information about groups offers prima facie evidence that the state has formally monitored them.

[9] Burial societies had a strong appeal, which rested upon the dread of working people for the pauper funeral of the nineteenth century. "Many who could not afford to insure themselves against both sickness and death in a normal friendly society nevertheless insured against the expenses of their funerals by subscribing to a so-called friendly society which existed solely for that purpose" (Gosden 1961: 58).

1792 with the customary triple aim of providing insurance against sickness and funeral expenses and of bringing members into closer social contact. Thirty years after its foundation it provided "that when a member is sick, lame or blind, and rendered incapable of working . . . he shall be allowed eight shillings per week during his inability to work" and "that upon the death of every free member, notice must be given to the stewards, who, at the next monthly meeting, shall pay to the widow or executor ten pounds" (Articles of the Amicable Society at Patrington, Hedon, 1822, cited in Gosden 1961: 17). Each member was also required to pay three-pence towards the cost of refreshment at each meeting. Publicans gladly offered their taverns as meeting sites, since many groups engaged in drinking. Additional benefits commonly included "medical attendance"—the right to take advice from a "medical officer" who was employed by the society on a contract basis (Gosden 1961: Ch. 6)—educational benefits (some groups, such as the Oddfellows, provided classes in a variety of subjects and published magazines that encouraged educational development of their readers), and, not least, entertainment. The societies held monthly meetings (generally in a pub), a gala annual feast (which many considered to be the most festive holiday of the year), and sometimes summer excursions. Members were initiated into the societies by elaborate ceremonies, participated in secret rites, and occasionally paraded publicly in expensive regalia.[10]

For most members such goods were unavailable elsewhere. Until the spread of commercial insurance to the middle and working classes in the late nineteenth century, friendly societies were the major source of health and life insurance in Britain. Free public education was not initiated until the early part of the twentieth century. And until the advent of cheap rail transport, the prospects of entertainment in provincial British towns were rather bleak: "There was very little organised entertainment as men have since come to know it, there were no annual holidays, thus the colour and amusement without which life was so dull and tedious were furnished on the nightly club nites or feast days" (Gosden 1961: 127).

Whereas the growth of British friendly societies was spurred by industrialization, the development of American fraternal associations occurred largely after the mid-nineteenth century and was instigated by waves of immigration. In contrast with the friendly societies, no centralized agency

[10] Why did friendly societies place so much emphasis on socializing and spend so much money on regalia? In addition to its effects on conviviality, required attendance at the monthly meeting enabled members to keep track of one another and thereby provided them with monitoring opportunities. Hardwick (1879: 152) sees the money spent on regalia as a form of advertising that attracts the attention of other potential members, and thus helps the society grow.

collected information about them. The evidence that survives about fraternal associations remains to be gathered from records in each large city of their constitutions, by-laws, and articles of agreement (Galey 1977 is the most useful current study; see also Cummings 1980).

Fraternal orders supplied virtually identical goods to those offered by the friendly societies, including death, sickness, and disability benefits; a place for socializing with other members (in this case, the members of one's own ethnic group); and a forum for a variety of cultural activities, as well as musical, dance, and sports events. Finally, instruction in a variety of subjects was given in the mother tongue, and some groups provided their members with education in the English language (which in the long run contributed to these groups' demise, since it lessened members' dependence on them).

As in the case of the friendly societies, the initial members of fraternal associations found it difficult to obtain such benefits elsewhere. Commercial life insurance was too expensive for most of the newly arrived immigrants (Stalson 1942; Kip 1953), who tended to be clustered in the working-class occupations (Hechter 1979). True, the immigrant church often acted as a source of comparable benefits, but to a significant extent it too must be regarded as an insurance group (Bodnar 1985: 120–30).

The goods produced in insurance groups (like those of rotating credit associations) hinge on the integrity of the central fund. In effect, insurance groups provide an immanent good: a sense of security that comes with the knowledge that the individual, or the family, is protected against some potential loss. This sense of security is only justified insofar as the group retains sufficient assets. Naturally, depletion of its assets erodes the members' insurance. The value of membership therefore directly depends on the existence of controls that insure the preservation (if not growth) of the group's assets.

Controls in Insurance Groups

There are a number of different kinds of threats to the integrity of the insurance fund. The first threat arises from the selection of members who have highly correlated risk. When a group's members run correlated (rather than independent) risk of loss, the insurance fund will be quite vulnerable to depletion. Imagine the case of a "sick club" whose members are all the same age. When everyone is twenty, the group's assets appear to be secure. The insurance fund is likely to grow since incidence of illness will be low. But once everyone reaches, say, the age of sixty, then it is likely that outflow due to the payment of benefits will exceed the inflow from premiums. Unless the group manages to attract a large proportion of new, younger members to subsidize the benefits of the aged, it will be unable to survive. The problem of correlated risk can generally be mitigated by *increasing the number of members:* thus the size of insurance groups is likely to be larger than that of rotating credit associations.

The second threat is that the officers who are responsible for the insurance funds can embezzle or abscond with them. The risk of this is greater in insurance groups than in rotating credit associations, for the fund is larger, and it is likely to be controlled by one person rather than a rotating committee of the whole. How can this problem be solved? The members of insurance groups are likely to select their officers with the greatest of care. Since these groups often emerge in densely connected networks (based either on residence, in the case of friendly societies, or on ethnicity, in the case of fraternal associations), much information is available concerning members' reputations. Yet selecting officers for their honesty and integrity is unlikely to provide sufficient assurance against fraud.[11] *State enforcement of laws against embezzlement and outright theft* is, therefore, virtually a precondition for the long-run survival of insurance groups.

If levels of contributions to the insurance fund are based on calculations that understate the true risk of loss, this too will soon deplete the group's assets, for members' premiums then will be inadequate to cover the (greater-than-anticipated) losses. Quite naturally, miscalculations were the source of widespread insolvency among early insurance groups. The problem was intractable until the development of adequate life and morbidity tables and the complement of *modern actuarial methods,* many of which were spurred by the experiences faced by the friendly societies.

Beyond these issues, the provision of insurance also hinges on members' compliance with rules that create the fund in the first place. The threats to insurance groups, in this respect, are several. Although members must regularly pay their premiums in order to maintain the insurance fund, noncontribution is simply not an issue since insurance benefits can easily be withheld from members who have failed to pay their premiums. The desire for insurance is a sufficient incentive for compliance with the obligation to contribute.

[11] Thus one leader of Oddfellows rather cynically observed: "I have often heard it argued that if the members would always be careful, and choose 'honest men' for their treasurers and officers, legal protection would become superfluous! Perhaps, if all mankind were all practical Christians, and gifted with the privilege of peeping into futurity, we might contrive to get on without any social compact whatever. But, unfortunately, I have never yet heard of a defaulting treasurer or trustee who was not, *at the time of his appointment,* regarded by those who selected him as a most exemplary individual! It is generally some exceedingly 'good character', some 'very nice person', or some 'highly respectable gentleman' whom nobody distrusts, that contrives to decamp with the funds of unenrolled Friendly Societies, or impudently demands 'something handsome' before he will transfer his trust to a properly-appointed successor" (Hardwick 1879: 104).

Of course, if members are allowed to collect on fraudulent claims, then the incidence of loss will be greater than anticipated actuarially. The incentive to make fraudulent claims can be weakened by employing the principle of indemnity, which limits the payment a member can receive to an amount that is no more than that actually incurred by the loss in question. In theory, this makes it impossible for members to profit by making a claim. Beyond this, fraud can only be forestalled by *investigating individual claims*, which, of course, involves monitoring expenditures. Insurance groups routinely engage in this kind of monitoring. For example, officers of the friendly society were obliged to visit any ill member to verify illness before any payment of benefits. Members who lived far from the meeting place had to supply a certificate signed by the parson (Gosden 1961: 139). Similarly, the members of ethnic fraternal associations established Sick Committees that were responsible for visiting sick and disabled members to verify illness, to report the members' conditions to the local lodge, and to arrange for payment of benefits (Galey 1977: 22).

The payment of benefits for all claims was subject to compliance with the society's rules, and noncompliance provided a basis for denial of benefits or for expulsion from membership (Galey 1977: 25). Thus, payment of the death benefit in fraternal associations was carefully regulated. The associations insisted on proof of death (usually it was necessary to obtain a physician's certificate), the deceased's membership certificate, and the beneficiary's claim submitted within one year of the member's death. If the member died by the hand of the beneficiary or gave false information on a membership certificate, cash payments were voided (Galey 1977: 25).

In addition to fraud, however, insurance groups face a distinctive problem, which has come to be known as moral hazard (Heimer 1985). Moral hazard involves risks that are partially under the control of the members themselves. To illustrate, drivers with comprehensive automobile insurance are more liable to be careless than those who have no such protection. Why? Insured drivers are not as motivated to be careful as uninsured drivers because the insurance company has agreed to bear the consequences of their carelessness. Whereas totalling a vehicle may have tragic consequences for the uninsured driver, the insured are likely to lose a lot less sleep. But if the mere fact of having insurance contributes to the carelessness of drivers, then automobile insurers can remain solvent only by devising means of curtailing moral hazard.[12]

How do insurance groups manage to do so? Generally, by resorting to

---

[12] For some kinds of losses the problem of moral hazard is insurmountable and commercial insurance cannot be provided at all. Hence one cannot buy insurance against divorce or getting poor grades in college: most people have little to gain by dying, but—if the price is right—it might well pay to get divorced or to settle for C's.

two different kinds of strategies. We have already encountered the first means in the case of rotating credit associations: the *selection of members who run a low risk of loss*. (One form of this is what insurance companies refer to as "underwriting," that is, setting differential premiums for more and less risky policyholders on the basis of their previous experience with loss.) This principle was recognized in the rules and regulations of most of the friendly societies:

> As there are . . . diversities of dispositions amongst men, which, though good in a general point of view, are wisely ordained, as they contribute to the happiness of the whole; yet, in select societies, discord and disorder may arise from an indiscriminate admission of members; to prevent which, as much as may be, this Society have determined to admit none but such as are recommended for sobriety.
>
> (Good Intent Society 1815)

Only people with low risk of disease or death were admitted to fraternal associations: membership was restricted to those of good physical and mental health. Proof of this had to be provided by a medical examination and certificate signed by a recognized professional physician or by the association's medical examiner. The associations also sought to admit only those of high moral character: prospective members were required to submit letters of reference from existing members.

The final means of controlling moral hazard in insurance groups is by instituting coverage only if the member complies with a variety of *prespecified conditions for voiding benefits* in order to reduce the risk of loss. In commercial insurance contracts, for instance, a factory may be granted insurance only after the owners have installed a sprinkler system. Similar strategies were employed by insurance groups. Some friendly societies legislated against intemperance: "Although they met in pubs, the Manchester Unity of Oddfellows made the propagation of temperance its specialty. Members were severely punished if seen intoxicated when in receipt of the sick allowance. Any member appearing in a lodge-room in a state of intoxication is subject to a fine" (Hardwick 1879: 150). In fraternal associations, sick benefits were not paid for losses or injuries resulting from certain kinds of behavior. For example, many societies did not pay benefits if sickness resulted from drunkenness, fighting, or practical joking (Galey 1977).

All told, individuals who have been deprived of insurance customarily provided by primordial groups—due to migration, war, or rapid socioeconomic change—are likely to demand new sources of insurance. This may lead them either to establish their own mutual insurance groups or to join associations started by entrepreneurs. Whether they are formed in a contractarian or entrepreneurial fashion, the resulting insurance groups will adopt a series of formal controls because members understand that their coverage depends entirely upon the integrity of the common fund. Rational individuals will hesitate to invest any amount of money in insurance groups whose controls appear to be inadequate to guarantee against depletion of the common fund from known hazards of any kind.[13] The greater the diversity of these known hazards, the greater the diversity of the resulting controls. Thus the same reason people join groups in the first place— namely, to gain access to valued joint goods—is also sufficient to account for the establishment of formal controls.[14]

The survival of both rotating credit associations and insurance groups therefore depends on the adoption of measures that provide security for their common fund. The existence of this fund, however, provides the insurance group with a collective good that, in principle, can be put to any number of uses. In contrast to the rotating credit association, the common fund is not regularly distributed to members. Instead, responsibility for banking, investing, and disbursing it is likely to be delegated to a small number of elected officers. What they choose to do (or are instructed to do) with the fund can have important implications for the development of other kinds of groups, for organization often begets new organization (R. Breton 1964).

BY-PRODUCTS OF INSURANCE GROUPS

The early-nineteenth-century parliamentary legislators' concern to register the friendly societies came from their appreciation that such groups are capable of engaging in collective action. Although they are likely to be formed by those with little in the way of capital stock, or even credit, insurance groups (and rotating credit associations) permit the poor to accumulate collective capital. This capital can be put to any number of uses that the membership will support, or at least tolerate. Therefore, once established, insurance groups can serve as the basis for the crystallization of quite different types of groups, including financial institutions, commercial insurance firms, churches, labor unions, and interest groups of various types.

The historical record reveals that some of these groups evolved into com-

---

[13] Of course, members may not know about some of the hazards of insurance groups, particularly those involving correlated risk and the necessity of actuarial methods. People invested in insurance groups well before these hazards were understood and before adequate measures were developed to mitigate them.

[14] I ignore the possibility that individuals may adopt controls merely because they desire them to bring regularity to their otherwise chaotic lives—as Durkheim sometimes was wont to imply. This is quite foreign to any rational choice conception.

mercial insurance firms or financial institutions. Over the course of time, local friendly societies and fraternal associations merged into national federations offering insurance at ever cheaper rates to an ever larger clientele. As these federated associations grew in size, the nature of their operations became transformed. Many ended up as offices for life insurance and sickness benefits that increasingly did business over the counter. Some of the federated societies began offering mortgages and other financial services to their members (this was the origin of many of the British building societies, for example).

As fraternal associations in the United States increasingly faced competition from commercial insurance companies, they were led to provide greater benefits to retain their clientele. Some provided benefits for special age groups—orphanages, scholarships for college-bound youth, summer camps for children and young adults, and homes for the aged (Galey 1977). Occasionally these facilities were later opened for the use of the public, as happened in the case of ethnic and religious hospitals. Fraternal associations were known to have spurred the development of some churches, and vice versa.[15]

Some of the assets of insurance groups were also diverted to political ends. So long as the membership did not collectively object, there was nothing to stop enterprising officers from taking advantage of their access to large sums of other people's capital by helping to produce certain kinds of public goods, for which they could subsequently take credit and enhance their prospective political careers. Thus during the 1920s and 1930s, several fraternal associations established funds whose monies were used to liberate the homeland or to assist the poor there (Galey 1977: 29). Being an officeholder of a fraternal association was an important asset to

[15] The absence of systematic data on immigrant fraternal associations, churches, and other institutions makes it difficult to understand their respective evolutionary patterns. Currently the best that can be done is to sift through secondary historical accounts. The *Harvard Encyclopedia of American Ethnic Groups* (Thernstrom, Orlov, and Handlin 1980) offers a compendium of such accounts for sixty-one major immigrant populations. Most of these accounts devote attention to the kinds of organizations that were first established by each type of immigrant group. In 35.8 percent of these groups, churches were the first organizations to develop; in 12.3 percent of them, fraternal associations (or mutual benefit societies) arose initially; whereas in 19.8 percent of these groups, social, cultural, and occasionally political organizations are mentioned as being the first kinds of groups to be established. (In 32.1 percent of the groups, it was impossible to determine the temporal priority of these types of groups.) It is probably safe to assume that when the *initial* group was considered to have social and cultural aims, it provided some insurance benefits (broadly construed) to its members, as well. Mutual benefit societies were established in all of the largest immigrant populations (including Afro-Americans) at some point in their history. Afro-Americans in the rural South organized church beneficial societies to provide insurance benefits (Frazier 1957: 375–76); in the urban North many of the fraternal associations that arose were independent of the church (Du Bois 1899).

the aspiring immigrant politician (Stolarik 1980; Renkiewicz 1980). Conditions for voiding benefits that were irrelevant to the protection of the common fund (and hence to the stated purpose of the insurance group) were often adopted. Pittsburgh's Greek Catholic Union, for example, penalized those who did not go to confession twice yearly. Other associations voided the benefits of or expelled members who had committed crime or treason against the United States, who failed to make Easter confessions, and—in the case of the Ukranian National Aid Association—who hired out as strikebreakers. Naturally, the adoption of this last rule was helpful to nascent trade unions.

This chapter began by noting that the development of groups that seek to provide public, rather than collective or private, goods has been difficult to explain from rational choice premises. Consider Mancur Olson's (1965) explanation of the initial development of trade unions (and, for that matter, farm organizations as well). Insofar as these groups sought to raise the wages of whole classes of workers, they aimed to produce a public good. Given this, the optimal strategy for any individual worker was to free ride and cash in on the successful efforts of union organizers and their credulous followers. How then did these groups emerge? Olson's explanation is that the early trade unions (in the days before the passage of closed-shop legislation) could lure members only if they provided them with desirable selective incentives, including insurance. In Olson's account, therefore, public-goods-seeking unions used insurance as a selective incentive to attract members; insurance groups are considered to be the by-product of trade unions.

The problem with this explanation is that selective incentives (like formal controls) are a second-order collective good. This means that they have to be produced. How is it that a group aiming to provide a public good can attract any rational members at all, let alone manage to produce selective incentives? As the material in this chapter demonstrates, the rise of insurance groups entails no such liability. Since they are formed for the provision of joint *private* goods, there is no initial free-rider problem. To obtain their insurance, members are led to adopt formal controls that protect the common fund. Once the fund is intact, it can be used in a variety of ways. There is no inherent reason why the members of an insurance group cannot convert their assets into a strike fund and reconstitute themselves as a trade union.

After observing that "people of the same trade seldom meet together, even for merriment and diversion, but the conversation ends in a conspiracy against the public, or in some contrivance to raise prices," Adam Smith argues that

> A regulation which enables those of the same trade to tax themselves in order to provide for their poor, their sick, their widows and orphans, by giving them a common interest to manage, renders such assemblies necessary.
>
> (Smith [1789] 1961: I, 144)

The existence of a link between insurance groups and the emergence of trade unions has been noted in several different countries. In their classic work on the origins of British trade unions Sidney and Beatrice Webb comment that

> Local friendly societies giving sick pay and providing for funeral expenses had sprung up all over England during the Eighteenth Century. Towards its close their number seems to have rapidly increased until, in some parts at any rate, every village ale-house became a center for one or more of these humble and spontaneous organisations. . . . So long as they were composed indiscriminately of men of all trades, it is probable that no distinctively Trade Union action could arise from their meetings. But in some cases, for various reasons, such as high contributions, migratory habits, or the danger of the calling, the sick and burial club was confined to men of a particular trade. *This kind of friendly society almost inevitably became a Trade Union.* Some societies of this type can trace their existence for nearly a century and a half. The Glasgow coopers, for instance, have had a local trade friendly society, confined to journeymen coopers, ever since 1752. The London Sailmakers' Burial Society dates from 1740. The Newcastle shoemakers established a similar society as early as 1719. On the occurrence of any dispute with the employers their funds, as [a] contemporary observer . . . deplores, "have also too frequently been converted into engines of abuse by paying weekly sums to artisans out of work, and have thereby encouraged combinations among workmen not less injurious to the misguided members than to the Public Weal."
>
> (Webb and Webb 1907: 23; emphasis added)

There was a direct connection between the existence of guilds (in large part insurance groups) and the emergence of trade unions in the Scandinavian countries (Galenson 1952: 107–15). Although Dutch unions emerged about four decades afer the legal dissolution of guilds in the Netherlands in 1798, these guilds survived as insurance groups (mutual aid societies) well into the twentieth century (Windmuller 1969: 5). L. G. J. Verberne (1959: 68–70) suggests that the continuation of these insurance groups stimulated the initial development of Dutch unions. Finally, American fraternal associations occasionally became transformed into trade unions (for example, Iorizzo and Mondello 1971: 78).

Thus Olson's causal order should be reversed: it is far more likely that trade unions were the by-product of insurance groups than vice versa. A systematic comparative investigation of the origins of trade unions might yield additional evidence that the establishment of insurance groups preceded that of public-goods-seeking groups such as trade unions.[16] The historical study of insurance groups may therefore help provide an answer to this key question in rational choice theory.

It is no mystery to understand why rational egoists participate in the production of formal controls, even if these are a collective good. They do so when such controls are necessary for their access to goods that they have no better means of obtaining. The mystery is why rational egoists would ever agree to produce *public* goods. This analysis tentatively proposes that groups devoted to the production of public goods must be built on the already existing edifice of the formal control system that sustains groups that produce *excludable* goods.

As such, it suggests something of a two-stage theory of institutional development. In the first stage, individuals form groups to attain joint *private* goods, like credit and insurance, but to do so they must also establish formal controls, which constitute a *collective* good. Once these controls are in place, a second stage becomes possible. The group's resources, now protected by the existence of formal controls, can be diverted (under a set of circumstances that needs to be investigated) to the production of further collective, or even *public*, goods.

Does the foregoing analysis mean that Parsons's famed Hobbesian problem is a chimera and that the development of social institutions can be satisfactorily accounted for by current rational choice theory? Such a conclusion would be premature. There is indeed a Hobbesian problem (see Gauthier 1986: 158–62), but Parsons's identification of it is mistaken. The voluntary establishment of formal controls in nonhierarchical groups is not difficult to explain in rational choice logic.[17] What *is* difficult to under-

---

[16]One of the reasons for the link between friendly societies and trade unions in Britain is that during the early part of the nineteenth century trade unions as such were frowned upon by the authorities and were unable to lead an open existence. Friendly societies, however, not only were permitted but also were granted certain legal privileges if they registered. Consequently many of the early one-trade societies might well have called themselves trade unions had circumstances been different (Gosden 1961: 71–72).

[17]The members of such groups often establish control systems on their own initiative. Three examples illustrate the forms that this process sometimes takes. Steven Cheung (re-

stand is why the rational members of large groups would ever abide by the controls they have consented to establish.[18]

ported by McManus 1975: 341) relates that on the Yangtze River in China, there is a section of fast water over which boats are pulled upstream by a team of coolies prodded by an overseer using a whip. On one such passage an American lady, horrified at the sight of the overseer whippping the men as they strained at their harness, demanded that something be done about the brutality. She was quickly informed by the captain that nothing could be done: "Those men own the right to draw boats over this stretch of water and they have hired the overseer and given him his duties." Similarly, although fifty-four members of the Berlin Philharmonic Orchestra revolted against their leader in 1882 and set themselves up independently as a self-governing cooperative, "the orchestra has always been willing to select stern podium dictators [von Bulow, Nikisch, Furtwangler, and von Karajan among them], the musicians' pride and desire for self-betterment has transcended any more comfortable inclinations" (Rockwell 1982: 26). Finally, worker-owned plywood factories in the United States Pacific Northwest hire outside managers and work under their direction on a day-to-day basis (Bernstein 1980: 15–18). For pioneering studies of the evolution of property rights in nonhierarchical societies—a parallel phenomenon—see Demsetz (1967) and Umbeck (1981).

[18] Like many other rational choice attempts to resolve the problem of social order, David Gauthier's (1986) ambitious effort to devise a Hobbesian solution cannot be judged a complete success. His analysis (which rests on the principle of "constrained maximization") suffers from such stringent common knowledge requirements that it can be applied only to the smallest of groups.

CHAPTER VII

THE LIMITS OF COMPENSATION IN CAPITALIST FIRMS

> The Sovereign can punish immediately any faults he discovers, but he
> cannot flatter himself into supposing that he sees all the faults he should
> punish.
>
> Alexis de Tocqueville

T HAT SANCTIONS may motivate compliance is undeniable. But they cannot magically be brought to bear on individual behavior. In order for
sanctions to influence behavior, two analytically separate processes have to
occur. On the one hand, compliance and noncompliance must be detected. On
the other, a stock of adequate sanctions must be available, and members must believe that not only will their behavior be sanctioned appropriately, but also that of others, especially if they do not comply. Together,
these processes constitute the mechanisms of control. Naturally, the greater
the probability of detection and the greater the magnitude of the sanction,
the greater the likelihood of compliance.[1]

Formal control mechanisms derive from planned social action and are
not self-reinforcing. Establishing and maintaining them is costly. Although members always have an interest in control (because it is a necessary condition for the production of the joint good), they may not always
institute it, precisely on account of these costs.[2]

Control costs tend to be higher in compensatory than in obligatory
groups. Recall that there are three ways to obtain the compliance necessary
to produce joint goods—through compensation, obligation, or some mix-
ture of these two means. Compensatory groups arise to produce marketable commodities that are consumed mostly by nonmembers. Since the
members of these groups do not receive any direct utility from the production of these goods, they must be compensated for the time they spend
producing them. Naturally, this compensation is most useful when it is

---

[1] This formulation is similar to that commonly used by deterrence theorists in criminology
(Gibbs 1981), although the sanctions referred to in that literature are exclusively negative.
[2] A more complete discussion of the evolution of formal controls can be found in Chaper 6.

provided in a highly fungible form (such as money wages) so that it can be exchanged for many other kinds of goods.

In contrast, obligatory groups exist in order to supply members with immanent goods, such as security or friendship, for which the number of close substitutes tends to be limited. Since immanent goods directly yield utility, members do not have to be compensated in order to undertake their production. Acceptance of corporate obligations, however, is the price for access to these goods. Because obligatory groups provide goods that are generally not as substitutable as fungible goods, they tend to entail more dependence than compensatory groups.

No matter what kind of goods a group produces, however, members would always prefer to be compensated for their compliance with production rules. Yet compensation tends to be limited to groups producing marketed commodities, for they alone have the ability to generate compensatory resources. Thus firms pay for their wage bill from sales revenues. Since non-profit-making groups cannot generate a continuous flow of compensatory resources, their survival hinges on their ability to provide members with immanent goods. This opens the door to obligation, which obviates the need for costly compensatory resources. If members are reluctant to make contributions to their group, however, then why do obligatory groups ever survive at all?

One reason is that, due to greater dependence, obligatory groups have lower sanctioning and monitoring costs. Since every group has one relatively costless sanction at its disposal—the threat of expulsion—then the greater the dependence of a group's members, the more weight this sanction carries. In the second place, monitoring and sanctioning are to some degree substitutable. If the value of the joint good is relatively large, the threat of expulsion can partly compensate for inadequate monitoring. The more one has to lose by noncompliance, the less likely one is to risk it (given the important caveat that the group's monitoring capacity is greater than zero).

Like that of obligatory groups, the survival of compensatory groups rests on their ability to reduce control costs to tolerable levels. They have an advantage over obligatory groups when it comes to generating sanctioning resources, but they must also find a way to reduce monitoring costs. In the face of particularly costly monitoring constraints, one strategy is to provide their members with immanent goods, in addition to pure compensation.

This chapter considers how these cost considerations affect the adoption of control systems in the exemplary type of compensatory group, the capitalist firm that produces one or many joint goods for profit. The firm is well suited to this task because its control systems are relatively transparent. This is due, in part, to differences of interest between employers and workers: "The workmen desire to get as much, the masters to give as little as possible" (A. Smith [1789] 1961: I, 74). Once the wage has been determined, this sets the stage for conflicts over work effort. Workers have an interest in shirking—they always prefer to use their time to satisfy their own ends rather than the employer's—but this threatens the firm's profitability (Marx [1867] 1965: I, 424). When the efficiency of labor (or the ratio of labor input to value produced) can be reliably estimated (see United Nations 1951; Homans 1965; and Pratten 1976), it is a reasonable indicator of the workers' rate of compliance with production rules.

Whether established by a single entrepreneur or by a group of producer-owners, firms institute formal controls so as to curtail the incidence of shirking and to promote maximum worker effort, among other things. Several different types of control systems have been employed in firms, and—unlike the control systems of groups that are not easily subject to research observation—much evidence is available about each.[3] Indeed, so much attention has been devoted to control in firms that a separate academic discipline was established to consider the issue—management science.

A brief tour through the history of management systems in capitalist firms reveals that the benefits they have offered their workers have changed fundamentally over time. Initially many of these enterprises relied entirely

---

[3] Evidence also exists for other kinds of organizations such as governments, armies, schools, and prisons. Information on formal control systems abounds for the military; the establishment of the Spartan hoplites is a notable early example. Monitoring on the Roman latifundia was carried out by *monitores*, or overseers (Weber [1922] 1946b: 261), whose job was similar to that of their counterparts on the slave plantations of the American South (Scarborough 1966; Fogel and Engerman 1974). Some of the most elaborate control systems arose in hydraulic societies, where cultivation was possible only with the aid of irrigation. The controller of the waterworks (whether he resembled Wittfogel's [1957] oriental despot or the democratically elected *cequier* of medieval Valencia [Glick 1970]) was the head of a control system that employed substantial sanctions; compliance provided the cultivator with access to water, whereas noncompliance could lead to the withdrawal of water rights. Among his other duties, the feudal lord sought to monitor production on the manor, and some (Kula 1976) have argued that the scattered strips characteristic of manorial production resulted from his desire to accurately monitor the output of his serfs. *Métayage* and other forms of sharecropping have been explained on the basis of control costs (Cheung 1969; Lucas 1979). The reason that concerns about control developed more completely in industry than in other institutional spheres is that economic production has different objectives than military or civil administration, and it operates with far more clear-cut criteria for failure and success. The primary objective of a large capitalist firm is to show a return on investment by the production and sale of goods and services. The continuing profit-and-loss record of a firm provides a reasonably precise criterion of its performance. Except in times of war, such clear-cut standards for the performance of a military corps or a government bureau are hard to find (Chandler 1962: 322).

upon piece-rates or time wages to motivate their workers to produce. As the tasks that workers performed became more complex, however, and monitoring costs increased thereby, firms known as internal labor markets began to supply their workers with a variety of immanent benefits— insurance and welfare benefits and, most important, the promise of a career—in addition to wages. The upshot is that some capitalist firms began to pursue a most unlikely goal—solidarity.

Just as employers will institute controls only when they are a worthwhile investment, so the particular type of control system resorted to should yield maximum profit.[4] Since the costs of control vary with the nature of the specific behaviors to be affected and with the kinds of sanctions utilized, these factors affect the types of controls that are likely to be put into place.

When the employer uses compensation to motivate worker compliance, then there must be a perfect correspondence between the workers' performance of a given task and their receipt of a wage. In standard neoclassical discourse the optimal wage is one that reflects the worker's marginal productivity. The simplest form of compensation occurs when the firm contracts to offer the worker a stated wage for the performance of some given task, which is an element in the set of the worker's possible behavior patterns (Simon 1957: 183–95). This contract assures the firm only that this task, and this task alone, however, will be carried out.[5] In order to motivate compliance with production rules, a compensation scheme depends upon the extensive monitoring of the worker's behavior.

But monitoring is a highly costly activity. The basic source of monitoring costs is the difficulty of measuring individual compliance. Individual compliance may be monitored by assessing input, output, or some combination of the two. These types of measurement incur different kinds of costs. In consequence, it is impossible to determine on an a priori basis what form of control is likely to be selected.[6] This depends on the characteristics of the activity that is to be controlled.

---

[4] I ignore the possibility that firms resort to control because employers enjoy the exercise of power for its own sake.

[5] If, due to changed circumstances, the firm would rather employ the worker to perform some other task, this particular contractual arrangement will not provide for it. The firm must either negotiate a new contract with the worker (one that offers a given wage for the new task), or it must resort to a type of arrangement that does not restrict the worker's compliance so narrowly, such as an authority relation (Simon 1957; Williamson 1975: Ch. 4). Any other kind of arrangement, however, violates the principle of strict compensation (which is analogous to direct reinforcement).

[6] For one of the few studies of the determinants of input-versus-output assessment, see Ouchi and Maguire (1975).

COSTS OF INPUT ASSESSMENT

The difficulty of measuring inputs is ultimately revealed at the level of technique: no devices for the measurement of human behavior exist that are designed with so perfect a knowledge of all the major sources of variation as may be found, for example, in the physicist's galvanometer. Such measures as do exist tap multiple processes and sources of variance that are unknown. Any instrument is therefore subject to an unknowable amount of error in a single measurement. The only way to increase the accuracy of behavioral measurement is through the simultaneous use of multiple, independent measuring processes (Webb, et al., 1969: 4), as well as by improving the accuracy of each.

To appreciate the costs of input assessment, it is essential to understand why these measurement problems occur. The basic reason is that, unlike Einstein's perception of God,[7] people are wont to act maliciously by covering their tracks. When people become aware that they are being scrutinized, they are likely to adjust their behavior in consequence (Selltiz et al. 1959: 97). If observation per se leads to behavioral adjustment, much greater adjustment, indeed strategic adjustment, occurs when subjects know that their observer is empowered to punish or reward them contingent on their performance (Leibenstein 1975: 598).[8]

Since members tend to resist being monitored (Day and Hamblin 1964), the best way of improving the accuracy of input measurement is through unobstrusive observation. A worker who is unaware of being observed has no incentive to work harder. Since measurement will not work as an instigator of change, a supervisor can obtain a better estimate of this person's "normal" working proclivities. Even unobtrusive observation, however, cannot assure perfect measurement.[9]

Employers may find it feasible to monitor the inputs of the members of small groups, but as the scale of a group increases—or the spatial distribution of its members[10]—it becomes vastly more difficult for any one per-

[7] In Morgenstern's (1951: 17–18) account, "The Lord God is sophisticated but not malicious."

[8] Further behavioral changes can be caused quite incidentally by the personal characteristics of the observer. Much social research has established that subjects tend to respond differentially to visible cues provided by observers and interviewers. Characteristics such as age, sex, race, and religion have all been shown to have demonstrable effects on the behavior of subjects, particularly interactions of age and sex. What is true of social research probably holds for all supervisory situations: the behavioral "distortions" arising from observation may depend, to an unknown degree, on just who the observer happens to be.

[9] Thus supervisors may vary over the course of their observations: different ones may see different things, and the length of time that they are on the job may affect their perception (E. Webb et al., 1969: 138–39).

[10] Input monitoring is not necessarily precluded in spatially dispersed groups. Forest rangers, for example, are required to keep extensive diaries of their activities when they are

son to do this.[11] In such circumstances, employers must use *agents* to monitor for them.

Agency Costs

Whenever employers—or, for that matter, any other *principals*—engage other people to perform some service on their behalf that involves the delegation of some decision-making authority, an *agency* relationship is established (Jensen and Meckling 1976; Holmstrom 1979; McDonald 1984). Agency relationships arise whenever persons must be placed in strategic positions within the group to detect the compliance of members. If both parties to the agency relationship are rational egoists, the principal will incur costs, for agents will not always act in the best interest of the principal but in their own best interest instead.[12] Principals incur agency costs when they attempt to motivate those engaged in input measurement. Agency costs consist of the resources devoted to compensating agents, as well as those necessary to enable principals to monitor their performance.[13]

In the factory, employers have two alternative means to monitor the workers' inputs. They can give the job to an inside contractor, who becomes a "residual claimant" (Alchian and Demsetz 1972: 782), or they can hire a salaried agent to do it for them.

Inside Contractors.   Inside contracting, a system that was widely employed in early factories (Nelson 1975; Clawson 1980), produces considerable labor efficiency, but it does so only at the price of high agency costs. Inside contractors exist in a bilateral exchange relationship with the company, doing all their work inside factory buildings owned by the company and using the company's machinery, equipment, and raw materials. They

---

in the field (Kaufman 1960). Essentially, they are required to monitor their own inputs. Entries from their diaries are subject to cross-checking by supervisors who have access to comparable reports by other forest rangers, but the accuracy of this kind of input assessment is difficult, if not impossible, to evaluate.

[11] The ubiquity of closed-circuit television monitors has, however, substantially reduced these costs in some settings.

[12] Adam Smith ([1789] 1961: II, 264–65) was an early commentator on agency costs: "The directors of such [joint-stock] companies, however, being the managers rather of other people's money than of their own, it cannot well be expected, that they should watch over it with the same anxious vigilance with which the partners in a private copartnery frequently watch over their own. Like the stewards of a rich man, they are apt to consider attention to small matters as not for their master's honour, and very easily give themselves a dispensation from having it. Negligence and profusion, therefore, must always prevail, more or less, in the management of the affairs of such a company."

[13] This usage differs from that of Jensen and Meckling (1976: 309), who define agency costs as synonomous with all control costs.

are company employees who receive a day wage as well as a certain amount for each completed piece. This amount is negotiated by the employer and the contractor. The greater the labor efficiency, the greater the contractor's profit will be. By providing contractors with an incentive to produce pieces for less than the negotiated price, thereby making them residual claimants, the system motivates contractors to obtain maximum labor efficiency from the workers. To this end, the firm grants contractors substantial powers to obtain compliance from the workers. Typically this involves complete authority over production in their areas, the right to hire and fire those employees without following any company rules or guidelines, unilateral control over employee wages, and, finally, control over work assignments and training.

This system produces labor efficiency, but the contractor often reaps much of the profit at the expense of the employer. In the negotiations over the piece-rate, the contractor's interest is to maximize the rate while the employer seeks to minimize it. An employer who has little intimate knowledge of the details of production—most crucially, of its costs—is at the mercy of the contractor's (over)estimates.[14] Further, in a period of rapid technological change, the contractor is likely to pocket all the benefits of labor-saving innovations for the duration of the contract (often a full year). In this situation contractors can amass a good deal of income, sometimes as much as high company managers and officials (Butterick 1952: 217).

Salaried Agents.   One alternative is to hire a salaried agent.[15] This arrangement might save the employer personnel costs, but it entails other difficulties. When effective measures of the performance of agents cannot be devised, principals are at risk of receiving little return on their monitoring investment, for the salaries of agents may end up purchasing negligible amounts of member compliance.

The problem can be illustrated in a host of different settings. First consider an extreme example: an organization where principals have maximum, and legally sanctioned, authority over highly dependent members (who have no right of exit)—the maximum-security prison (taken from Sykes 1958). For the moment, think of the prison as a group made up of principals (the prison officials), agents (the guards), and members (the

---

[14]Additionally, the contractor may be rough on the owner's equipment.

[15]It is also possible to reward informants who bring forth evidence about individual noncompliance, but since this provides them with an incentive to slander, it requires verifying *their* information. For other problems with information from secret sources, see Wilensky (1967: 66–69).

prisoners). In this group the prison officials have great power at their disposal: if any principals should be able to obtain compliance (here, obedience to prison rules and regulations), surely these should be able to do so.[16] Yet despite the broad powers of prison officials, the actual behavior of the inmate population differs markedly from that which is called for by official demands and decrees. Far from being omnipotent rulers who have crushed all signs of rebellion against their regime, the principals are engaged in a continuous struggle to obtain order, and it is a struggle that they frequently fail to win.

Agency costs are a major cause of this failure: officials cannot rely on the guards to enforce the regulations systematically. Instead, the guards frequently appear to be corrupted by the very prisoners they are supposed to be controlling. When the officials evaluate the guards in terms of the conduct of the prisoners they control, it is in the guards' best interest to make deals with the prisoners in their power. In effect, guards buy "compliance or obedience in certain areas at the cost of tolerating disobedience elsewhere" (Sykes 1958:54–57). The root of the difficulty lies squarely with the principal's reliance on the behavior of the prisoners under the guard's control as evidence in evaluating the agent's performance. Guards have many different means (both legal and illegal) of affecting the comportment of their prisoners, and those who are rational will do so by enriching themselves at the expense of both prisoners and officials.[17]

A strikingly similar tale can be told about the foreman in a capitalist factory. By paying the dependent foreman less than the more autonomous inside contractor to supervise inputs, a firm would realize savings in personnel costs. Yet what the firm saves on this account is likely to be dissipated by a decrease in labor efficiency on the shop floor. As a company employee on a time wage, the bulk of the foreman's income is not contingent on the performance of the workers. Despite the fact that good pro-

---

[16]The one power they do not have is, of course, the marginal power of putting the noncompliant member in jail (although they do have discretion over assignment to solitary confinement). Prison inmates are not, to be sure, typical members of social groups. Most are held involuntarily and have little desire to comply with the principal's dicta. But, as I have been at pains to argue, routine compliance is a burden on the rational members of any group, and thus is something that each would prefer to evade. From this perspective, the members of many groups occasionally are wont to feel that they too are (unwitting) prisoners. Of course, actual prisoners are especially reluctant to comply. Yet, as Foucault (1979) notes, with some justification, the demand for compliance in prisons has much in common with its quest in other kinds of rehabilitative institutions, like schools and factories.

[17]The agency problem also lies at the root of the famous Iron Law of Oligarchy (Michels [1911] 1962). Michels wryly noted the fact that the parliamentary representatives of the European social democratic parties (the agents, in this example) seldom carried out the revolutionary demands of their working-class constituents (the principals), upon whom they depended for reelection. For another illustration of agency costs, see the discussion in Chapter 4 of the live-and-let-live system of trench warfare in World War I.

duction records doubtlessly increase the foreman's security and provide an occasional bonus, the foreman has less of an incentive to drive the workers than the inside contractor and is more likely to make deals with them. The net result is lower labor efficiency.

The fundamental difficulty with agency relationships is that they raise a second-order monitoring problem. Principals employ agents to monitor members, but unless the agents are themselves monitored, the principals' interests will be compromised. Like all control costs, the costs of monitoring agents are variable; they depend in good part upon the structure of given institutional arrangements.

From the employer's point of view, therefore, each type of input assessment has potential shortcomings. While inside contractors provide high labor efficiency, much of the resultant gain is liable to accrue to them alone. But it is not necessarily less costly to replace contractors with foremen. In spite of foremen's lower remuneration, the system diminishes labor efficiency by putting them at greater risk of being influenced by the very workers they supervise.

The accuracy of monitoring and the magnitude of sanctions are each necessary but insufficient conditions for the attainment of compliance. Compliance cannot be assured unless these separate activities are linked so that the appropriate sanction is invariably allocated to every individual on the basis of performance. Improper or inefficient sanctioning can also erode compliance. Several factors affect the efficiency of sanctioning by interfering with the linkage between information about monitoring and the dispensation of given sanctions. Thus, it matters whether monitoring and sanctioning are carried out by the same person, by different individuals, or—in the extreme case—by different offices. To the degree that such a functional division of labor exists, the units performing each function will pursue their parochial interests more vigorously than their corporate responsibilities, unless they are motivated otherwise. And the longer the delay between performance and sanctioning, the less effective the sanction will be (Wilson and Herrnstein 1985: Ch. 2). Finally, to the degree that sanctioning is not perceived as a certainty, compliance will decrease.[18] These are some of the reasons for the inefficiencies of bureaucratic management.[19]

[18] The clearest evidence comes from research in criminology. Thus, "the most consistent finding in deterrence research is that higher levels of certainty of punishment are associated with lower levels of crime. This pattern has been regularly reported in experimental studies, in studies relating sanction structures to crime rates across different jurisdictions, and in studies relating individual perceptions of sanctions to self-reported criminality" (Minor 1978: 25).

[19] This is by no means to deny that under certain conditions agents can be effectively constrained from exploiting their principals. As was seen in Chapter 5, this is the rationale for the use of roll-call voting in legislatures. Note that a competitive labor market for agents—especially an external one—also can serve the same purpose (Fama 1980).

In light of these facts, perhaps monitoring costs are better minimized by the assessment of outputs rather than inputs.[20] Whereas accurate input assessment requires *continuous* observation, all that accurate output assessment requires is evidence about individual rates of output combined with quality-control procedures. This might appear to be less costly for two reasons. For one thing, it is evident that continuous monitoring is more labor-intensive than the intermittent variety: more agents have to be employed to observe inputs than to assess outputs. For another, the supervisors' ability to monitor inputs is limited by their understanding of the actions taken in the performance of a given task. To the degree that this task is complex, supervisors therefore must possess specialized knowledge in order to monitor inputs effectively. A lay hospital administrator could continuously monitor operating room activity without in the least constraining the quality of a surgeon's performance. This need for specialized knowledge is a source of further agency costs.

For these reasons it would seem that firms always should prefer to measure outputs rather than inputs. But frequently output assessment is not the most effective monitoring strategy. Despite the costs of agency, therefore, firms often find it advantageous to supervise inputs.

COSTS OF OUTPUT ASSESSMENT

Among the many reasons why firms may choose to monitor inputs rather than outputs, one is of fundamental importance. To the degree that output does not accurately reflect individual performance, the firm that relies solely on assessments of it to allocate sanctions will not be in a position to reward compliance and punish noncompliance. In these circumstances, the rational member's incentive to routinely comply is weakened, and, as a consequence, rates of free riding and shirking will increase within the group.

Output is a poor indicator of individual performance when individual members are faced with nonstandard conditions and materials, when the task to be controlled is performed by a subset of members who act as a team, or when the attributes of the output itself are costly to measure.

---

[20] Just as the distinction between principals and agents sometimes may be ambiguous (D. Friedman 1986)—that is, the same legislator may be an agent with respect to voters but a principal with respect to a regulatory agency—this may also be true of the distinction between inputs and outputs. Thus in the prison example above, the prisoners' behavior can be regarded as the prisoners' input, or—from the point of view of principals—as an output of the guards.

The Lack of Standard Conditions and Materials

A unique product—a single piece of output like a major symphony, paint-ing, or book—can hardly be the basis for the assessment of its producer's performance, since no one can determine just how long it *should* have taken to produce. It would be folly to suppose that Brahms was shirking merely because it took him several years to write his first symphony. How much time should it have taken Marx to write *Das Kapital,* or Picasso to paint *Les Demoiselles d'Avignon?* Output can only be used as an accurate indicator of individual performance when output of similar quality is produced from standard materials by several different individuals working in equivalent circumstances. To the extent that these stringent conditions are not met, differences in individual rates of output cannot be reliable in-dicators of differences in individual performance. Deviations from stan-dard conditions tend to discourage compliance, since one person might be rewarded over another merely because of more efficient equipment or more pleasant working conditions—in other words, because the job is easier rather than the performance better.

One of the more celebrated systems of output assessment is the monitor-ing of data production in the physical and natural sciences. The highest rewards in science depend on establishing priority for original discoveries. It would appear that scientists have an incentive to report false data, if this would allow them to obtain credit for an original discovery (Babbage [1830] 1970). A high rate of fraudulent data production would discourage scientific enterprise. To forestall this, researchers are obliged to comply with norms forbidding the promulgation and publication of fraudulent data, among other things. Since scientific production is highly de-centralized, however—and on this account much too costly for input as-sessment—it would appear to be exceedingly difficult to enforce com-pliance with these standards. Despite this daunting situation it is often held that there is relatively little fraud in the annals of the exact sciences (Merton 1973).[21] This exemplary record is not due to the exalted moral qualities of individual scientists, but rather to the possibility of the effec-tive monitoring of output.

---

[21]In their rather sensationalist account, Broad and Wade (1983) argue, however, that the incidence of fraud in the annals of science has been underestimated. According to them, even scientists of the stature of Ptolemy, Newton, Galileo, Mendel, and Millikan on occasion mis-represented their data to portray their theories in better light. The increasing scale of contem-porary science, and the concomitant proliferation of specialized journals, makes the problem of monitoring scientific research considerably more difficult. If my analysis is correct, the incidence of scientific fraud should rise sharply. In addition, as the Lysenko episode in the Soviet Union illustrates, fraud will increase if political authorities become committed to par-ticular scientific theories and employ stronger inducements on their behalf than those avail-able to the scientific community.

The control system in modern science is based upon conventions, established by scientific societies and their journals, that compel the authors of papers to provide enough information about their methods of generating results to enable readers anywhere to reproduce these results in the privacy of their own laboratories. Since there is competition between laboratories for funding and status, scientists' research claims are always subject to the severest scrutiny of their expert colleagues (Merton 1973: 276). Mistaken speculative claims derived from real data are tolerated, if seldom committed; faking the data is not. Scientists who stand accused of the promulgation of fraudulent data have no future in their profession. The sanction against faking the data takes its force from the many years of specialized training that scientists must endure in order to practice their trade. As professional disgrace renders this investment useless, the consequences of proven fraud are serious.[22]

Teamwork

If a single piece of output is the joint product of a team of interdependent workers, it cannot provide clues as to which members of the team complied with group standards (for example, by performing efficiently) and which did not (Bentham 1843). This anonymity provides an incentive for the team member who prefers to shirk to do so, for the cost of shirking is equally borne by all members of the team. Thus teams of rational workers are likely to produce at suboptimal levels in the absence of supervision of their individual inputs. Manual freight-loading offers a standard example. As Armen Alchian and Harold Demsetz (1972: 779) put it: "Two men jointly lift cargo into trucks. Solely by observing the total weight loaded per day, it is impossible to determine each person's marginal productivity. . . . The output is yielded by a team, by definition, and it is not a sum of separable outputs of each of its members." In this case the agency costs that are incurred by supervision of inputs may be more than offset by a corresponding increase in output.

Costs of Measuring the Quality of Output

Often a firm desires to know not merely that a task has been carried out, but that it has been carried out conscientiously. Because the quality of an output is costly to measure (Akerlof 1970), a control system depending

---

[22] This sanctioning mechanism only holds in fields that employ precise measurement and standardized data that allow each scientist's results to be checked and double-checked by others. While this is indeed the situation in the physical and natural sciences, it is rarely approached in the social sciences.

solely on output assessment provides rational members with an incentive to maximize the rate of their production at the expense of its quality. The firm that cannot detect output of low quality will bear a cost if it is subsequently discovered; hence the incentive to invest in the measurement of output, or quality control.

But the measurement of anything is costly (Barzel 1982). Think of the costs involved in measuring the properties of a familiar object like an apple. Some of the apple's attributes (such as its weight) can be measured rather accurately at slight cost, but others—such as its taste, nutritional value, and ability to stay fresh—are much more difficult to assess. Sellers often resort to costly practices such as giving product warranties or establishing brand names in order to compensate buyers for their inability to measure the properties of certain commodities and thereby to convince them that the item is of a high standard of quality. Quality control can be so expensive—depending on the nature of the piece produced and the state of available technology—that in some cases it is less costly to resort to input than output assessment.[23]

Although it is costly to assess the quality of a simple commodity like an apple, imagine how much more costly it is to assess the quality of the performance of a given task. It is often relevant to determine not only that the task was performed, but also that it was performed in a certain way, with a certain attitude (Williamson 1975). Personnel managers, football coaches, and graduate professors all express a good deal of interest in the spirit of their respective charges. The point is that to the degree goods and services are multidimensional, the costs of measuring them substantially increase.

The Dissipation of the Group's Capital Stock

Output assessment also has a tendency to dissipate the group's capital stock. In this kind of monitoring system individuals have an incentive to increase their output, but to the degree that their performance depends on equipment that is owned by the employer (or by the group as a whole), they will be motivated to overutilize this equipment. It is rational for truck drivers who are paid by the piece delivered to drive their company-owned rigs into the ground in order to maximize their wages. While this practice

---

[23] The demise of the putting-out industry offers a classic example of the disadvantages of output assessment. Merchants soured on the system when they discovered that the workers substituted low-priced yarn for the high-priced material that had been extended to them (Landes 1969). Marglin (1974) argues—controversially—that considerations of control were key factors in the victory of the factory over putting-out and other decentralized forms of industrial organization. Although a desire to reduce control costs may provide part of the reason for the growth of factory organization it is hardly the only such consideration.

undoubtedly increases their personal productivity, it erodes the firm's re-sources. By circumventing rules designed to keep vehicles in proper run-ning order, overzealous drivers reduce the utility of their trucks to the firm as a whole. Similarly, mimeograph and duplicating machines are fre-quently overutilized by party members anxious to gain influence within their organization.

Some of these points can be exemplified by considering the fate of the most extensive attempt to utilize output assessment in the history of the capitalist firm, namely scientific management.

Scientific Management

The aim of scientific management is not merely to minimize shirking on the shop floor, but to get the workers to produce more than either they, or their bosses, think is possible. Its novelty lies in the realm of monitoring labor performance. Production is monitored in four separate ways: through stopwatch time study, functional foremanship, production controls, and refinements to existing systematic management procedures.

The difficulty with previous output assessment (or piece-work) schemes lay in setting the proper production goals so as to achieve maximum labor efficiency. The traditional approach to setting production goals had been by rule of thumb (Norton, [1932] 1968: 47; Nelson 1980: 8), but this could hardly maximize labor efficiency. To do that, it was necessary to determine optimal, yet feasible, rates of individual output. Were these established, then the piece-rate could have been used to induce workers to perform op-timally. But how could such optimal outputs ever be established? The an-swer appeared to be stopwatch time study.

The first requirement of time study is the measurement of individual output: teamwork, which encourages shirking by raising the cost of moni-toring individual performance, is to be avoided if at all possible (F. Taylor [1911] 1947b: 52–53). Then each worker's task is analyzed kinestheti-cally and broken down into standardized component units (Abruzzi 1956: 28–29). Next, a "first-class" worker is selected for study and instructed to perform each unit task while being timed (sometimes overtly, sometimes covertly) by a stopwatch. Often several workers are studied, and the differ-ent observations are averaged. These data are transformed by a rating pro-cedure presumed to represent what production performance ought to be. Allowances are then made for fatigue and delays of different types. What finally emerges is a specific expectation of individual output, with all waste motions eliminated. Time study enables employers to specify a large daily task for workers in standard conditions. Once each worker's task is defined, it is easy to reward success with high pay, and to offer inferior pay for failure.

Scientific management also strikes at the position of agents. The problem with foremen (F. Taylor [1903] 1947a: 93) is that their duties are so varied and call for such special information and ability that it is very difficult to find suitable persons to do them. The alternative is to subdivide a single foreman's work among eight workers ("functional foremanship"). By restricting the scope of their responsibilities, functional foremanship reduces the training costs of foremen. In addition,

> it becomes entirely practicable to apply the . . . leading principles of management to the bosses as well as to the workmen. Each foreman can have a task assigned him which is so accurately measured that he will be kept fully occupied and still will be able to perform his entire function. This renders it possible to pay him high wages when he is successful by giving him a premium similar to that offered the men and leave him with low pay when he fails.
>
> (Taylor [1903] 1947a: 105)

Cost accounting procedures are the final monitoring device in scientific management (for a survey of early developments in the United States, see Garner 1954). They permit managers to gauge the productivity of entire departments, rather than of individual laborers.[24]

Taken as a whole, this system represents a concerted attempt to decrease the cost of output assessment in industrial production. Its greatest success is in continuous-process production (Woodward 1965; Kelley 1982), where standard materials and conditions are most often found. In other types of production, however, its effectiveness is more limited.

Scientific management spurs resistance because it challenges the powers of various entrenched interests within the factory. Functional foremanship

---

[24] That scientific management dramatically increases the employers' control over the labor process is a fact that has been the leitmotif of recent Marxist industrial sociology (Braverman 1974; Marglin 1974; Stone 1974; Clegg and Dunkerly 1980; and Clawson 1980). Following Marx ([1867] 1965: I, 331), who argues that the control exercised by the capitalist is "rooted in the unavoidable antagonism between the exploiter and the living and laboring raw material he exploits," this literature often sees capital's desire to control the labor process as motivated by its impulse to secure an ultimate victory over the proletariat. Isn't it more reasonable to suggest that one of the important reasons for the desire for control has less to do with the grand issue of class struggle, and more with the prosaic one of output assessment? After all, controls are as necessary in worker-owned cooperatives—such as the plywood factories described by Bernstein (1980)—as they are in more traditional firms. As Lenin's well-known advocacy of scientific management suggests (Bendix 1956: 206–7), the appeal of Taylorism was by no means limited to ardent capitalists (for a discussion of Gramsci's alternative, see Clegg and Dunkerly 1980: 106–22).

is merely a polite way to describe a radical dilution of the foreman's authority. As a result foremen often stood in the way of innovations in cost accounting and production control procedures (Chandler 1977: 274–75). Scientific management was also anathema to skilled workers, for its emphasis on radical specialization and management control rendered many craft skills superfluous. In the steel industry, where skilled workers were well organized, it took the Homestead strike to break their power so that new management procedures could be established (Stone 1974). By the same token, however, the increasing de-skilling of factory labor contributed to the development of industrial unions (Hoxie 1915: 129). This resistance raised the employers' costs of adopting scientific management procedures.

Another problem is that rate-setting is not amenable to "scientific" solutions. Once workers appreciate that time-study engineers are there to set piece-rates, they attempt to outwit them by deliberate acts of sabotage (Matthewson 1931; Whyte 1955: 14–27). When workers have little opportunity to move up a job ladder, and time study is used as a rate-setting device, what results is a two-person zero-sum game between the observed and the observer (Abruzzi 1956: 19–20, 50–53). Rate-setting then becomes the outcome of bargaining processes between workers and management. The game works like this: the workers present a biased impression of the job requirements to protect lenient rates, while they protest stringent ones. Management redesigns jobs in such a way that the rates become more stringent. As in any bargaining situation, the ultimate rate is determined by the relative power of the respective players, rather than by any "scientific" procedures.[25]

If workers think that the rate for a particular job is too low, they engage in output restriction, but they work hard at jobs with favorable rates (Roy 1952). Their work behavior seems to be determined by a complex calculus in which the actual piece-rate plays some part, but relieving boredom and socializing with their comrades also tend to be salient. Although the existence of output restriction provided the rationale for scientific management in the first place, it is obvious that the medicine is not up to the cure. Scientific management increases the scope for output assessment in the factory and thereby reduces monitoring costs. It does so, however, at the expense of increased wages. Further, when managers do not employ sufficiently high wages, workers will prefer leisure or social activity to hard labor (Dalton 1948).

---

[25] Ironically, unionization—a movement that was given strong impetus by the adoption of scientific management—has significantly strengthened labor's hand in the rate-setting game, to the detriment of stringent rates.

What then determines whether firms will adopt input or output assessment? Output assessment is always favored save in those situations where there is a lack of standard conditions and materials, high amounts of teamwork, high costs of measuring the joint product, and potential dissipation of the capital stock. Output assessment is limited when it comes to the performance of complex, nonroutine tasks—the kinds of tasks that are particularly costly to monitor. When monitoring costs rise, the advantages of input assessment grow.

How then do firms attain control in the face of high monitoring costs? The fact that there may be more labor efficiency on the shop floor than analyses based solely on considerations of supervision would suggest (Roy 1952; Burawoy 1979) provides a hint. Compliance may result not merely from the desire to gain rewards or avoid punishment, but also from access to certain kinds of *immanent* goods. Some of these—like the social contact engendered in cooperative labor—may be merely the unintentional by-products of the work setting. Thus, workers who have fatiguing, repetitive jobs often create competitive games amongst themselves to relieve their boredom and help pass the time of day (nevertheless, for a skeptical note, see Kelley 1982).

Some firms, however, extend immanent goods to their workers intentionally in an attempt to win their loyalty and commitment. Many modern capitalist firms do not rely strictly on compensation as a control strategy. By providing immanent goods in addition to compensation, these firms are able to rely, to some extent, on *obligation* to produce the joint good. Indeed, for Sombart (1953: 36) the capitalist firm is an organization that is not so radically different from the *Gemeinschaft*-like groups that preceded it in the history of production. Like families, tribes, and corporate village communities, the capitalist firm also must attain compliance to production rules. To reach this goal, it sometimes has to inspire a certain amount of esprit de corps and trust.[26]

THE INTERNAL LABOR MARKET AS A
QUASI-OBLIGATORY GROUP

We have seen that for tasks that are complex or interdependent or nonroutine, monitoring is extremely costly. Under these circumstances compensation is unlikely to produce optimal levels of compliance. Yet many such tasks do get accomplished in firms. How can this be explained? One

[26]Similarly, recent studies in industrial organization (Williamson 1975; A. Breton and Wintrobe 1981) have emphasized the importance of trust as a determinant of firm success.

solution to the problem of costly monitoring is for the employer to provide workers with immanent goods, so that their dependence on the firm, and their willingness to accept some obligation to fully comply with its production rules, increases. These immanent goods—such as insurance, welfare benefits, and the prospect of a career—must be offered to workers in addition to compensation. And it is precisely these kinds of goods that the internal labor market offers that other kinds of firms do not.

An *internal labor market* is an administrative unit within which the pricing and allocation of labor are governed by a set of administrative rules and procedures rather than determined by supply and demand (Doeringer and Piore 1971: 1–2). Its distinctive feature is that most of the jobs within it are filled by the promotion or transfer of workers who have already gained entry to the firm. Consequently, these jobs are shielded from the direct influences of competitive forces in the external market. Internal labor markets generally have a differential job structure, some formal means of disseminating information about vacant positions, and a system of on-the-job training.

The classic example of the internal labor market in industry is the large Japanese corporation with its lifetime employment, seniority-plus-merit wage system, and high level of firm welfare benefits (Dore 1973; Cole 1973). "Japanese-style" management has been making inroads in the United States and other Western countries (Ouchi 1981). The increasing popularity of internal labor markets in contemporary firms suggests that this form of industrial organization may be profitable, at least under present economic conditions. Does the apparent success of internal labor markets owe anything to high labor efficiency?

The consensus of the literature is that it does,[27] and that the value of the immanent goods provided by the firm is the reason. By holding out the promise of promotion within the firm's hierarchy, contingent on maximum labor efficiency, the internal labor market serves to tie the interests of the workers directly to those of the firm in a continuing way (Williamson 1975: 77). The system works best if the alternative firms to which the worker might otherwise turn for a promotion are also internal labor markets. In this case (and Japan provides the best example) the worker simultaneously faces high rewards for compliance and little prospect of upgrading or even of maintaining his job outside the firm—hence, very high exit costs. Such a system of internal labor markets increases the depen-

---

[27] This conclusion is, however, not firmly established. The high degree of cultural homogeneity and stratification by gender among permanent employees in Japan undoubtedly allows greater scope for social sanctions than exists in comparable Western corporations.

dence of employees and thereby makes it feasible to obtain compliance from them in the absence of continuous monitoring.[28]

To appreciate how the internal labor market operates, take the case of Polaroid, an American firm with a strong internal labor market. During the late 1970s the company had highly differentiated job descriptions, and each job was divided into seven pay steps. To qualify for promotion, workers were judged on their work habits, attendance, attitude, and other personal characteristics (Edwards 1979: 143). The highest steps for each job were reserved for workers who "set examples to others in methods and use of time" and who suggested ways of "improving job methods" and "increasing the effectiveness of the group." These workers needed to show cooperation, enthusiasm, and the right kind of attitude in order to advance. Supervisors had to provide special justification for outstanding ratings. The step system at Polaroid provided up to a 30 percent increase in pay contingent on individual performance. In addition, seniority was rewarded: every employee who stayed at the job for five years earned an extra 5 percent. Finally, if layoffs were required, the company established an elaborate bumping system in which seniority was the major criterion.

The key instrument of the internal labor market in producing labor efficiency is the value of its immanent benefits. By offering each worker the possibility of a career, rather than a dead-end job, it encourages individual responsibility, resourcefulness, and conscientious performance. The prospect of receiving these goods—in conjunction with their relative scarcity elsewhere—means that termination from the firm becomes a severe sanction. Given the severity of this sanction, the firm need not engage in continuous, on-the-spot monitoring. It can use less intrusive methods and less frequent spot-checks. The threat of blocked mobility (or, worse, termination) is sufficient to help reduce monitoring costs.

Nevertheless, the costs of providing workers with careers as well as extensive fringe benefits are substantial; they cannot be sustained by marginal firms and are threatened in declining markets.[29] After all, a policy that rewards seniority is very different from one that makes rewards con-

---

[28] Bendix (1956: 211) presents a similar argument on behalf of bureaucracy in general.

[29] Evidently, the internal labor market is a device that enables employers to hold on to their labor. It is well-suited for firms that train their workforce, for it helps them to preserve this investment (Doeringer and Piore 1971). At the same time it provides an incentive for workers to develop firm-specific skills that have low value in the external labor market. For these reasons, the internal labor market is associated with a highly skilled labor force. As such it is found in conjunction with external labor markets that cover "peripheral" segments of the economy. In Japan, for example, only about 35 percent of the labor force is employed by corporations having internal labor markets (for explanations of the development of Japanese internal labor markets see Cole 1971; Dore 1973).

tingent on the individual worker's marginal productivity. By giving higher pay to older workers, internal labor markets pay a premium for the stability, loyalty, and dedication of their work force, for older workers are usually less productive than younger ones (Edwards 1979: 152).[30]

All told, firms will always invest in control, but how much and what kind depend on the nature of the good being produced and the opportunities for monitoring and sanctioning. Whether monitoring is based on input or output assessment depends to a significant degree on the nature of the relevant task.[31] Costs involved in measuring compliance and mobilizing resources for sanctioning are the major constraints on the adoption of any control system. Thus there is no single solution to the problem of control; the most effective strategy in one situation may prove to be relatively costly in another.

To the degree that production is nonroutine or involves teamwork, this weighs against monitoring by output assessment. Yet each form of input assessment—inside contracting and foremanship—has its liabilities. Inside contracting can attain high labor efficiency, but only at the price of large agency costs. Whereas foremanship reduces agency costs, it is unable to provide high levels of labor efficiency. Despite this, some form of input assessment is preferable so long as the employer cannot inexpensively monitor individual output.

Efficient monitoring is scientific management's rationale. By using elaborate techniques of output assessment in conjunction with the differential piece-rate, the firm hopes to reduce its agency costs and spur labor efficiency on the shop floor. In certain industries (particularly those employing continuous-process production) this hope is frequently realized. But elsewhere the firm meets higher costs due to the resistance of individual workers, their unions, and agents. Finally, the growth of plant bureaucracy necessary to administer scientific management imposes further costs.

By offering its workers a valued immanent good—in particular, the prospect of a career—firms with an internal labor market can overcome

[30]The costs of a seniority policy may, however, be borne by systematically underpaying young workers and overpaying older ones (Lazear 1979). Thus, the granting of what amounts to tenure in the internal labor market may not be any more costly for the firm than a system that compensates workers according to their marginal productivity—given the existence of a finite termination date, that is, mandatory retirement.

[31]Sometimes this calculation is far from easy. Ouchi and Maguire (1975) report that one of the major determinants of the form of monitoring adopted in their sample of retail department stores is company policy: one company consistently favors input assessment, the other just as consistently favors output assessment. The authors provide no convincing explanation of this difference in policies.

the inherent difficulties of monitoring complex, nonroutine tasks. Therefore, it is reasonable to consider the internal labor market as a quasi-
obligatory group. Due to the immanent goods it supplies to its workers, it
provides greater monitoring economies than pure compensatory groups.

Even so, this form of organization is not well suited to all types of firms.
Because it requres substantial resources to make the offer of a career cred-
ible, the internal labor market is best suited for well-established large
firms. Further, its advantages depend partly on the supply of skilled labor,
on the importance of company-specific skills in the enterprise as a whole
(Williamson 1981), and on the competitiveness of the labor market, which
affects workers' dependence. As these factors vary, so the value of the internal labor market to the firm waxes and wanes.

Thus, by its focus on control, the theory of group solidarity gives a systematic account of what otherwise appears to be a hodgepodge of control
strategies in the firm. Every group—whether compensatory, obligatory, or
both—faces the problem of control in the production of joint goods. Given
the ingenuity of human beings in evading those who would seek to control
their behavior, these solutions are never stable; the struggle over control is
a constant feature of groups attempting to survive.

CHAPTER VIII

ECONOMIZING ON CONTROL COSTS
IN INTENTIONAL COMMUNITIES

The protruding stake is hammered down.

Japanese proverb

SO LONG AS joint production is based on the performance of simple, independent, and largely repetitive tasks, compensation is adequate to provide compliance. When monitoring becomes very costly, however, even firms are likely to resort to solidarity to ensure their survival. They do this by offering workers immanent goods that increase their dependence. But if dependence lowers control costs, then are controls really needed in obligatory groups? The issue is controversial.

Normativists are willing to grant the necessity of controls in compensatory groups, but they downplay their significance in obligatory groups, or *Gemeinschaften*. To understand why, we must probe the meaning of the concept of *Gemeinschaft*. By it is meant

something that goes far beyond mere local community. . . . [I]t encompasses all forms of relationship which are characterized by a high degree of personal intimacy, emotional depth, moral commitment, social cohesion and continuity in time. Community [that is, *Gemeinschaft*] is founded on man conceived in his wholeness rather than in one or another of the roles, taken separately, that he may hold in a social order. It draws its psychological strength from levels of motivation deeper than those of mere volition or interest, and it achieves its fulfillment in a submergence of individual will that is not possible in unions of mere convenience or rational assent. Community is a fusion of feeling and thought, of tradition and commitment, of membership and volition. . . . Its archetype is the family, and in almost every type of genuine community the nomenclature of the family is prominent. . . . Fundamental to the strength of the bond of community is the real or imagined antithesis formed in the same social setting by the non-communal relations of competition or conflict, utility or contractual assent. These, by their relative impersonality and anonymity, highlight the close personal ties of community.

(Nisbet 1966:47–48)

Free riding should hardly be expected to occur in such a setting. Compliance in the *Gemeinschaft* is achieved not by some control system that enforces members' obligations, but instead by an entirely different mechanism—the internalization of norms. From the normativist point of view, controls should be virtually superfluous in obligatory groups.

From the perspective of the group solidarity theory, however, rational egoists should be just as willing to evade their corporate obligations in the family or the community as in the workplace. If there is less free riding in the family than the firm, then this ultimately has to be explained by the family's greater control capacity. As the control capacity of any kind of group varies—even the type of group that sociologists regard as a *Gemeinschaft*—so should its compliance.

No doubt some part of the family's control advantage derives from the high dependence of its members. Yet this raises an important question about the development of compliance in obligatory groups. Since the firm can attain compliance for tasks whose monitoring costs are relatively high by increasing its members' dependence, then why must obligatory groups— whose members tend to be dependent in the first place—also have to be concerned with the costs of control? Because the production of some kinds of joint goods requires much more extensive compliance than that required for the maximization of profit. To the degree that a group imposes extensive obligations on its members, its control costs will tend to increase and thereby place a constraint on its survival.

This chapter will show, first, that—despite normativist claims—controls are necessary for the survival of even the most highly solidary groups, and second, that the costs of these controls can be economized by the adoption of particular institutional arrangements. The effects of two such arrangements—roll-call voting and the internal labor market—have already been discussed at some length. But these examples far from exhaust the list of feasible economizing arrangements. Some of the arrangements to be discussed have a faintly coercive ring about them. A good number of the examples are drawn from workplaces and other settings not typically considered to be solidary. Yet if the solidarity theory is correct, then such economizing arrangements also should be found in profusion in those groups with the most extensive obligations as well. This view stands in stark contrast to the normativist claim that compliance in the *Gemeinschaft* is achieved in more voluntaristic—and mysterious—ways.

To these ends, the chapter explores the effects of different institutional arrangements on solidarity in one notably obligatory kind of group, the intentional community.[1] By *intentional community,* I refer to a group, the bulk of whose members are not cemented by kinship or marriage and who choose to live together for an indefinite period of time. Moreover,

> it intentionally implements a set of values, having been planned in order to bring about the attainment of certain ideals, and its operating decisions are made in terms of those values. Its primary end is an existence that matches the ideals. All other goals are secondary and related to ends involving harmony, brotherhood, mutual support, and value expression. . . . [U]nlike monastic orders, which may serve the interests of a wider church community, or businesses, which are concerned with the interests of the market or of absentee owners such as stockholders, [it] operates to serve first and foremost its own members; any benefits it provides for the outside are generally secondary and based on the need to support its own. . . . Maintaining the sense of group solidarity is as important as meeting specific goals.
>
> (Kanter 1972: 2–3)

Intentional communities are quintessential obligatory groups whose members seek to produce joint goods—like a sense of community, friendship, love, and the feeling of security—all of which flow from the existence of social harmony. Not surprisingly, intentional communities are often considered as exemplary instances of the *Gemeinschaft*. Oriented to the pursuit of noninstrumental goals, their members interact on a primary group basis and are organized in terms of nonspecific, generally interchangeable roles (Vallier 1959).

The principal threat to the production of social harmony comes from rational egoism in any of its manifestations. Members consent to the establishment of controls to reduce the risk of individualistic behavior in work, in play, in the allocation of resources, in all aspects of community life. The extensiveness of these controls cannot be overemphasized. Many intentional communities seek compliance in thought as well as deed. According to an ex-member of one such group,

> there is a drastic difference from the demands on the personality made in civil life. There only outward conformity is demanded. I think that few total

---

[1] A very similar story can be told about the attainment of solidarity in another classic *Gemeinschaft* site, tribal society. For evidence to this effect that is consistent with much of the above analysis, see Michael Taylor (1982).

institutions demand so much conformity down into the private recesses of feeling. In a concentration camp, officer candidate school, even POW camp *cum* brainwash, you can still gripe, provided you obey—and if not publicly, then privately, and if not gripe, than at least *feel* opposed. It is difficult to convey the degree to which the Bruderhof demanded and got conformity in the most private attitudes and feelings.

(quoted in Zablocki 1971: 238)

Though these communities seek high solidarity, that not all of them manage to achieve it is an understatement. The residue of communal breakdown pervades the contemporary scene as well as the historical record. Do variations in control capacity account for the differential solidarity of these groups?

Intentional communities have arisen in many different historical eras and countries (Zablocki 1980: 19–41). Although there is a voluminous literature on specific communities, sources of systematic data are scanty. However, several comparative studies of intentional communities do exist (among them, Nordhoff [1875] 1965; Spiro 1956; Talmon 1972; Kanter 1972; Erasmus 1977; and Zablocki 1980). Together with case studies of individual communities, these works offer sufficient evidence to inquire into the dynamics of compliance in such groups.

In the face of the now-familiar measurement quandary, longevity is often used as a proxy for levels of community solidarity. The more solidary the members, the higher their compliance with corporate obligations and the longer their community should survive as a separate entity. In this regard, Rosabeth Kanter's *Commitment and Community* (1972) stands out as the most important study. Ninety-one intentional communities were founded in the United States between 1780 and 1860. Of these, eleven "successful" communities survived for at least twenty-five years. Seventy-nine other "unsuccessful" groups did not meet this criterion. Kanter investigates the social characteristics of nine of the successful and twenty-one of the unsuccessful groups in order to determine whether any subset of these characteristics tended to distinguish longer-lived communities from shorter-lived ones. To the degree that longevity is a function of solidarity, the characteristics that are associated with group survival should also promote solidarity.

It turns out that a large number of factors do differentiate the successful communities from the unsuccessful ones, including hierarchy, cultural homogeneity, group rewards, obligatory confession, limits on privacy, and public sanctions. These and other community characteristics will be assessed in terms of their potential for economizing on the costs of monitoring and sanctioning.

Monitoring poses groups with a fundamental problem. In order to attain joint goods, most (if not all) members must comply with production rules. But rational members would prefer to consume the good without complying, if their noncompliance can be concealed from their comrades. Therefore, one way of reaping monitoring economies is by extending the opportunity to observe members' performance of their obligations.

Increasing Visibility

The less chance members have to be alone, the less difficult it is to observe their behavior. For this reason the fictional rulers of Oceania in Orwell's *1984* installed telescreens throughout their realm. But actual groups have ample, if less technically sophisticated, means of observation at their disposal. Among these is increasing the visibility of their members' activities.

Architecture.   In the first place, visibility can be enhanced by placing people in certain kinds of physical structures. Since the literature on intentional communities tends to ignore considerations of architecture, illustrations must come from other settings. The most famous example is Jeremy Bentham's eighteenth-century design, the Panopticon—a circular, glass-roofed prison with cells in tiers around the wall facing a central rotunda. A few guards placed in the rotunda could keep the prisoners under constant surveillance (Foucault 1979). Although Bentham's structure was never adopted in England, its influence can be seen in such maximum-security prisons as those located at Breda, in Holland, and at Joliet, in Illinois.

The architecture of nineteenth-century American women's colleges (Horowitz 1984) provides a less draconian instance. Whereas men's colleges were designed to create a cluster of buildings arranged around a common, the earliest women's colleges (Vassar and Wellesley) were fashioned after seminaries, like Mount Holyoke. These women's colleges were a single building where students lived, studied, worked and prayed—subject to close supervision all the while, so as to protect their femininity.

Finally, consider the layout of government offices. Whereas high-ranking American bureaucrats are accustomed to having their own offices or having desks in private areas carved out by partitions, their Japanese counterparts often have their desks in full view of their coworkers. In Japanese offices a greater proportion of the individual's acts are visible—and hence subject to monitoring—than they are in comparable American ones.[2]

Public Rituals.   Visibility also can be promoted by adopting rituals that require members to perform certain acts in public. Oral examinations for doctoral candidates provide an example that is familiar to all academics. Hence, it should be no surprise that obligatory attendance at public meetings is a staple of communal life. The most important ritual held by Seattle's Love Israel Family—a three-hundred-person commune I observed over the course of several years—is public baptism. At the Amana and Economy communities religious meetings were the principal recreations (Nordhoff [1875] 1965: 400). Amana's meetings were held three mornings a week and every evening. The Shakers held meetings every night, though not all of them were religious (Nordhoff [1875] 1965: 142).

The Specificity of Obligations.   Compliance is more easily observed when people are required to meet highly specific obligations rather than nonspecific ones. In age-graded societies, for instance, it is simple to determine which youngsters fail to pay their elders sufficient respect (Goffman 1967). In the Japanese and Korean languages deference is expressed in verb endings, and in the Romance languages it is expressed in polite and familiar forms of address. Not only do these practices reinforce status distinctions, but they also highlight verbal violations of deference norms. If all members sharing some visible characteristic X (say, women) are precluded from engaging in activities of type Z (driving), then it is child's play to monitor anyone with characteristic X who is deviant in this respect. The more that visible characteristics such as age and sex govern individual behavior, the lower the costs of observation. When obligations are specific, it is easier to engage in something akin to output assessment.

Mechanisms of Preference-Revelation

Although architecture, public rituals, and the specificity of obligations do affect visibility, members still may resist complying when it comes to their less visible obligations. A certain man may shirk the moment his boss turns his back, and he may cheat on his wife while at an out-of-town convention. Both boss and wife might be made better off if they were apprised of his inclinations. It follows that any means of encouraging members to

[2] The role of architectural arrangements on legislative behavior is mentioned in footnote 6 in Chapter 5.

reveal their true preferences and feelings also helps reduce monitoring costs.

Consensual decision-making is one such mechanism. The process usually entails long meetings where people are supposed to let their hair down; in the course of the meeting they gradually come to reveal their true feelings about the issues at hand. As a result private attitudes are made public. Some (Pateman 1970) have argued that consensual decision-making tends to commit members to the ensuing collective decisions. Even so, this commitment entails another kind of cost—considerable time and exposure to superfluous information (Buchanan and Tullock 1962).

Consensual decision-making is found disproportionately in the successful intentional communities. Often community decisions require unanimous consent. For example, decision-making in the Bruderhof, a long-lived contemporary commune in New York State, is based on the notion that a "right decision" exists:

> The right decision is right for the entire group and for each member, equally. But no person acting alone can ever find this right decision. For this reason, everyone in the Bruderhof has a duty to become involved in every decision and to speak his mind if any relevant thought occurs to him, even if it contradicts the entire rest of the Brotherhood.
>
> (Zablocki 1971: 155)

Obligatory confession is a far more straightforward means of revealing preferences. Like many other successful intentional communities (Kanter 1972: 112), the Bruderhof does not rely on norms of self-disclosure alone. All individuals must participate in a program of confession (or "pastoral counseling") by members of the hierarchy who are skilled diagnosticians of attitudinal failings, and who also serve as constant observers of all individuals. Usually, members are given strong incentives to reveal past deviant activity. Those who voluntarily admit to wrongdoing are treated more leniently than those who try to conceal it and are later discovered.

Positive Sanctions.   All these means of increasing visibility discourage the behavior of would-be deviants. But visibility can sometimes be promoted in quite a different fashion. Although deviants have an incentive to conceal their behavior, the compliant have precisely the opposite incentive: they have an interest in publicizing their good deeds. This means that one of the solutions to the problem of visibility can rest with a sanctioning mechanism because the use of positive sanctions—a commonplace in nearly all groups—will lead the compliant to apprise others of their exemplary behavior.[3]

Unfortunately, there is a catch: the prospect of being rewarded also motivates deviants to publicly misrepresent their behavior. To the degree that members are able to offer convincing evidence of their compliance—evidence that is unavailable to the deviant wolves in sheep's clothing—the use of positive sanctions can increase visibility. Without such unequivocal evidence, however, all self-reported compliance must be subject to (costly) scrutiny.

Sharing the Monitoring Burden

Whereas arrangements that increase visibility make it easier to observe members—a task that is more or less difficult given the characteristics of the group—no member will undertake this responsibility without being motivated to do so. Groups can delegate the monitoring task to individual agents, but this is likely to entail high costs. If the burden of monitoring could be shared among the entire membership, then agency costs could be avoided. The rub is that rational members will only engage in monitoring on the group's behalf if they have a sufficiently large incentive to do so.

Group Rewards.   Any allocation scheme that rewards members on the basis of the total level of group compliance offers one source of such incentives. Every individual still is interested in shirking or free riding, since the rest of the group, but not the individual, will bear the consequences of noncompliance, and the larger the group, the greater the disincentive to comply. But no one in such a group has an interest in letting any of the others evade corporate obligations, since to the degree that others do not comply, each individual's share of the group reward is diminished.[4] Therefore collective rewards promote a sort of monitoring cost-sharing not found in groups where individual reward structures prevail.[5]

---

[3] I owe this point to Herbert L. Costner.

[4] As Douglas Heckathorn (1985) points out, collective punishment also can promote monitoring economies. This occurs when an entire group is punished for the behavior of one of its members. In such cases, monitoring costs are reduced for two reasons. First, the monitoring agent need not know the identity of the culprit, but merely the group to which that person belongs. Second, this kind of punishment provides all members with an incentive to monitor each other informally. Collective punishment is, however, a strategy that is highly sensitive to group size. It fails in excessively small groups, because the odds of punishment are too remote to justify control costs. Yet if the group is too large, punishment becomes inevitable, and as a result, the group will either be faced with massive defections or with the prospect of revolt against the monitoring agent.

[5] For evidence that profit-sharing enterprises have higher productivity than comparable firms without such group rewards, see Cable and FitzRoy (1980) and Bernstein (1980). If

As it happens, most of the successful intentional communities (Kanter 1972: 94–95; 104; Zablocki 1971; Erasmus 1977: 140) have communal rather than individual private property rights. This means that each member's level of consumption is determined by the productive effort of the collectivity as a whole. Indeed, sometimes the passion for communalism extends beyond the distribution of property to include proscriptions against monogamy and the obligation to engage in various forms of collective sexual activity (Kanter 1972: 12–13, 50–51).

Limiting Privacy.   Groups can also make rules requiring members to spend much of their time in group activities. The higher the number and density of interactions among members, the greater the opportunity to directly observe each other's behavior. Proscriptions against secrecy and limits on privacy—over and above the prohibition of private property—are frequent in intentional communities.[6] Members are expected to respond with methodical compliance to the community's demand for information about every aspect of their life (Zablocki 1971: 194). Secrecy is the most serious sin of all. Yet there is a difficulty here. Groups that rely on rules of this sort are likely to encounter enforcement dilemmas: either members will comply only when it suits them or agents must engage in monitoring to insure compliance. Any strategy that rests on monitoring to reduce monitoring costs can hardly be cost-effective.[7]

Rewarding Informants.   Of course, rewards can be provided to informants who bring forth evidence about another member's noncompliance.

---

group rewards promote productivity, however, why have worker-owned firms and cooperatives fared so poorly in capitalist societies (for the British evidence, see D. Miller 1981)? Apparently because these gains are more than offset by economic disadvantages that also flow from cooperative ownership. On the one hand, cooperative firms will not take on enough labor to reach efficient size; on the other, they are likely to have suboptimal levels of investment (for reasons discussed by Meade 1972; Clayre 1980; and D. Miller 1981, among others). Due to these considerations, cooperatively owned productive units are most likely to survive in capitalist industries where small-scale production is technically efficient, labor-intensive production methods dominate, and technological change is slow. The printing, footwear, clothing, and plywood industries—each of which has witnessed some successful cooperatively owned firms—seem to share these characteristics. The Basque cooperatives at Mondragón (Thomas and Logan 1982; Saive 1980; Bradley and Gelb 1981, 1983) are exceptional in this regard. The success of the Mondragón cooperatives appears due, in part, to the establishment of their own financial and credit institutions.

[6] Posner (1980) offers a parellel discussion of the role of privacy in primitive society.

[7] This is the principal objection to one possible solution to the solidarity problem. Laver (1981: 62–69) argues that if it were possible to enforce one very general norm—say, a norm that members should always obey the law—then this would serve to reduce a whole host of specific compliance problems, which are unlikely to be resolved, to a single compliance problem, enforcement of this one norm. Why it should be more feasible to enforce one general norm than a host of specific rules is unclear.

As the Oneida did before it (Kanter 1972: 15), the Bruderhof rewards informants who discern and admonish wrongness in any other member (Zablocki 1971: 228–29). But this raises questions about the reliability of informants. Since they have an inducement to slander, resources must be spent to verify the informants' stories.[8] This too entails second-order monitoring costs.

Gossip. Sometimes evidence about noncompliance comes to the group's attention without remuneration, as if by magic. People have a great tendency to gossip about their fellows. This testifies to their willingness to engage in horizontal monitoring. Gossip can be a source of considerable information—generally of an invidious sort—and it is provided with few costs. In the kibbutz, gossip is virulent:

> Everyone here judges, everyone is judged, and no weakness can succeed for long in escaping judgment. There are no secret corners. You are being judged every minute of your life. That is why each and every one of us is forced to wage war against his nature. To purify himself. We polish each other as a river polishes its pebbles. . . . Gossip is simply the other name for judging. By means of gossip we overcome our natural instincts and gradually become better men. Gossip plays a powerful part in our lives, because our lives are exposed like a sun-drenched courtyard.
>
> (Oz 1973: 9)

And as one young member of the Bruderhof recounts, gossip made him "constantly on the lookout, constantly doing things for the look, for the effect. . . . To me it was two different lives. When I got to school (outside the community) I acted one way. The second I got on the bus to go home, I changed myself and acted a completely different way" (Zablocki 1971: 227).[9]

In the absence of formal judicial processes, gossip can assume great importance. There are no trials or rules of evidence in the intentional community, nor is anyone ever excused on a technicality. This means that pun-

---

[8] For other problems with information derived from secret sources, see Wilensky, (1967: 66–69).

[9] Zablocki (1971: 227) notes that "As a visitor [to the Bruderhof] I had the impression of great freedom from surveillance. I felt that nobody watched or cared about my movements, whether I came on time or slightly late to work, how much food I ate, etc. I also perceived this as true for everybody else. To some extent, it is true. The atmosphere of the Bruderhof is very relaxed; no one tries to present an appearance for the benefit of others. People do not work as if they had somebody watching them. Yet coexisting with all of this, is the consciousness that one's actions and even one's thoughts, are somehow public."

ishment is ordinarily more certain for a transgression than it is in more bureaucratic settings. One's fellows are likely to rush to judgement without waiting for a trial and without attention to all the niceties of the law. Hence members will strive to avoid even the *appearance* of noncompliance because they will have no chance to prove that they are innocent.

Why do rational egoists provide this kind of information without payment, let alone promulgate it? One reason flows from the skewed distribution of status in most groups. By demonstrating that they have intimate knowledge of influential people—particularly knowledge that these individuals attempt to conceal from public view—members may hope to enhance their status in the eyes of their associates. Malicious gossip about others is a way of putting them down. In a small group, putting another down is a way of enhancing one's own standing in the group, especially if the invidious gossip is about a highly esteemed person.[10] Since the gossip's motivations are somewhat akin to the professional informer's, the reliability of his information cannot be assumed, but must be verified. The resources that must be spent to assess the quality of gossip may be sufficient to offset the cost of receiving the information.

Minimizing Errors of Interpretation

Observation invariably produces data, but sometimes these data must be interpreted to determine whether or not compliance has occurred. Interpretation is not needed when all that counts is the proper performance of a simple task. But many other things are relevant to assess compliance in certain groups—including the intentions of members. When this is the case, these assessments require some degree of interpretation. What are white teachers in a racially integrated high school to make of the fact that one of their black students gives them a "high five"? Is this a sign of respect, or is it a disrespectful act that should be punished? The teachers must judge. It stands to reason that errors of interpretation are more likely in groups whose members do not share a common cultural idiom. As a consequence, the greater the cultural homogeneity of a group, the greater the likelihood of minimizing such errors.

Thus it may be significant that 67 percent of the long-lived communities in Kanter's (1972: 104) sample of intentional communities were ethnically homogeneous, as against 15 percent of the unsuccessful ones.[11] Many of

---

[10] There are undoubtedly other motives to gossip, as well. For instance, shoptalk is a way of establishing understandings between two strangers in the same profession. The role of gossip in primitive societies has been analyzed extensively by anthropologists (for a critical survey of this literature, see Merry 1984).

[11] This finding could, however, also lend support to a normative interpretation.

the nineteenth-century United States communes were German (including the Harmony Society, Amana, Zoar, and Saint Nazianz); the Icarian Commune was French; while other groups were composed entirely of native-born Americans. Cultural homogeneity is partly the result of selective recruitment patterns. These rest on the basis of the initial members' networks of relatives and friends (Snow and Machalek 1984).[12]

SANCTIONING ECONOMIES

Sanctioning in obligatory groups introduces its own difficulties. Unlike compensatory groups—which can generate wages by marketing their goods—obligatory groups have no built-in means of accumulating sanctioning resources. True, all such groups can employ the threat of expulsion as an ultimate sanction, but this threat cannot be overused, or the group will soon begin to unravel. Sanctions of less severity are, therefore, helpful in the struggle to maintain regular compliance. How then can groups obtain the resources necessary to reward the compliant and punish the noncompliant? Garnering these resources is costly, and this cost also constrains the group's quest for solidarity. Here again it is essential to recognize that the costs of sanctioning are not constant, but variable.

Symbolic versus Material Sanctioning

The analysis of sanctioning is more problematic than that of monitoring because material and symbolic sanctions have different characteristics. By *material sanctions*, I refer to pecuniary ones, as well as all other goods that primarily have exchange value. *Symbolic*, or *social, sanctions* include such intangibles as honor, shame, prestige and so forth. Material and social sanctions warrant separate treatment because they differ with respect to both the breadth of their appeal and their relative costs of production.

Material sanctions affect the widest spectrum of individuals and groups because they can be converted into many different utilities. Since social

[12] It is not at all obvious why people join intentional communities, since in most instances they provide a lower standard of living and less individual freedom than is available in the host society. The benefits that such communities can offer prospective members need not be universally attractive. At a minimum, membership in such a group provides relief from loneliness (which appeals to the lonely), a heavy dose of direction (which appeals to those with low self-esteem—see Zablocki 1971: 178–79, 239), and, often, escape from economic insecurity (which appeals to the economically insecure—see Nordhoff [1875] 1965). Thus the Amana society assumed the debts of the people who joined. Yet, the benefits of membership often have an extremely narrow appeal: the Shakers, for example, allowed physically unattractive women with reduced marital prospects the chance to lead stable, respectable, and celibate lives in nineteenth-century America. And Seattle's Love Israel Family offered young musicians and artists the opportunity to perform in these roles without having to compete in the tightest of labor markets.

sanctions only affect individuals who already share specific values (such as the value of being esteemed by a specific set of people), their appeal tends to be limited to relatively homogeneous groups. The effectiveness of symbolic sanctions depends on the distribution of values (or preferences) among members: it has an inherently subjective dimension. To hold a high position in the Hell's Angels or an urban street gang is not everybody's idea of a reward. To the degree that people do not share the same values, they cannot be motivated by the same symbols. Hence, a second precondition for symbolic sanctioning is cultural homogeneity (Spiro 1984).

Unlike material rewards, symbolic sanctions are readily available because they can be generated within the group (J. Q. Wilson 1973: 30–55). Symbolic sanctions are only likely to be effective, however, in groups that satisfy an essential precondition. This is hierarchy, which serves as the source of most such sanctions. Elevation within the group hierarchy is a private good to members just as demotion is a private bad. Status cannot be bestowed indiscriminately, however, for the greater the number of recipients, the lower the value of the reward (Oliver 1980). Emily Dickinson's poem tells why:

> Success is counted sweetest
> By those who ne'er succeed.
> To comprehend a nectar
> Requires sorest need.

It follows that the use of symbolic sanctions not only presupposes the existence of hierarchy, but also perpetuates it over time.

Although groups can emerge in one of two quite distinct ways, in principle it is easy to see how *hierarchy will tend to evolve in either scenario*. The first scenario is contractarian. Individuals with an interest in access to some jointly produced good band together. They have no interest in devising controls—all they want is access to the good. Either rules are instituted to produce and allocate the good, or members will exit the group, and it will perish. But the mere existence of such rules will inevitably lead to disputes. Some of these disputes will concern the interpretation of these rules; others will result from accusations that a particular member is free riding or not contributing a fair share. In order to resolve such disputes, members will probably designate a given member as an adjudicator. This leads to agency problems. The agent will try to extract a maximum return for his service by extending central controls (this is because he is the center). Whatever the initial discretion of the agent, his power will grow relative to that of the members, unless his autonomy can be effectively constrained.

Groups are also formed by entrepreneurial action. An entrepreneur (like a commune guru or a political boss) perceives that he may get returns by supplying collective goods and offers himself as a provider—say, by designing a set of rules and organizational procedures to attain these goods. He reserves control functions for himself (and his own staff) and serves as the residual claimant. His returns (which are extracted by central controls) are limited only by the members' dependence. Thus, whether a group's roots are contractual or entrepreneurial, some degree of hierarchy is likely to evolve.

In this respect it is notable that whereas many long-lived intentional communities have elaborate communal ideologies—as well as communal property rights—most are strongly hierarchical. The nineteenth-century American authority on communes, Charles Nordhoff, once observed that "the fundamental principle of communal life is the subordination of the individual's will to the general interest or general will: practically, this takes the shape of unquestioning obedience by the members toward the leaders, elders, or chiefs of their society" (Nordhoff [1875] 1965: 392). In some groups leaders take extraordinary privileges and require their members to use special terms of address. Often leaders demand the right to name their successors. Many communities have an extensive spiritual hierarchy, compelling members with lesser moral status to defer to those who have more.

The Bruderhof, for instance, has at least nine formally distinct hierarchical statuses (Zablocki 1971). The Elder (*Vorsteher*) is at the top of the pyramid. Following him, in descending order, are the Servants of the Word; Stewards, Witness Brothers, and Housemothers; married Brotherhood members; single "decision-making" Brotherhood members; "non-decision-making" Brotherhood members; novices; older teenagers and long-term guests; and children, guests, and members who are on exclusionary probation. Whatever the names given to the ranks among members of intentional communities, they are distinguished by the degree of information available to those in each rank and by the scope of their participation in decision-making.

Naturally, the specific directives emanating from the hierarchy vary across groups. One indicator of the pervasiveness of hierarchy in long-lived intentional communities is that most of the successful groups insist that their members wear uniforms (Kanter 1972: 112). In this case, hierarchy is used to minimize the distinctions between individual members of the same status—much as occurs in the military.

Public Sanctioning

Public sanctions are more cost-effective than private ones. When a member is publicly admonished for a transgression, others may be dissuaded from committing the act. Hester Prynne's scarlet letter was intended to deter other young Salem women from committing adultery. When one Arab child sees another lose a hand after being caught with a stolen loaf of bread, he may think twice about stealing from the baker.[13] This demonstration effect holds for positive sanctions as well: groups that celebrate their heroes are likely to have a continuing supply of them. Public sanctioning multiplies the effect of a single sanction many times over (J. F. Scott 1971: 158).[14]

Public admonishment is commonplace in intentional communities. Oneida employed the technique of mutual criticism (Nordhoff [1875] 1965: 287–301) long before its adoption by the Chinese during the Cultural Revolution. In addition to the daily evening meetings where problems were aired, members periodically submitted themselves to criticism by a panel of from six to twelve judges. The subject was expected to receive the criticism in silence and confess to it in writing. The Rappites at Harmony conducted weekly "mutual improvement" meetings (A. Williams

[13] Or, nowadays, from the supplier of electrical cable: "KHARTOUM—Two thieves convicted of stealing electrical cables had their right hands and left legs cut off by order of an Islamic court Monday and became the first criminals to undergo cross-limb amputation since the introduction of Islamic law last September, the Sudan News Agency said. Amputations in Sudan are carried out by government doctors who have been trained in Saudi Arabia where criminal amputations are commonplace.

"Convicted criminals are usually drugged and sedated and then blindfolded while a doctor amputates the limb with a surgical scalpel and saw. The victims are then taken to a hospital to recover from the shock. The amputation procedure usually takes less than 15 minutes" (*International Herald Tribune* 1984: 4). In this light, it would be interesting to explore the secular trend in public punishment historically. Systematic evidence on this question appears to be thin. Newman (1978: 123) claims that (at least in western Europe) prior to the seventeenth century the most frequently used punishments were private, economic ones like fines, confiscations, and restitution. Thereafter, public executions, beheadings, and other spectacular instances of public sanctioning became popular. As Foucault (1979) has noted, these punishments were largely abandoned in the nineteenth century. He explains this by shifts in *mentalités*, but it is far simpler to argue that such public displays became too costly to the rulers of the western European states because they threatened to incite crowds to participate in rebellious collective action. The decline of public corporal punishment and execution does coincide neatly with the development of professional policing, and hence with the state's ability to provide increased private sanctioning. Whatever the explanation, however, it is not entirely clear whether public sanctioning actually has declined since this dramatic era or merely has changed its form. The attention devoted to the criminal justice system by the media suggests that public knowledge of the costs of illegal and/or deviant action may be at historically high levels in Western societies.

[14] Durkheim (1901) also placed emphasis on public sanctioning in his explanation of social order. He claimed that public sanctioning reinforces the group's commitment to the violated norm. My argument is different—that public sanctioning deters potential deviants from future noncompliance. Whereas both arguments predict an association between public sanctioning and heightened compliance, the explanations for this association are very much at odds.

1866: 41), and mutual confession was practiced at Amana at annual meetings (Shambaugh 1932: 247). Sanctioning in the Bruderhof begins with informal ridicule, and when this proves ineffective, more formal public sanctioning occurs.

Increasing Exit Costs

Practices that increase exit costs put teeth into threats of expulsion and ostracism. Groups can raise exit costs in three different ways: by purposely locating in a venue that is isolated (Jonestown, Guyana) or near hostile neighbors, by requiring members to invest money or goods that cannot be reclaimed on exit, or by restricting members' extra-group affiliations. When exit costs are high, rewards such as advancement up the ladder of status come to have greater value.

The force of community sanctions ultimately flows from the dependence of members. The most serious sanction of all in the intentional community—as it is in tribal society—is expulsion, but the severity of this punishment depends entirely on the value of alternatives outside group boundaries. Most successful intentional communities do attempt to limit their members' extra-group affiliations. Often members are required to surrender their goods on entry (Kanter 1972: 82), and once having thus "invested" in membership, exiting from the group is more costly. Not all the investment need be material. Members invest their time and energy in the intentional community. They invest in a certain kind of on-the-job training: mastering the community's jargon, learning the rules, abiding by status distinctions.[15] Rarely do these investments have value outside the group.[16] Since most successful groups forbid contact with ex-members, the publicized social costs of exit are also extremely high: "All the people that matter to you will be cut off from you forever. A member is often not even sure if his own spouse will come with him" (Zablocki 1971: 281).

Finally, compliance can only be assured when members receive rewards for compliance, and punishment for noncompliance. In order to make members appreciate the consequences of their actions, sanctioning should follow closely on the heels of the behavior in question. To the degree that sanctioning is not determined by monitoring or that the delay between behavior and sanctioning is long, subsequent compliance will be harder to attain (J. Q. Wilson and Herrnstein 1985: Ch. 2). Long ago, Beccaria

[15] Jargon appears in all kinds of solidary groups, not least among academics sharing a disciplinary niche. For revealing discussions of jargon and group solidarity, see Lifton (1961: 429–30), who analyzes the treatment of Chinese political prisoners in the 1950s, and Mitford (1977), who spoofs the jargon of the Communist Party of the United States.

[16] These investments promote what Williamson (1981) terms "asset specificity."

and Bentham emphasized not only the promptness of sanctions but also the perceived probability of being sanctioned at all as determinants of compliance.

There is nothing automatic about the process of sanctioning. It too requires effort; it too consumes resources. Like monitoring costs, sanctioning costs are reduced in small groups, where the familiar bureaucratic lament that the right hand does not know what the left hand is doing is not often heard. The fact that intentional communities are relatively small groups, groups whose members generally know one another by sight, therefore contributes to their control capacity.[17]

Once it is appreciated that the costs of control are variable, it becomes obvious that these costs will be lower in some circumstances than in others. Groups that are able to realize control economies should have enhanced prospects of attaining solidarity. In general, monitoring costs are minimized by arrangements that promote visibility, give members an incentive to monitor each other, allow for minimal errors of interpretation, and provide positive sanctions. Sanctioning costs are lowered to the degree that groups employ both symbolic and public sanctioning, institute high exit costs, and limit group size. The efficacy of several of these arrangements (for example, symbolic sanctioning) depends on preconditions like hierarchy and cultural homogeneity, but other arrangements (for example, those that increase visibility) decrease control costs across the board. (Table 8 summarizes the various kinds of arrangements.)

Some of these arrangements may affect both a group's monitoring and sanctioning capacities. I have already noted that, in addition to its sanctioning effects, the use of positive sanctions will sometimes bring about monitoring economies. And while an institution like consensual decision-making may reduce monitoring costs by revealing members' private feelings, at the same time it may also operate as a mechanism of persuasion and sanctioning. It would seem that the precise role of an economizing institution can only be determined by a detailed analysis of particular cases.

There is no inherent limit to the number of institutional arrangements that can reduce control costs. Hence no enumeration of them can ever be exhaustive. The factors discussed above are merely illustrative; the reader is invited to imagine other, more subtle economizing arrangements. Al-

---

[17]The small scale of preindustrial social life was a major factor in its high degree of solidarity. Few persons in the western European ancien régime, for example, "ever found themselves in groups larger than family groups, and there were not many families of more than a dozen members in any locality" (Laslett 1984: 7).

TABLE 8. Institutional Arrangements That Economize on Control Costs

Monitoring Economies			Sanctioning Economies		
Increasing Visibility	*Sharing the Monitoring Burden*	*Minimizing Errors of Interpretation*	*Symbolic Sanctioning*	*Public Sanctioning*	*Increasing Exit Costs*
1. Architecture 2. Public Rituals 3. Specificity of Obligations 4. Preference-Revelation 5. Positive Sanctions	1. Group Rewards 2. Limits on Privacy 3. Rewards to Informants 4. Gossip	1. Cultural Homogeneity	1. Awarding Differential Prestige	1. Public Sentencing 2. Media Coverage of Criminal Proceedings	1. Geographical Isolation 2. Required Investment on Entry 3. No Extra-Group Affiliations

though these arrangements should result in lower control costs, they may have other effects that members regard as deleterious.

To this point, it is clear that the survival of intentional communities is associated with particular kinds of institutional arrangements. But this association leaves two important questions begging.

First, are all of these institutional arrangements equally important in this regard, or are some more significant than others? It would be a difficult and thankless task to determine the relative efficacy of each of these factors as determinants of group survival. No doubt the answer depends on a host of specific community characteristics—including size, previous history, the nature of the environment, and so forth. Nevertheless, some insight into this problem is provided by a recent study by John Hall (1983). In a multivariate reanalysis of Kanter's data on American communes, Hall found that only four factors were strongly and independently associated with longevity: a common ethnic background and/or foreign language spoken by members ($\beta = .447$), hierarchical authority based on differential moral status ($\beta = .358$), obligatory confession ($\beta = .295$), and the wearing of uniforms ($\beta = .320$). Other practices—including the existence of community property rights and irrevocable financial contribution required on entry—did not significantly contribute to communal longevity.

Second, why are practices such as the wearing of uniforms, obligatory confession, and the establishment of high exit costs associated with group survival? In Kanter's (mostly implicit) normativist view arrangements of this sort are "commitment mechanisms" that contribute to group longevity by strengthening an individual's identification with the group. The key to the commitment process is that it binds the individual to the group (cf. H. Becker 1960; Etzioni 1975; and Collins 1975): "A person is committed to a group or to a relationship when he himself is fully invested in it, so that the maintenance of his own internal being requires behavior that supports the social order" (Kanter 1972: 66). Thus, commitment does for the intentional community what control does for the capitalist firm. The committed member

> internalizes community standards and values and accepts its control, because it provides him with something transcendent. This commitment requires, first, that the person reformulate and re-evaluate his identity in terms of meeting the ideas set by the community. For this to occur, the group must first provide ways for an individual to reassess his previous life, to undo those parts of himself he wishes to change, and to perceive that identity and meaning for him lie not in an individualistic, private existence but in acceptance of the stronger influence of the utopian group.
>
> (Kanter 1972: 73)

But this is hardly the only possible interpretation of the findings. *The practices that have been found to be associated with community longevity may not attest to the community's hopes about building commitment through identification but, instead, may reveal its doubts that such identification is likely to develop at all.* Perhaps community survival is promoted through an entirely different kind of mechanism. Groups employing arrangements to reduce control costs may succeed not because of the internalization of new norms, but rather because they curb members' egoistic tendencies toward free riding and deviance.[18]

The group solidarity theory suggests not only that the free riders should plague intentional communities, but that the problem of controlling them should be especially troublesome there. Like the leaders of all groups, the leaders of the intentional community seek compliance, yet they face especially difficult obstacles in this quest. On the one hand, the group demands highly extensive obligations. On the other hand, compensatory resources are scarce, and, insofar as they stimulate competition between members, individual rewards undermine the community's raison d'être—the very harmony that members seek to produce.

This peculiar combination of constraints and demands makes the intentional community particularly vulnerable to free riding. Why else are disputes over inequalities of work effort so frequent (Erasmus 1977: 144–45, 160–62; Kanter 1972: 25)?[19] Why else is deviance such a pervasive concern?

Bruderhof life is a continuing struggle between the ego inclinations of the individual and the call to a Christian communal life. Most of the effort of the Bruderhof system of social control therefore goes into correcting deviance. . . . The Bruderhof is much more concerned with an individual's underlying attitudes, in most cases, than with his overt behavior. It follows from this that "good" behavior may be rebuked if the underlying attitudes are wrong and that "bad" behavior may be condoned if it is thought that the behavior is not indicative of a bad attitude. An example of the former is reported by a woman who was a long-term serious guest at the Woodcrest Bruderhof. She was told that her behavior was too perfect. The Brothers felt that she was a sharp observer of, and adapter to, her environment. They asked her if she wasn't just noticing what sort of actions would evoke favor-

[18] Similarly, why is the common ethnicity of members the strongest determinant of group survival? This could be due either to identification mechanisms (as specified in the normativist account) or to dependence mechanisms (as specified in the theory of group solidarity) or to some combination of the two.

[19] The status of members of the kibbutz depends heavily on their labor efficiency; shirking is "spotted immediately" and "jeopardizes the respect of one's fellows" (Spiro 1956: 85).

able responses, and then exhibiting these actions. When she admitted that she had been doing that, she was told that she would never advance in the life that way.

(Zablocki 1971: 223–24)

Since the only means of curtailing free riders and deviants countenanced in the theory of group solidarity is control, this implies that arrangements that yield economies of control should pervade the most successful groups.

Are hierarchy, confession, and mutual surveillance commitment mechanisms that encourage members to internalize community norms and thereby identify with the collective, or are they arrangements that permit these groups to reap economies of control so as to better curtail potential deviants?

These two possibilities have quite different empirical implications. If such practices do in fact build member commitment, then in the long run the more successful the community is, the more superfluous its commitment mechanisms will become—at least for old hands. (They may still be necessary for new inductees, though.) Therefore, commitment mechanisms should be most pervasive in the initial stages of community development, when collective identification is at its nadir. But as this identification grows, the role of commitment mechanisms should diminish apace; only relatively unsuccessful groups should have to rely on them.[20] The principals of groups whose members are predisposed to act in the corporate interest anyway have no reason to expend resources on control, when these could be diverted to other, more productive uses. After all, committed members do not need to be controlled in order to comply with group obligations; by definition, they will do so voluntarily.

If these practices provide economies of control, however, then they should be a necessary condition for group survival in communities of all ages. Older, well-established communities should be as vulnerable to free riding as neophyte communities are. Groups that cannot muster sufficient resources to maintain the requisite control capacity will be at the mercy of their egoistic members and will invariably dissolve as a result. From this point of view, the most successful groups should be those with the greatest profusion of economizing arrangements.

Kanter's data clearly demonstrate that hierarchy, confession, mutual surveillance, and similar factors are overwhelmingly found in the longest-lived groups, but such arrangements occur hardly at all in the short-lived

[20] It might be objected that these institutions are required to help transmit community values across the generations. But why does socialization not do this job naturally, in the absence of such stringent controls?

ones. If these practices constitute commitment mechanisms, then it can only be concluded that they are remarkably ineffective ones. Is it not more sensible to regard them as means to curtail free riding and deviance among those who would otherwise be tempted to transgress? The intentional communities that employ such arrangements are the most likely to survive precisely because they reap the benefits of control economies.

Even though these controls are relatively economical, they still remain costly to produce. Subsidizing formal controls in obligatory groups is a challenge. Compensatory groups can use their profits to offset the cost of central controls, but communes are not profit-making. How then do intentional communities manage to defray the costs of their controls? One possible answer is socialization, but as the previous analysis indicates, this is no substitute for formal controls. Another possibility is for the group to be expansionist, relying on the continual ingestion of new members and appropriation of their assets. Since the opportunity of expansion is always finite, however, this strategy is necessarily subject to diminishing returns. There is a more permanent solution: to the degree that members forsake the labor market (as they must do in communes), they also give up their ability to demand a market price for their work. As a result, they are willing to work for below-market wages (French and French 1975: 203–21). This gives the intentional community a comparative advantage in the production of labor-intensive goods over more conventional producers, who are compelled to compete for their labor in the marketplace.[21]

Overall, it appears that control mechanisms proliferate in obligatory groups just as they do in compensatory ones. Further, the obligatory groups that employ the greatest number of economizing arrangements are likely to be the longest-lived. If the same mechanisms that produce compliance in the *Gemeinschaft* do so in the *Gesellschaft*, clearly the meaning of this hallowed sociological distinction needs to be reevaluated. The *Gemeinschaft* is more solidary than the *Gesellschaft*, not because it entails more extensive normative internalization or promotes greater commitment, but because its institutional arrangements permit its members' behavior to be controlled more economically.

[21] Due to its low labor costs, Jim Jones's People's Temple could operate nursing homes in California much more cheaply than commercial providers (Hall 1987).

CHAPTER IX

CONCLUSION

D IFFICULT AS IT is to analyze, the concept of group solidarity is fundamental to social science. Solidarity varies with the proportion of
members' private resources that are contributed to collective ends. Sociologists have always appreciated its significance; for them individual compliance to group norms constitutes the very basis of social order. Although
some other social scientists have relegated the concept to darker corners of
their intellectual realms, or ignored it altogether, this neglect is short-
sighted. After all, solidarity underlies the stability of institutions as important as markets and states. It increases both the likelihood of the optimal
provision of public goods (including the free market itself) and of collective action. Likewise, it is the key cog in the Marxist engine of social
change, for according to Marxists history is unfolded through the struggles
between solidary classes. Therefore without a theory of group solidarity,
sociologists cannot explain the dynamics of social order; economists cannot explain the stability of markets, or of the property rights underlying
these markets; and Marxists cannot explain the transformation from *Klasse
an sich* to *Klasse für sich*.

Despite the fact that the evidence that has been used in support of the
group solidarity theory is far from conclusive, this book shows how a small
set of behavioral assumptions can elucidate macrosociological processes by
taking both social structures and individual actors into account. The explanations of solidarity in political parties, rotating credit associations and
insurance groups, capitalist factories, and intentional communities derive
not from particularistic analyses but principally from the illumination that
is cast upon each case by the general theory.

In order to properly assess the theory, however, new kinds of evidence
must be collected that expressly measure dependence, control mechanisms,
and the solidarity of groups. Given such evidence, the theory could be applied to groups of all kinds, for any factor that increases the members'
dependence and facilitates the control capacity of a group should pro-

mote the compliance of its members thereby. To illustrate the range of future research the theory might suggest, I will briefly sketch a few of its implications.

MARKETS AND GROUPS

Since there is likely to be competition among the providers of joint goods, the groups most likely to survive are those that can reap the greatest monitoring and sanctioning economies. Yet that groups are selected on the basis of their productive efficiency raises a deeper issue by far. Formal controls consume resources that otherwise could be marshalled toward directly productive ends. If such nonproductive expenditures were forgone, more goods could be provided in the aggregate. Can the productive activities of a large number of individuals be organized in the absence of formal controls? Is there an alternative to joint production in groups?

The answer, of course, is yes. Activity can be organized impersonally, in response to *markets* where faceless buyers and sellers meet to exchange standardized goods at equilibrium prices.[1] Market transactions entail a full quid pro quo, and there is no leftover business or outstanding balance (Ben-Porath 1980: 2). When the environment "selects" the fittest organisms, or when the competitive market "disciplines" firms with respect to their efficiency, these are examples of market principles at work.[2]

In contrast to groups, which are made up of individuals who are engaged in activities that are coordinated by formal controls, markets link persons who are engaged in independent and divergent activities. In fact, the greater this divergence of activities is, the greater the gains from trade and the resulting efficiency of the market.

Not only do markets permit coordination among large numbers of producers in the absence of central controls, but the productive output in

---

[1] This immediately raises the difficult question of how an individualistic theory can account for the genesis of markets themselves. There seem to be two leading ideas. The first emphasizes that market efficiency depends upon a number of technical requirements—including the development and enforcement of private property rights, large numbers of buyers and sellers, as well as other factors affecting transactions costs—that did not hold for most of human history (Weber [1924] 1981). On the other hand, some writers (Polanyi [1944] 1957; Anderson and Tollison 1985) have argued that the establishment of free markets in labor and land (represented, in Britain, by events such as the repeal of the Speenhamland labor laws and the Corn Laws) was a means of increasing the wealth of powerful interest groups. In essence, this argument holds that the rise of markets depends on the prior existence of solidary groups. The unintended consequence of the establishment of these markets, of course, is that the members of these groups were then subjected to a variety of new uncertainties, impelling them to seek protection from the very creature they brought into being.

[2] "The real and effectual discipline which is exercised over a workman, is not that of his corporation, but that of his customers. It is the fear of losing their employment which restrains his frauds and corrects his negligence" (A. Smith [1789] 1961: I, 144).

markets will, in general, exceed that in groups. This greater output is possible because markets provide coordination, allocation, and disincentives for free riding endogenously—without formal controls—and therefore at minimal social cost. Coordination is achieved in markets via prices, which are the signals that guide individuals to action without centralized information and controls.[3] Goods are allocated in markets according to the law of supply and demand. Finally, by forcing actors to bear the consequences of their own behavior, markets provide incentives for optimal performance.[4] This does away with the free rider problem.

Altogether, then, markets will elicit the production of goods in the absence of formal controls (save for those required to enforce the underlying rules of the game).[5] In contrast, however, the production of goods in large groups requires formal controls. Some amount of productive resources must be forgone in order to provide for these controls: the upshot is that fewer goods can be provided. But if so, then why do groups exist at all?

Part of the answer is that markets are an historical novelty. Their efficacy depends upon individual private property rights in land and labor, as well as in a stable political authority capable of enforcing these rights. Lacking these supports, market exchange is impossible and all joint production must occur in groups. This logic suggests that the growth of markets should have destabilizing consequences for many preexisting groups. Indeed, the rise of the market is accompanied by the demise of a host of different kinds of groups—the traditional extended family, kinship groups and lineages, guilds, and so forth.

But if this is the whole story, then why don't all groups simply disappear

---

[3] "The chief cause of the wealth-creating character of the game is that the returns of the efforts of each player act as the signs which enable him to contribute to the satisfaction of needs of which he does not know, and to do so by taking advantage of conditions of which he learns only indirectly through their being reflected in the prices of the factors of production which they use" (Hayek 1976: 115).

[4] In markets, producers receive resources according to the nature of their individual performance. The greater the productivity, the greater the reward and vice versa. As Alchian and Demsetz (1972: 778) note, "in many situations markets yield a high correlation between rewards and productivity. If a farmer increases his output of wheat by 10 percent at the prevailing market price, his receipts also increase by 10 percent. This method of organizing economic activity meters the *output directly*, reveals the marginal product and apportions the *rewards* to resource owners in accord with that direct measurement of their outputs. The success of this decentralized, market exchange in promoting productive specialization requires that changes in market rewards fall on those responsible for changes in *output*."

[5] Whereas enforcement costs must be incurred to maintain *all* allocation rules (including those inherent in market allocation), there is no reason to believe that any one rule has an advantage over any other in this respect. As Demsetz (1967), for example, points out in his study of the development of property rights among the Labrador Indians, the costs of establishing and enforcing the property rights—in other words, the minimal state—necessary for the market order sometimes outweigh the benefits. A similar argument might account for the paucity of markets during the feudal era.

in market societies? In the first place, because markets are not well suited for the production of certain kinds of goods. Among these are goods (like automobiles) that are assembled from large numbers of intermediate products. Such goods conceivably could be produced in markets—each individual producer of an intermediate good would contract with an entrepreneur who would be responsible for assembling them into the final product and marketing it. The cost of designing and enforcing all of these individual contracts, however, is likely to exceed the cost of instituting formal controls. This kind of argument has often been used to explain the prevalence of firms in market societies (Coase 1937; Alchian and Demsetz 1972; Williamson 1975; North 1981).

Further, many immanent goods—like love and friendship—cannot be produced through the impersonal market mechanism at all (Ben-Porath 1980). One cannot purchase friendship or love; these goods have to be earned, and, once earned, they cannot be exchanged. This explains the prevalence of affective groups linking kin and friends in market societies. The rise of the market has no direct implications for the survival of affective groups; it may, however, have strong indirect effects on their composition by virtue of influencing patterns of geographic and social mobility.

In the second place, markets create a demand for the formation of new kinds of groups. Unlike traditional insurance groups, which arise to reduce the risk of physical and natural losses, these new groups arise to shield their members from consequences that are unleashed by the market itself. This leads to a preference for goods allocation in groups rather than in markets.

In its pristine form, the market allocates resources according to individual performances. In general, the greater the value of the actor's performance, the greater the resultant rewards. In groups, however, members receive resources from some central agency, which can allocate them according to one of a wide variety of principles—among them, equality and need. Whereas allocation in the market always occurs on the basis of individual performance, groups have no set allocation rule. Hence, whenever actors prefer resource allocations on any basis (seniority, equality, or individual need) other than that of their own performance, they are led to form and/or join groups (Cook and Hegtvedt 1983). Why might actors prefer allocation rules of this sort?

There are a host of possible reasons. Some people do not feel their performance can be competitive—and hence suspect that they will do worse under a system of market allocation than under an alternative system. Individuals who have low initial endowment of human capital (due to birth into a disadvantaged family) or lower-than-average skills may believe that they have a low probability of ever reaching the norm. The course of an actor's productivity is likely to vary over the life course. Productivity tends to reach a peak either in late adolescence or in middle age and declines thereafter, yet the demand for income increases monotonically to late middle age. If rewards were solely a function of effort, individuals would have the least earning power at precisely that period when their income needs are greatest. There are other reasons as well. Some people may be altruists who prefer to see the poorer made better off. Others may prefer a life-style that expresses many facets of their personality—not just that single facet for which they have a comparative advantage in the labor market. By "choosing a smaller pond," others can attain a local reputation (for example, as an artist or musician) that they might not be able to earn in a more global community.

Whereas the preceding reasons for choosing goods allocation in groups are limited (and in some cases idiosyncratic), there is a far more fundamental reason, one that affects actors regardless of their market position. *Allocations in groups can provide predictable rather than stochastic resource flows.* Resource allocation in markets is necessarily stochastic: it depends not only upon factors within the actors' control (such as their own performance), but also upon those that are beyond their control and are fundamentally unpredictable, such as the performance of others in the market (which is unknowable) and shifts in technology or in aggregate demand (which may place a high value on actors' performance at one point in time, but a low one thereafter). Individuals whose only source of resources is markets, then, are likely to experience income and welfare fluctuations.

Yet risk-neutral and risk-averse actors will place a value on the predictability of resource flows (Owen and Breautigam 1978: 36–42).[6] Altogether,

---

[6]Of course, some actors are risk-seekers. Schumpeter (1950: 73–74) notes that a defining characteristic of the entrepreneur is the tendency to *overestimate* the likely success of risky ventures. Adam Smith ([1789] 1961: I, 120) even believes that this is true of "the greater part of men." Isn't it more likely, however, that the vast bulk of agents have a more realistic appraisal of their success in markets? The issue of preferences about risk has been a major theoretical battleground, at least since the von Neumann–Morgenstern formalization of expected utility theory. The fact that people both gamble (seek risk) and insure (avoid risk) has raised serious issues about nature of utility schedules. There seem to be two kinds of responses to these difficulties. Some (M. Friedman and Savage 1948; Allais and Hagen 1979; Kahneman and Tversky 1979; and Machina 1983) have tried to fit complicated new curves that are consistent with the latest behavioral evidence. Others (Simon 1983; Heiner 1983; Brenner 1983) challenge the traditional behavioral assumptions of rational choice and seek to substitute modified ones. An unanswered question is what difference any of this makes for aggregate-level behavior. If we assume that people seek maximum utility by attempting to gain control over their environment, then they are always liable to be simultaneously concerned with wealth maximization and the protection of their current assets. Only those whose safety is assured (those who have enough resources to self-insure), however, are liable to engage in relatively costly gambles. Buying a $1 lottery ticket—even if this is an unfair gamble—is relatively costly for only an infinitesimal percentage of the adult American population.

then, the prevalence—or threat—of market-based allocation produces a countervailing demand for insurance against fluctuations in income and welfare. And due to the problem of moral hazard, commercial insurance cannot be provided against such losses. (Some of these kinds of insurance can be provided without resort to groups: thus the stock and futures markets reduce uncertainty with respect to the supply of some kinds of goods, as does vertical integration (Arrow 1971: 135, 140).

How is the demand for this new kind of insurance met? Individuals vary systematically in their opportunities to obtain insurance against market induced uncertainty. Individuals have at least five separate ways of obtaining insurance, most of which do *not* require membership in insurance groups. They can *self-insure*—that is, place their assets in several separate holdings so as to spread the risk of future losses. If they live in the right country (and in the right era), they can receive insurance provided as a public good by the *state*. Whereas the best example is the insurance benefits of the contemporary welfare state (Dryzek and Goodin 1986), preindustrial states occasionally offered important insurance benefits as well (Polanyi [1944] 1957). Those who work for the right employer (private or public) can receive job tenure as an immanent benefit.

Those who lack the opportunity to attain insurance against market fluctuations through these means have but one possible alternative source: to join or form some insurance group. The demand for membership in such groups, therefore, should be highest among the most disadvantaged—those who cannot effectively self-insure or land a job in the primary sector of the labor market. Insurance groups are unlikely to select members, however, who cannot pay their way by providing dues, labor, or other services. Thus the aged and infirm are not likely to be admitted as members. The membership of insurance groups should, therefore, primarily consist of *productive* members of the following categories: youth, the able-bodied unemployed, and those facing discrimination, such as ethnic minorities.

Insurance, however, is a necessary but insufficient determinant of patterns of group affiliation. It explains why actors join *some* kind of insurance group but not necessarily *which* one they will join. People with strong left-wing political commitments are not at much risk of joining a right-wing group simply because it offers insurance at a marginally lower cost. Members are only likely to shop around when they are indifferent between the goods provided by different groups—as some blacks were with respect to competing fraternal orders (Light 1972; see also Weber [1922] 1968: 347–48). Since selection rules are so frequently employed to control moral hazard in all insurance groups, chances are that both the initial members and all subsequent recruits will be selected from kin and friendship networks of the current group members.

The consequences of market expansion on patterns of group solidarity are complex. Efficient markets lower the dependence of group members by providing lower-cost alternatives to many group-produced joint goods. The solidarity of traditional groups such as the extended family, the guild, and the corporate peasant village cannot be sustained in the face of this lowered dependence. Yet since efficient markets are the source of a new type of uncertainty, they foster the development of new dependencies, and therefore new insurance groups as well.

I would argue that this dialectic is clearly visible in the recent rise of feminist groups in the United States. Due largely to exogenous macroeconomic forces, both the rate and type of female labor force participation increased after World War II (Sweet 1973; Keyserling 1979). Whereas most females had entered the labor force temporarily, after this date many women entered the competitive labor market on a more permanent basis, and the proportion of married to unmarried women in the labor force rose. The greater demand for female labor tended to reduce these women's dependence on their husbands. Rates of divorce began to rise. But these new entrants to the labor market were faced not only with the opportunities of the market but with its uncertainties as well. Those women who were barred from joining trade unions, professional associations, internal labor markets, or other existing groups that offer some insurance against market-induced uncertainty (due either to discrimination or to being disproportionately clustered in female occupations) demanded their own insurance. In order to obtain it, they spontaneously formed consciousness-raising groups, cooperative day-care centers, and other kinds of supportive groups in many different localities (Fulenwider 1980; Deckard 1983). These groups can be seen as a direct analogue to the friendly societies and fraternal orders formed by the new male entrants to the labor market from the late eighteenth century onward (Chapter 6). As in the case of these earlier insurance groups, these local feminist insurance groups soon federated into the National Organization for Women. This organization's very success in providing women with new opportunities to gain entry into existing insurance groups has undercut the demand for its services.

THE FAMILY

The theory may also be able to shed light on the effects of different family structures upon children's behavior. The comportment of children ranges all the way from habitual compliance with familial obligations to outright rebellion and delinquency. Since the family is a group that normally boasts an extremely high control capacity, the theory implies that these different outcomes may be affected by variations in the dependence of children.

The diminishing dependence of family members has been among the most significant social changes in modern history. It is by now well appreciated that as wives' opportunities for employment and welfare have expanded beyond the boundaries of the household, rates of divorce have increased. The effects of divorce—and its resultant variations in custodial arrangements—on the dependence of children, however, have received less attention. Children's dependence on their parents is a function of their costs of exiting the home. If the parents have little to offer their children materially or emotionally, their dependence will be low. In this case, as has become all too evident in large American cities, the street may actually provide a better alternative residence. Yet given equal material and emotional resources, children's dependence may also vary with different family structures.

Consider the following possibilities: the two-parent household, the single-parent household, and two households, each headed by a single parent. If dependence were the only issue, the theory would suggest that the single-parent household would elicit the greatest degree of compliance from the child, for exit costs would be prohibitively high. In such a household, the child has only one source of needed benefits. The two-parent household should evince nearly as much compliance as the single-parent household, for still the child has no alternative household to consider.

The contrasting case is the one in which the child is simultaneously a member of two different households. Divorce often provides children with the choice between residence in the mother's or the father's home. When these children have no marked preference for either household, and when the parents are unwilling to collude to limit their mobility, the children will not be highly dependent on either parent. If parents respond by competing for the residence of the children, the obligations they impose on them are likely to be lower than those in the other two types of households.

The upshot is that parents in this situation may demand less of their children and have great difficulty obtaining compliance with familial obligations. Due to their lower dependence, the children of divorce should have high rates of noncompliance (for supportive evidence, see Hetherington, Cox, and Cox 1978; Mitchell 1985: 105). Similarly, Rutter (1971) reports that, in comparison with boys from intact two-parent families or those who have lost a parent through death, delinquency rates are nearly double for boys whose parents have divorced or separated. Dependence, however, is not the only issue. While single-parent households might be the ones in which the child's dependence is the greatest, control is also a serious problem. One monitor simply is not as effective as two. Variations in control capacity therefore may provide some hints about the greater delinquency of the children of divorce.

If the family has maximum solidarity when its members abide by extensive obligations, then this illustrates how the consequences of divorce can be far more profound than the mere dissolution of a marriage.

CLASS AND STATUS SOLIDARITY

Groups can form around any single common interest. In principle, left-handedness, shortness, fatness, intelligence, and even red hair (as in Conan Doyle's story "The League of Red-Headed Men") each could be responsible for the development of solidary groups. Empirically, however, solidarity seldom occurs on these bases; it is most likely to be found, instead, among individuals who have a common status or class position (Weber [1922] 1968: 302–6). Status groups are made up of individuals who share a certain amount of social honor (or prestige)—usually defined by religion, mother tongue, or ethnic background (for a treatment of homosexuals as a status group, see FitzGerald 1986). Classes, on the other hand, are made up of individuals having the same relation to the means of production, a common socioeconomic status, or both.

Why does solidarity so often crystallize around factors like class and status, as against those like height, weight, or hair color? The structuralist answer to this question is that in most societies status and class determine much more about an individual's life chances than factors like height, weight, or hair color. Being left-handed may affect one's ability to start on a baseball team, but it is simply irrelevant for the attainment of many other ends. Being born black or poor, however, may affect one's ability to attain any number of ends. When one's life chances are seen to be independent of one's membership in a social category, the psychic significance of the category tends to recede (Hechter 1978). If engaging in collective action is the only way for people to improve their life chances, then they will do so.

The structuralist explanation is inadequate, however. First, it cannot account for those cases where a group's position in the stratification system gives its members every reason to participate in collective action, and yet no collective action occurs. Scholars of ethnic and race relations are often surprised by the absence of ethnic groups acting on their own behalf, as well as by the eruption of ethnic collective action among previously dormant groups (Hechter and Friedman 1984). Second, the structuralist explanation offers no guidance in those cases where people are simultaneously stratified along two or more dimensions, such as race and class. What kinds of groups (if any) will be formed by people who are *both* poor and black? Will these individuals be motivated to coalesce along the lines of race, class, or some combination of the two?

The theory of group solidarity might provide a new solution to these old and thorny issues by its emphasis on questions of dependence and control. It claims that, whenever possible, individuals will always consider alternative sources of goods. Regardless of their position in the stratification system, people demand education for their children, good jobs, insurance, and welfare benefits. Their position in the stratification system will certainly affect their opportunities to obtain these goods in the marketplace. To the degree that demanded goods (like life and health insurance) are attainable in the market, the motive for group formation diminishes. Similarly with goods attainable from the state. If the state provides many such goods (education, unemployment benefits, health insurance and social security), then this also diminishes the motive to form many kinds of groups.[7]

Thus, solidary groups are most likely to emerge when demanded goods are not attainable from the state or in the market. But will this solidarity tend to be on the basis of race or class? Sometimes the allocation of goods is discriminatory, both in the market and in the state sector. When welfare benefits are allocated at the local level, blacks may be denied goods to which they are legally entitled. Similarly, the labor market may pay blacks less for the same work than whites. To the degree that the allocation of goods is discriminatory, solidary groups are likely to form among those individuals so affected. This explains why discrimination will sometimes be the ostensible basis for solidarity.

Why it is that the disadvantaged do not always manage to coalesce and engage in collective action to better their position, however, has long been a puzzle. Since the disadvantaged are always potentially dependent, the answer does not lie here. As the group solidarity theory demonstrates, dependence alone is an insufficient cause of solidarity; control capacity is also necessary. Whereas dependence sets the general contextual parameters for group formation, it does not account entirely for the emergence and solidarity of groups. If the state or the market cannot provide demanded goods, what kinds of problems must individuals overcome to produce them for their own consumption?

The success of groups in producing joint goods is determined largely by

---

[7]To the degree that an individual's ability to receive state-derived entitlements requires legal assistance, then groups can offer such assistance as an incentive to membership. The People's Temple is merely one of a number of groups that have taken advantage of this opportunity in recent American history (Hall 1987). Under these conditions the growth of the welfare state may actually *contribute* to the viability of such client-oriented groups.

their capacity to preclude free riding. Thus, research attempting to understand the differential salience of race and class in the formation and solidarity of groups would need to focus on the determinants of each kind of group's control capacity. This, in turn, depends upon the existence of monitoring and sanctioning economies. But how does this emphasis help to predict whether solidarity is likely to be based on race or class? Monitoring economies come from three sources. Visibility is enhanced when members are phenotypically distinct, and when their interaction tends to be dense and multiplex. Monitoring is also facilitated by dense and multiplex ties, for these promote informational exchange (and hence the effectiveness of reputation and gossip). Finally, cultural homogeneity helps to minimize errors of interpretation. Sanctioning economies come in part from increasing exit costs. Geographical isolation and the absence of extragroup affiliations therefore also enhance control capacity.

A focus on control capacity—particularly on the attainment of monitoring economies—therefore provides an initial clue as to why racial groups often seem to have an advantage over all other kinds of groups in the production of joint goods. At the same time, consideration of the joint effects of dependence and control sheds light on the failure of some racial groups to attain solidarity. The divisive effects of welfare (which make poor black men and women differentially dependent, for instance) and programs like affirmative action (which make lower- and middle-class blacks differentially dependent), together with geographic and occupational dispersion (which decreases control capacity) are obstacles to the attainment of solidarity among blacks.

In this way, research suggested by the theory of group solidarity would point to an entirely different approach to the problem of the relative salience of status and class. Rather than treating an aggregate's position in the stratification system as the sole predictor of its likely solidarity, attention would be paid first to the determinants of dependence and of control (for some supportive evidence see R. Breton 1964; Foster 1974; Bonacich and Modell 1980; Hanagan 1980; and Reitz 1980).

SOLIDARITY IN THE NATIONAL SOCIETY

Although the theory is pessimistic about the prospects of attaining solidarity in large groups, nevertheless it should be easier to attain in the presence of institutional arrangements that promote control economies. To illustrate the point, it may be useful to consider the theory's implications in the largest of social groups, namely, in national societies. Large and diverse as they may be, national societies can also be likened to groups with different degrees of solidarity. If high rates of crime, divorce, and industrial absenteeism can be regarded as indicators of low solidarity, then levels of solidarity vary widely between societies. There seems little doubt that among industrial capitalist states, Japan has attained the highest level of solidarity.

In a period when capitalist societies are generally portrayed as chronically anomic and ungovernable, the extent of this social order is exceptional. The general Japanese "tendency to confine social relations as far as possible to family or pseudo-family relations" (Dore 1958: 135) imbues the harshest of *Gesellschaft* settings with a soft affective glow. *Gemeinschaft*-type relations have been noted in government bureaucracy as well as in economic institutions like labor unions (Shirai 1975) and banks (Rohlen 1974). Even scientific research groups in Japan differ from their Western counterparts. In Japan "the research group is a *Gemeinschaft* entity, 'everyone's group', 'our group', not the director's personal following. But a European research group is the leader's property: it is a *Gesellschaft* unit in which group members do no more than play their assigned roles in order to complete the director's work" (Nakane 1970: 76). The literature speaks with a single voice about the importance of group solidarity in Japanese daily life (Doi 1973).

How can this relatively high degree of Japanese social integration be explained? Since the inhabitants of most advanced countries place a high value on their citizenship, cross-national rates of dependence are roughly constant. Therefore, the group solidarity theory would suggest that the answer is due to considerations of control. Perhaps Japan is endowed with a peculiar set of institutional arrangements that yield economies of control. This explanation contrasts sharply with most of the popular accounts of Japanese exceptionalism—many of which emphasize its Confucian legacy (for an example, see R. Smith 1983: 9–36).

That Japanese institutional arrangements differ sytematically from those of the West is also well-known. According to the anthropologist Chie Nakane (1970: 40–42), hierarchy lies at the base of all Japanese social organization, but it is a distinctive kind of hierarchy comprised of personal links between a superior and one or a small number of subordinates. The elementary building block of all social groups and organizations is a hierarchical network of the type shown in the accompanying figure. The key point about this structure is that *b* and *c* are linked only through the superior, *a*. This means that *b* and *c* cannot unite to form a coalition against *a*, for they have no relationship with each other.

The name given this type of relationship—which traditionally held between patron and client, landowner and tenant, or master and disciple—is *oyabun-kobun*. These terms continue to be used today to describe the type of relationship existing between the senior and junior members of groups of all kinds. Essentially, the *kobun* receives benefits from his *oyabun*, such as help in securing a job or a promotion, or advice about an important decision. In turn, the *kobun* is ready to offer his services whenever the *oyabun* requires them. Most Japanese, whatever their position in the social structure, are involved in many different relationships of this sort.

This pattern of hierarchy also appears at the organizational level. Many business transactions are effectively internalized. The economy is dominated by a small number of vast enterprises—no more than thirty of them, analogues of the prewar *zaibatsu*, a term literally meaning "financial cliques"—which collectively control the bulk of investment opportunities (Caves and Uekusa 1976: 494–503).

Below these huge firms are many smaller enterprises that survive largely by filling niches as subcontractors to the industrial giants. Each subcontractor tends to have a relationship with only one large firm. Even though the subcontracting company is external to the large firm, it is constrained to deliver its product on time and with sufficient quality by the prospect of losing the right to do business with the larger firm in the future. In other words, the price of maintaining a relationship with the giants is the subcontractor's ability to meet, or exceed, the firm's expectations time and again.

Repeated instances of noncompliance on the part of the subcontractors will cause the large firm to terminate the relationship. Since the few large firms share information to a much larger degree than is common in the West (partly because there are so few of them), there is a good chance that the small company may never be able to establish a subcontracting relationship with any of the other large firms. In this environment, the dependence of subcontractors on the large firm is so strong—the Japanese call them *parent-child* relationships (Nakane 1970: 96)—that moral hazard can be precluded without extensive resort to detailed contracts and lawyers.

Given this hierarchical organizational principle, it follows that social life in Japan is quintessentially concerned with ranking. Juniors must always defer to their seniors. No situation is as awkward in Japan as when the appropriate order is ignored or broken—when, for example, an inferior sits at a seat higher than that of his superior. Thus hierarchy makes it very easy to know what everyone is supposed to be doing. The clarity of expectations could only be possible given Japan's extreme cultural homogeneity. Strict and well-defined role-obligations in and of themselves reduce monitoring costs. The process starts in earnest when children enter school and don uniforms that can be readily used to identify their schools and grade levels.

I have previously mentioned the typical Japanese office, which, by virtue of its lack of partitions, gives principals maximum opportunities to monitor subordinates. Is there a more general tendency in Japanese architecture to limit private spaces and thereby increase visibility? The general tendency for Japanese groups to engage in diffuse rather than specific activities also contributes to visibility. Quality control circles in factories (Cole 1979) are a case in point. But large companies provide recreational facilities and other benefits for the families of employees as well. As a result the worker's entire family becomes drawn into the corporation's networks. Another device that increases the principal's opportunity to monitor members is employed extensively in Japan, namely, consensual decision-making (Nakane 1970: 145).

Larger groups and organizations tend to be built upon concatenations of hierarchical dyads as shown in the accompanying figure. Naturally, the principal (who occupies position a) has a supreme role in this structure. Individuals b and c are his agents, but so far as d, e, f, and g are concerned, they are principals. The fact that most Japanese groups are based on cumulated dyadic relations has significant implications for monitoring costs. Whatever the size of the group, any principal is responsible for monitoring only a limited number of subordinates. In this way, large groups are confederations of extremely small and intimate ones.

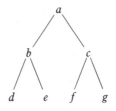

This kind of organizational structure would appear vulnerable to one particular control liability. Since it is based on the proliferation of agents, what keeps agency costs from skyrocketing? Part of the answer may be group rewards that are generated in competition with similar types of groups or organizations: "Because competition takes place between parallel groups of the same kind, the enemy is always to be found among those in the same category. (In other societies such groups could be linked by cooperative ties which would represent a totally opposite kind of strength in relations)" (Nakane 1970: 87–88). Hence steel producers, import-export firms, and universities all engage in internecine competition. In this competition there are two fundamental rewards—the ranking of the organization as a whole, which each member regards as a highly salient personal attribute; and the member's share of the pecuniary gains, in the form of bonuses, which are contingent on the group's superior performance (Vogel 1979: 149–50). Together, these induce group members to monitor one another's behavior.

Ranking hierarchies are found in every field, and even those outside the particular institutional sphere are frequently apprised of the ratings. This system of rankings also produces significant sanctioning economies. Members who are motivated to excel for their share of group prestige need not be plied with extensive pecuniary rewards. Moreover, most members have high exit costs, since seniority is the most important determinant of the member's structural position and does not transfer from one group to the next.

Finally, the importance of small groups in all levels of social life probably leads to significant sanctioning economies. The intimacy of Japanese social relations makes it an easy matter to provide sanctions that are appropriate to given behaviors. But there is also a high degree of public order. Japanese police seem to be particularly effective in deterring crime. Here, as well, the explanation lies in the Japanese tendency to break large groups into small, manageable ones. Police decentralization is one of the factors responsible for the low crime rate (Ames 1981: 45). Another is the relatively high per-capita expenditure on policing.

Cursory as this survey of Japanese social life is, it is at least consistent with the view that economies of control are responsible for the high level of solidarity found there. Control is so effective in Japan that "a person is forever under a kind of surveillance to make sure he or she will come up to the standards required" (Clifford 1976: 13).

If this is so, then why don't other societies take advantage of these control economies? Perhaps because the mechanisms so effectively exploited in Japan depend on the concatenation of hierarchical dyads that permeate the social structure, as well as on a high degree of cultural homogeneity. In this respect Japanese institutions are unique. The control arrangements that work so well in Japan are unlikely to be as effective on foreign soil. Any complete explanation of Japanese solidarity would, of course, have to account for the historical evolution of these distinctive institutional forms.[8]

[8]Murakami (1984: 20; based on Murakami, Kumon, and Sato 1979) claims that distinctive institutions evolved in Japan on account of intensive rice paddy cultivation (its irrigation required high levels of cooperation among producers), the traditional mode of Japanese warfare

Should Japanese institutional arrangements become less hierarchical—perhaps due to a deconcentration of corporate resources, a growth of inter-firm labor mobility, or increasing opportunities for females in the labor force—it follows that this high level of social solidarity should decrease.

If correct, this analysis of the Japanese case shows how the group solidarity theory can account for social order despite the high costs of control and the absence of the internalization of prosocial norms. The key to this explanation lies in the fact that every person belongs to multiple small groups, each of which has a relatively high control capacity. To the degree that these groups all have a stake in preserving the social order—and in Japan, the hierarchical nesting of social groups tends to provide all groups with just this interest—in effect each group assumes some of the burden of control that tends to fall on the shoulders of the state in other societies.

However promising the group solidarity theory may appear to be, we should not be blind to its weaknesses. If the analysis is correct, then stable groups and social orders can be maintained only in the presence of institutions that promote dependence and control. There are a multitude of different kinds of institutions that can fulfill this requirement, but the theory has little to say about their relative merits. In order to resolve this problem a great deal more attention must be paid to the internal dynamics of groups. Although it suggests that the members of groups have a division of productive responsibility and recognizes the importance of leaders, the theory offers little insight into the means by which these responsibilities are decided. For example, both capitalist and socialist communities have institutions that promote dependence and control, yet these have quite different implications for the realization of ends such as economic growth or social stability.

At a more basic level, the theory does not seem capable of accounting for the kind of solidarity that is so often celebrated in our own experience, and in imaginative literature as well. I refer to the spontaneous fellow-feeling that mysteriously comes to the fore from time to time in families, communities (often in the aftermath of disaster), unions, political parties, and other groups, only to disappear thereafter as suddenly as the morning dew. Whether this kind of sentiment is amenable to analysis by the blunt instruments of modern social science is a question that remains open. Nor is the theory capable of explaining instances of spontaneous collective action that occur in the absence of control mechanisms (see Paige 1975: 50–58; Popkin

---

(frequent, but local and small-scale, using lightly armored samurai who also participated in agricultural production), and an extreme degree of cultural homogeneity.

1979: 266). (Whether a fine-grained analysis of such events actually would reveal a complete lack of control mechanisms is, at least to my mind, questionable.)

Yet, in common with nearly all other rational choice theories, the group solidarity theory suffers from a problem that is deeper by far. Individual preferences are a key cause of dependence on groups, but the theory has little to say about what determines the nature and strength of these preferences. There is a growing awareness of the problem of preference-formation among rational choice theorists, but as yet no solution is at hand.

In much rational choice theory preferences are denied an independent role in the determination of behavior.[9] Most research in economics and experimental psychology—and this is even true of a good deal of recent empirical sociology—has simply ignored internal states. This practice entails no special difficulty as long as it is safe to assume that individual utility schedules remain constant over time; that each person's discrete preferences stand in a transitive relation to one another; and that these preferences are independent of the actor's immediate environment. But economists themselves recognize that these are highly questionable assumptions.[10] Preferences of all types differ from group to group, and from society to society. To the extent that they do, it is not likely that explanations discounting their role will prove to be very accurate.

Similar difficulties crop up with learning theory. Just as economists assume the existence of stable preferences from one situation to another, behavioral psychologists assume that reinforcers are constant from situation

[9] See Stigler ([1942] 1966: 38–39) for a standard treatment of the issue. But his cavalier dismissal of the problem of preferences is no longer so fashionable. John Cross (1983: 26) comments: "Economists are often very free with casual assurances that it is acceptable to use the preference function as an exogenous determinant of behavior, because one can always 'go to the psychologists' to get the appropriate specification. This amounts to an assertion that the quantitative specification of the utility function is a problem that economists can legitimately ignore on the grounds that it is a central issue in someone else's professional field." This sense of propriety quickly disappears, however, when economists believe that their explanations of the central problems of another discipline are superior to those that are advocated by its practitioners.

[10] There has been a rapidly growing awareness of the problem of preference formation both among economists and other social scientists. Economists concerned with the effects of neglecting preferences for positive reasons include Schumpeter (1954); von Weiszäcker (1971); G. Becker (1976); Hammond (1976); Hayakawa and Venieris (1977); and Kapteyn, Wansbeek, and Buyze (1980). Welfare economists, moral philosophers (Sen and Williams 1982; Elster 1983), and other social scientists concerned with utilitarian theories of public policy are concerned with preference formation for normative reasons. Nevertheless, positive *theories* of preference formation are few and far between. For discussions of the origin of preferences, see Hirshleifer (1977), whose emphasis is biological, and Douglas (1979), whose emphasis is cultural; neither of these discussions, however, does justice to the complexity of the issues involved. Emerson's (1987; see also D. Friedman 1987) interesting attempt to create a new theory of value was cut short by his premature death.

to situation (this is known as "the empirical law of effect"). Some experimentalists are concerned that this law does not hold widely (Rachlin 1980; Timberlake and Allison 1974). Behaviorists also know that preferences do not remain constant in different situations (Garcia and Koelling 1967). Experiments (notably by Hursh 1980) have shown that preferences (as measured by past choices) can vary systematically with specific environmental conditions.[11]

This is not to argue that by evading the problem of preference formation economists and learning theorists have accomplished little, for such a claim would be as ridiculous as it is false. The analysis of human behavior by economists as a function of changing relative prices, or by learning theorists as a function of changing patterns of reinforcement, is a fundamental achievement of modern social science. By denying the salience of internal states, however, both these approaches also leave certain questions open, among them questions about the production of solidarity. As my brief remarks on the family suggest, preference formation itself may be as much a consequence of solidarity as its cause.

Finally, although the theory does provide an explanation of the evolution of institutional arrangements that promote solidarity, this account cannot be regarded as anything but elementary. Few problems in social science are as significant, and as intractable, as the problem of institutional development. Progress on this key research frontier awaits the development of more sophisticated theories—ones that explain the actual sequence of institutional development "as it goes on, under its own steam, in historic time, producing at every instance that state which will of itself determine the next one" (Schumpeter 1950: 44).[12]

Whereas a conflict between methodological individualism and sociology has long been assumed, that conflict was created by a set of peculiar historical events (Camic 1979: 539–40) and is not intellectually defensible.

[11] As the economist John Cross notes, "The inadequacy of this concept of 'reinforcer' has been apparent to psychologists for some time. In response, a number of models have been devised in which one interprets experimental conditions in terms of the constraints they impose on behavior. . . . All of these models have a strongly economic flavor, and, in effect, their authors are turning to ordinalist utility models to provide an alternative to the cruder presumption that any biological need under conditions of deprivation constitutes a 'reinforcer.' From the point of view of scientific rigor, this is a great step forward, and of course economists may be pleased to find that the analytic models that are familiar to them are proving to be useful in other fields as well, but the existence of such a trend makes it clear that the psychology profession is not yet in a position to provide significant new insights into the character of preferences under any but the simplest kinds of situations" (1983: 27).

[12] For examples of attempts to provide such endogenous models of change, see Hernes (1976), Schelling (1978), and Schotter (1981).

Solidarity and social order derive not from the biology or personalities of individuals, but from the socially conditioned reactions of individual actors to their circumstances. The path to the development of coherent theory lies in combining a concern for individual action with an appreciation for the structural constraints that these actors face.

Sociologists and rational choice theorists often assume that there is an antinomy between their two types of intellectual discourse. This is a most unfortunate view. At worst, it justifies and promotes a supercilious ignorance of the literatures of sister disciplines in the social sciences. Whereas sociologists command knowledge of a wide array of social and institutional structures, rational choice theorists are masters at explaining how individuals behave in the face of different constraints. Sociologists deceive themselves by treating rational choice with indifference or—what is more common—with contempt. Without some highly elaborated model of individual behavior (of which rational choice is the leading candidate), sociologists cannot properly understand the behavioral consequences of different social structures, for such an understanding requires the establishment of a link between structural constraints and individual dispositions. The same holds for those rational choice theorists who wrongly assume that they have nothing to learn from sociologists. Without appreciating and analyzing the immense variety of successful social institutions in world history, rational choice theorists can be justifiably condemned as parochial apologists for the status quo.

In combination, rational choice and sociology offer the best current hope of fusing individual and structural levels of analysis into a logically consistent whole that yields empirically falsifiable propositions. Many critical intellectual pursuits lie ahead: we must take cognizance of the significance of individual preferences and of the complexity of institutional development. Little progress can be expected if rational choice theorists always cling to their favorite, unrealistic behavioral assumptions, and if sociologists continue to dismiss methodological individualism out of hand. These tasks call for a marriage of the social sciences, not for a perpetuation of shopworn disciplinary prejudices and other idols of the tribe.

BIBLIOGRAPHY

Abruzzi, Adam. 1956. *Work, Workers and Work Measurement*. New York: Columbia University Press.

Akerlof, George A. 1970. "The Market for 'Lemons': Quality Uncertainty and the Market Mechanism." *Quarterly Journal of Economics*, 84, (3): 488–500.

Alchian, Armen. 1950. "Uncertainty, Evolution and Economic Theory." *Journal of Political Economy*, 58, (3): 211–21.

Alchian, Armen, and Harold M. Demsetz. 1972. "Production, Information Costs and Economic Organization." *American Economic Review*, 62, (5): 777–95.

Allais, M., and O. Hagen. 1979. *Expected Utility Hypotheses and the Allais Paradox: Contemporary Discussions of Decision under Uncertainty with Allais' Rejoinder*. Dordrecht: D. Reidel.

Ames, William L. 1981. *Police and Community in Japan*. Berkeley: University of California Press.

Anderson, Gary M., and Robert D. Tollison. 1985. "Ideology, Interest Groups, and the Repeal of the Corn Laws." *Zeitschrift für die gesamte Staatswissenschaft*, 141, (2): 197–212.

Ardener, Shirley. 1962. "The Comparative Study of Rotating Credit Associations." *Journal of the Royal Anthropological Institute of Great Britain and Ireland*, 94, (2): 201–29.

Arrington, Leonard J. 1958. *Great Basin Kingdom: An Economic History of the Latter-day Saints*. Cambridge: Harvard University Press.

Arrow, Kenneth J. 1970. *The Limits of Organization*. New York: Norton.

———. 1971. *Essays in the Theory of Risk Bearing*. Chicago: Markham.

———. 1972. "Models of Job Discrimination." In A. H. Pascal, ed., *Racial Discrimination in Economic Life*, pp. 83–102. Lexington, Mass.: D. C. Heath.

Axelrod, Robert. 1984. *The Evolution of Cooperation*. New York: Basic Books.

Axelrod, Robert, and William D. Hamilton. 1981. "The Evolution of Cooperation." *Science*, 211, (4489): 1390–96.

187

Babbage, Charles. 1970. *Reflections on the Decline of Science in England.* New York: Augustus M. Kelley. [Originally published 1830.]

Bandura, Albert. 1971. *Social Learning Theory.* Morristown, N.J.: General Learning Press.

Bane, Mary Jo. 1975. *Economic Influence on Divorce and Remarriage.* Cambridge, Mass.: Center for the Study of Public Policy.

Banfield, Edward. 1958. *The Moral Basis of a Backward Society.* Glencoe, Ill.: Free Press.

Banton, Michael. 1983. *Racial and Ethnic Competition.* Cambridge: Cambridge University Press.

Barry, Brian. 1970. *Sociologists, Economists, and Democracy.* Chicago: University of Chicago Press.

Barth, Fredrik. 1962. "The System of Social Stratification in Swat, North Pakistan." In Edmund Leach, ed., *Aspects of Caste in South India, Ceylon, and North West Pakistan,* pp. 113–46. London: Cambridge University Press.

Barzel, Yoram. 1982. "Measurement Cost and the Organization of Markets." *Journal of Law and Economics,* 25, (1): 27–48.

Baumol, William, John Panzer, and Robert Willig. 1982. *Contestable Markets and the Theory of Industry Structure.* New York: Harcourt Brace.

Becker, Gary S. 1974. "A Theory of Social Interactions." *Journal of Political Economy,* 82, (6): 163–91.

———. 1976. *The Economic Approach to Human Behavior.* Chicago: University of Chicago Press.

———. 1981. *A Treatise on the Family.* Cambridge: Harvard University Press.

Becker, Howard S. 1960. "Notes on the Concept of Commitment." *American Journal of Sociology,* 66, (1): 32–40.

Bendix, Reinhard. 1956. *Work and Authority in Industry.* New York: John Wiley.

———. 1960. *Max Weber: An Intellectual Portrait.* New York: Doubleday & Co.

Ben-Porath, Yoram. 1980. "The F-Connection: Families, Friends, and Firms and the Organization of Exchange." *Population and Development Review,* 6, (1): 1–30.

Bentham, Jeremy. 1843. *The Works of Jeremy Bentham.* Vol. 4. Published Under the Supervision of his Executor, John Bowring. London: Simpkin Marshall & Co.

Berkowitz, S. D. 1982. *An Introduction to Structural Analysis: The Network Approach to Social Research.* Toronto: Butterworth & Co.

Bernstein, Paul. 1980. *Workplace Democratization: Its Internal Dynamic.* New Brunswick, N.J.: Transaction Books.

Berreman, G. D. 1972. *Hindus of the Himalayas: Ethnography and Change.* Berkeley: University of California Press.

Blalock, Hubert M., and Paul Wilken. 1979. *Intergroup Processes: A Micro-Macro Perspective*. New York: Free Press.

Blau, Peter M. 1964. *Exchange and Power in Social Life*. New York: John Wiley.

Blumstein, Phillip, and Pepper Schwartz. 1983. *American Couples*. New York: William Morrow.

Bodnar, John. 1985. *The Transplanted: A History of Immigrants in Urban America*. Bloomington: Indiana University Press.

Bohm, P. 1972. "Estimating Demand for Public Goods: An Experiment." *European Economic Review*, 3, (2): 111–30.

Bonacich, Edna, and John Modell. 1980. *The Economic Basis of Ethnic Solidarity: Small Business in the Japanese American Community*. Berkeley: University of California Press.

Bonnett, Aubrey W. 1981. *Institutional Adaptation of West Indian Immigrants to America: An Analysis of Rotating Credit Associations*. Washington, D.C.: University Press of America.

Boudon, Raymond. 1981. *The Logic of Social Action*. Translated by David Silverman. London: Routledge & Kegan Paul.

Bouglé, C. 1971. *Essays on the Caste System*. Cambridge: Cambridge University Press.

Bradley, Keith, and Alan Gelb. 1981. "Motivation and Control in the Mondragón Experiment." *British Journal of Industrial Relations*, 19, (2): 211–31.

———. 1983. "The Replication and Sustainability of the Mondragón Experiment." *British Journal of Industrial Relations*, 21, (1): 20–33.

Brady, David. 1973. *Congressional Voting in a Partisan Era*. Lawrence: University of Kansas Press.

Braverman, Harry. 1974. *Labor and Monopoly Capital*. New York: Monthly Review Press.

Brennan, Geoffrey, and James M. Buchanan. 1980. *The Power to Tax: Analytical Foundations of a Fiscal Constitution*. Cambridge: Cambridge University Press.

Brenner, Reuven. 1983. *History: The Human Gamble*. Chicago: University of Chicago Press.

Breton, Albert, and Ronald Wintrobe. 1981. *The Logic of Bureaucratic Conduct*. Cambridge: Cambridge University Press.

Breton, Raymond. 1964. "Institutional Completeness of Ethnic Communities and the Personal Relations of Immigrants." *American Journal of Sociology*, 70, (2): 193–205.

Broad, William, and Nicholas Wade. 1983. *Betrayers of the Truth: Fraud and Deceit in the Halls of Science*. New York: Simon and Schuster.

Buchanan, James M. 1965. "An Economic Theory of Clubs." *Economica*, 32, (125), new series: 1–14.

———. 1975. *The Limits of Liberty*. Chicago: University of Chicago Press.

Buchanan, James M., and Gordon Tullock. 1962. *The Calculus of Consent.* Ann Arbor: University of Michigan Press.

Burawoy, Michael. 1979. *Manufacturing Consent.* Chicago: University of Chicago Press.

Butterick, John. 1952. "The Inside Contract System." *The Journal of Economic History,* 12, (3): 205–21.

Cable, John, and Felix FitzRoy. 1980. "Co-Operation and Productivity: Some Evidence from West German Experience." In Alasdair Clayre, ed., *The Political Economy of Co-Operation and Participation,* pp. 141–59. Oxford: Oxford University Press.

Cain, Bruce E., John A. Ferejohn, and Morris P. Fiorina. 1983. "The Constituency Component: A Comparison of Service in Great Britain and the United States." *Comparative Political Studies,* 16, (1): 67–91.

———. 1984. "The Constituency Service Basis of the Personal Vote for U.S. Representatives and British Members of Parliament." *American Political Science Review,* 78, (1): 110–25.

Camic, Charles. 1979. "The Utilitarians Revisited." *American Journal of Sociology,* 85, (3): 516–50.

Caves, Richard E., and Masu Uekusa. 1976. "Industrial Organization." In Hugh Patrick and Henry Rosovsky, eds., *Asia's New Giant: How the Japanese Economy Works,* pp. 459–524. Washington, D.C.: Brookings.

Cebula, Richard J. 1980. "Voting With One's Feet: A Critique of the Evidence." *Regional Science and Urban Economics,* 10, (1): 91–107.

Chandler, Alfred D., Jr. 1962. *Strategy and Structure.* Cambridge: MIT Press.

———. 1977. *The Visible Hand.* Cambridge: Harvard University Press.

Cheung, Stephen N. S. 1969. *The Theory of Share Tenancy.* Chicago: University of Chicago Press.

Cialdini, Robert B. 1984. *Influence: How and Why People Agree to Things.* New York: William Morrow.

Clawson, Dan. 1980. *Bureaucracy and the Labor Process.* New York: Monthly Review Press.

Clayre, Alasdair, ed. 1980. *The Political Economy of Co-Operation and Participation.* Oxford: Oxford University Press.

Clegg, Stewart, and David Dunkerly. 1980. *Organization, Class and Control.* London: Routledge & Kegan Paul.

Clifford, William. 1976. *Crime Control in Japan.* Lexington, Mass.: Lexington Books.

Coase, Ronald H. 1937. "The Nature of the Firm." *Economica,* n.s. 4, (16): 386–405.

Cohen, G. A. 1978. *Karl Marx's Theory of History: A Defence.* Princeton: Princeton University Press.

Cole, Robert E. 1971. "The Theory of Institutionalization: Permanent Employment and Traditions in Japan." *Economic Development and Cultural Change,* 20, (1): 47–70.

————. 1973. "Functional Alternatives and Economic Development: An Empirical Example of Permanent Employment in Japan." *American Sociological Review*, 38, (4): 424–30.

————. 1979. *Work, Mobility and Participation: A Comparative Study of American and Japanese Industry.* Berkeley: University of California Press.

Coleman, James S. 1966. "Individual Interests and Collective Action." *Papers on Non-Market Decision-Making*, (1): 49–62.

————. 1973. *The Mathematics of Collective Action.* Chicago: Aldine.

————. 1982. *The Asymmetric Society.* Syracuse, N.Y.: Syracuse University Press.

————. 1986. "Social Theory, Social Research, and a Theory of Action." *American Journal of Sociology*, 91, (6): 1309–35.

Collard, David. 1978. *Altruism and the Economy: A Study in Non-Selfish Economics.* Oxford: Oxford University Press.

Collins, Randall. 1975. *Conflict Sociology.* New York: Academic Press.

————. 1981. "On the Microfoundations of Macrosociology." *American Journal of Sociology*, 86, (5): 984–1014.

————. 1986. "Is 1980s Sociology in the Doldrums?" *American Journal of Sociology*, 91, (6): 1336–55.

Cook, Karen S., and Karen A. Hegtvedt. 1983. "Distributive Justice, Equity, and Equality." *Annual Review of Sociology*, 9: 217–41.

Cope, Thomas, and Donald V. Kurtz. 1980. "Default and the Tanda: A Model Regarding Recruitment for Rotating Credit Associations." *Ethnology*, 19, (2): 213–31.

Crane, Wilder, Jr. 1960. "A Caveat on Roll-Call Studies of Party Voting." *Midwest Journal of Political Science*, 4, (3): 237–49.

Cross, John G. 1983. *A Theory of Adaptive Economic Behavior.* Cambridge: Cambridge University Press.

Cummings, Scott, ed. 1980. *Self-Help in Urban America: Patterns of Minority Business Enterprise.* Port Washington, N.Y.: Kennikat Press.

Dahrendorf, Ralf. 1959. *Class and Class Conflict in Industrial Society.* Stanford, Calif.: Stanford University Press.

Dalton, Melville. 1948. "The Industrial Rate Buster." *Applied Anthropology*, 7, (1): 5–18.

Day, R. C., and Robert L. Hamblin. 1964. "Some Effects of Close and Punitive Styles of Supervision." *American Journal of Sociology*, 69, (5): 499–510.

Deckard, Barbara Sinclair. 1983. *The Women's Movement.* New York: Harper & Row.

Demsetz, Harold. 1967. "Toward a Theory of Property Rights." *American Economic Review*, 57, (2): 347–59.

Dex, Shirley. 1985. "The Use of Economists' Models in Sociology." *Ethnic and Racial Studies*, 8, (4): 516–34.

Doeringer, Peter, and Michael Piore. 1971. *Internal Labor Markets and Manpower Analysis.* Boston: D. C. Heath.

Doi, Takeo. 1973. *The Anatomy of Dependence*. Translated by John Bester. Tokyo: Kodansha International.

Dore, Ronald P. 1958. *City Life in Japan*. Berkeley: University of California Press.

———. 1973. *British Factory/Japanese Factory*. Berkeley: University of California Press.

Douglas, Mary. 1979. *The World of Goods: Towards an Anthropology of Consumption*. New York: Norton.

Downs, Anthony. 1957. *An Economic Theory of Democracy*. New York: Harper & Row.

Dryzek, John, and Robert E. Goodin. 1986. "Risk-Sharing and Social Justice: The Motivational Foundations of the Post-War Welfare State." *British Journal of Political Science*, 16, (1): 1–34.

Du Bois, W. E. Burghardt. 1899. *The Philadelphia Negro*. Philadelphia: University of Pennsylvania Press.

Dugdale, G. 1932. *Langemarck and Cambrai*. Shrewsbury, England: Wilding and Son.

Dumont, Louis. 1970. *Homo Hierarchichus: The Caste System and Its Implications*. Chicago: University of Chicago Press.

Durkheim, Emile. 1901. "Deux Lois de l'évolution pénale." *L'Année Sociologique*, 4, (1): 65–95. [An English translation of this paper, by T. A. Jones and A. Scull, is in Steven Lukes and Andrew Scull, eds., *Durkheim and the Law*, pp. 102–32 (New York: St. Martin's, 1983).]

———. 1938. *The Rules of Sociological Method*. 8th ed. Edited by George E. G. Catlin. Translated by Sarah A. Solovay and John H. Mueller. Chicago: University of Chicago Press. [Originally published 1895.]

———. 1951. *Suicide*. New York: Free Press. [Originally published 1897.]

———. 1961a. *The Elementary Forms of Religious Life*. Translated by Joseph Ward Swain. New York: Collier. [Originally published 1912.]

———. 1961b. *Moral Education: A Study in the Theory and Application of the Sociology of Education*. Translated by Everett K. Wilson and Herman Schnurer. New York: Free Press. [Originally published 1925.]

———. 1974. "The Determination of Moral Facts." In *Sociology and Philosophy*, pp. 35–63. Translated by D. F. Pocock. New York: Free Press. [Originally published 1906.]

Duverger, Maurice. 1963. *Political Parties*. New York: John Wiley.

Eden, Frederick Morton. 1801. *Observations on Friendly Societies for the Maintenance of the Industrious Classes during Sickness, Infirmity, Old Age and other Exigencies*. London: J. White and J. Wright.

Edwards, Richard C. 1979. *Contested Terrain*. New York: Basic Books.

Elster, Jon. 1979. *Ulysses and the Sirens: Studies in Rationality and Irrationality*. Cambridge: Cambridge University Press.

———. 1983. *Sour Grapes: Studies in the Subversion of Rationality*. Cambridge: Cambridge University Press.

------. 1985. *Making Sense of Marx*. Cambridge: Cambridge University Press.

Embree, John F. 1939. *Suye Mura: A Japanese Village*. Chicago: University of Chicago Press.

Emerson, Richard A. 1962. "Power-Dependence Relations." *American Sociological Review*, 27, (1): 31–41.

------. 1987. "A Theory of Value." In Karen A. Cook, ed., *Social Exchange Theory*, pp. 1–26. Beverly Hills: Sage Publications.

Epstein, Leon D. 1964. "A Comparative Study of Canadian Parties." *American Political Science Review*, 58, (1): 46–59.

------. 1967. *Political Parties in Western Democracies*. New York: Praeger.

Erasmus, Charles J. 1977. *In Search of the Common Good: Utopian Experiments Past and Future*. New York: Free Press.

Etzioni, Amitai. 1975. *A Comparative Analysis of Complex Organizations*. 2d ed. New York: Free Press.

Fama, Eugena F. 1980. "Agency Problems and the Theory of the Firm." *Journal of Political Economy*, 88, (2): 288–307.

Ferejohn, John A. 1977. "On the Decline of Competition in Congressional Elections." *American Political Science Review*, 71, (1): 166–76.

Festinger, Leon, Stanley Schachter, and Kurt Back. 1950. *Social Pressures in Informal Groups*. New York: Harper & Row.

Finer, Herman. 1949. *The Theory and Practice of Modern Government*. Rev. ed. New York: Henry Holt and Co.

Fiorina, Morris P. 1974. *Representatives, Roll Calls, and Constituencies*. Lexington, Mass.: D.C. Heath (Lexington Books).

------. 1980. "The Decline of Collective Responsibility in American Politics." *Daedalus*, 109, (3): 25–45.

Fireman, Bruce, and William A. Gamson. 1979. "Utilitarian Logic in the Resource Mobilization Perspective." In Mayer Zald and John D. McCarthy, eds., *The Dynamics of Social Movements*, pp. 8–44. Cambridge, Mass.: Winthrop.

FitzGerald, Frances. 1986. "The Castro." *The New Yorker*, July 21: 34–70.

Fogel, Robert W., and Stanley Engerman. 1974. *Time on the Cross*. Boston: Little, Brown.

Foster, John. 1974. *Class Struggle and the Industrial Revolution: Early Industrial Capitalism in Three English Towns*. London: Weidenfeld and Nicolson.

Foucault, Michel. 1979. *Discipline and Punish: The Birth of the Prison*. New York: Vintage.

Frazier, E. Franklin. 1957. *The Negro in the United States*. 2d ed. New York: Macmillan.

French, David, and Elena French. 1975. *Working Communally: Patterns and Possibilities*. New York: Russell Sage Foundation.

Freud, Sigmund. 1961. *Civilization and Its Discontents*. New York: Norton. [Originally published 1930.]

Friedman, Debra. 1983a. *Why Workers Strike: Individual Decisions and Structural Constraints*. Ph.D. dissertation, Department of Sociology, University of Washington.

———. 1983b. "Why Workers Strike." In Michael Hechter, ed., *The Microfoundations of Macrosociology*, pp. 250–83. Philadelphia: Temple University Press.

———. 1986. "The Principal-Agent Problem in Labor-Management Negotiations." In Edward J. Lawler, ed., *Advances in Group Processes*, vol. 3, pp. 87–104.

———. 1987. "Notes on a Theory of Value." In Karen A. Cook, ed., *Social Exchange Theory*, pp. 27–34. Beverly Hills: Sage Publications.

Friedman, M., and L. Savage. 1948. "The Utility Analysis of Choices Involving Risk." *Journal of Political Economy*, 56, (4): 279–304.

Frolich, Norman, Joe A. G. Oppenheimer, and Oran Young. 1971. *Political Entrepreneurship and Collective Goods*. Princeton: Princeton University Press.

Froman, L. A., and R. B. Ripley. 1965. "Conditions for Party Leadership: The Case of the House Democrats." *American Political Science Review*, 59, (1): 52–63.

Fulenwider, Claire Knoche. 1980. *Feminism in American Politics: A Study of Ideological Influence*. New York: Praeger.

Galenson, Walter. 1952. "Scandinavia." In Walter Galenson, ed., *Comparative Labor Movements*, pp. 104–72. New York: Prentice-Hall.

Galey, Margaret E. 1977. "Ethnicity, Fraternalism, Social and Mental Health." *Ethnicity*, 4, (1): 19–53.

Gamble, Sidney D. 1944. "A Chinese Mutual Savings Society." *Far Eastern Quarterly*, 4, (1): 44–52.

Gamson, William. 1964. "Experimental Studies of Coalition Formation." In Leonard Berkowitz, ed., *Advances in Experimental Social Psychology*, vol. 1, pp. 82–110. New York: Academic Press.

Garcia, J., and R. A. Koelling. 1967. "A Comparison of Aversions Induced by X-Rays, Toxins, and Drugs in the Rat." *Radiation Research*, 7, Supplement: 439–50.

Garner, Samuel Paul. 1954. *The Evolution of Cost Accounting to 1925*. University, Ala.: University of Alabama Press.

Gauthier, David. 1986. *Morals By Agreement*. Oxford: Clarendon Press.

Geertz, Clifford. 1966. "The Rotating Credit Association: A 'Middle Rung' in Development." In Immanuel Wallerstein, ed., *Social Change: The Colonial Situation*, pp. 420–46. New York: John Wiley. [Originally published in *Economic Development and Cultural Change*, 10, 3, (1962): 24–263.]

———. 1982. "The Way We Think Now: Toward an Ethnography of Modern Thought." *Bulletin of the American Academy of Arts and Sciences*, 35, (5): 13–34.

Gibbs, Jack P. 1981. *Norms, Deviance, and Social Control: Conceptual Matters*. New York: Elsevier.

Giddens, Anthony. 1979. *Central Problems in Social Theory: Action, Structure and Contradiction in Social Analysis*. Berkeley: University of California Press.

Gildin, Hilail. 1983. *Rousseau's "Social Contract": The Design of the Argument*. Chicago: University of Chicago Press.

Glick, Thomas F. 1970. *Irrigation and Society in Medieval Valencia*. Cambridge: Harvard University Press.

Goffman, Erving. 1959. *The Presentation of Self in Everyday Life*. New York: Anchor.

———. 1967. *Interaction Ritual*. New York: Anchor.

Good Intent Society. 1815. Rules and Regulations to be Observed by the GOOD INTENT SOCIETY, instituted at Newcastle Upon Tyne, July 12, 1813, for the relief of each other in distress and for Other Good Purposes therein contained. . . . Newcastle. Pamphlet in British Museum.

Gosden, P. H. J. H. 1961. *The Friendly Societies in England, 1815–1875*. Manchester: Manchester University Press.

Granovetter, Mark. 1985. "Economic Action and Social Structure: The Problem of Embeddedness." *American Journal of Sociology*, 91, (3): 481–510.

Greenstein, Fred I., and Elton F. Jackson. 1963. "A Second Look at the Validity of Roll-Call Analysis." *Midwest Journal of Political Science*, 7, (2): 156–66.

Groves, Theodore, and John Ledyard. 1977. "Optimal Allocation of Public Goods: A Solution to the 'Free Rider' Problem." *Econometrica*, 45, (4): 783–809.

Habermas, Jürgen. 1983. *The Theory of Communicative Action*. Boston: Beacon.

Hall, John R. 1983. "Social Structure and Commitment: A Reexamination of the Kanter Thesis." Department of Sociology, University of Missouri. Mimeograph.

———. 1987. *Gone from the Promised Land: Jonestown in American Cultural History*. New Brunswick, N.J.: Transaction Books.

Hamilton, William D. 1964. "The Genetical Evolution of Social Behavior, I." *Journal of Theoretical Biology*, 7, (1): 1–51.

Hammond, Peter J. 1976. "Endogenous Tastes and Stable Long-Run Choice." *Journal of Economic Theory*, 13, (2): 329–40.

Hanagan, Michael P. 1980. *The Logic of Solidarity*. Champaign, Ill.: University of Illinois Press.

Hannan, Michael T., Nancy Brandon Tuma, and Lyle Groeneveld. 1977. "Income Maintenance and Marital Events: Evidence from an Income Maintenance Experiment." *American Journal of Sociology*, 82, (6): 1186–1211.

Hansen, John Mark. 1985. "The Political Economy of Group Membership." *American Political Science Review*, 79, (1): 79–96.
Hardin, Russell. 1982. *Collective Action*. Baltimore: Johns Hopkins University Press (for Resources for the Future).
Hardwick, Charles. 1879. *The History, Present Position and Social Impor-
tance of Friendly Societies*. 3d rev. ed. London: John Heywood.
Hayakawa, Hiroaki, and Yiannis Venieris. 1977. "Consumer Interdepen-
dence via Reference Groups." *Journal of Political Economy*, 85, (3):
599–615.
Hayek, Friedrich A. 1976. *Law, Legislation and Liberty*. Vol. 2 of *The Mi-
rage of Social Justice*. Chicago: University of Chicago Press.
Heath, Anthony. 1976. *Rational Choice and Social Exchange*. Cambridge:
Cambridge University Press.
Hechter, Michael. 1975. *Internal Colonialism: The Celtic Fringe in British
National Development, 1536–1966*. Berkeley: University of California
Press.
———. 1978. "Group Formation and the Cultural Division of Labor."
American Journal of Sociology, 84, (2): 293–318.
———. 1979. "The Position of Eastern European Immigrants to the
United States in the Cultural Division of Labor: Some Trends and Pros-
pects." In Walter L. Goldfrank, ed., *The World-System of Capitalism:
Past and Present*, pp. 111–30. Beverly Hills: Sage Publications.
Hechter, Michael, ed. 1983. *The Microfoundations of Macrosociology*. Phila-
delphia: Temple University Press.
Hechter, Michael, and William Brustein. 1980. "Regional Modes of Pro-
duction and Patterns of State Formation in Western Europe." *American
Journal of Sociology*, 85, (5): 1061–94.
Hechter, Michael, and Debra Friedman. 1984. "Does Rational Choice
Theory Suffice? Response to Adam." *International Migration Review*,
18, (2): 381–88.
Hechter, Michael, Debra Friedman, and Malka Appelbaum. 1982. "A
Theory of Ethnic Collective Action." *International Migration Review*,
16, (2): 412–34.
Heckathorn, Douglas. 1985. "The Dynamics of Conformity and Revolt in
Collective Incentive Systems: A Rational Choice Approach." Paper pre-
sented at the annual meetings of the American Sociological Association
in Washington, D.C.
Hefferline, Ralph F., and Brian Keenan. 1963. "Amplitude-Induction
Gradient of a Small-Scale (Covert) Operant." *Journal of the Experimental
Analysis of Behavior*, 6, (3): 307–15.
Hefferline, Ralph F., Brian Keenan, and Richard A. Harford. 1959. "Es-
cape and Avoidance Conditioning in Human Subjects without Their
Observation of the Response." *Science*, 130, (3385): 1338–39.
Heimer, Carol A. 1985. *Reactive Risk and Rational Action: Managing*

Moral Hazard in Insurance Contracts. Berkeley: University of California Press.

Heiner, Ronald A. 1983. "The Origins of Predictable Behavior." *American Economic Review*, 73, (4): 560–95.

Hernes, Gudmund. 1976. "Structural Change in Social Processes." *American Journal of Sociology*, 82, (3): 513–47.

Hetherington, Mavis, Martha Cox, and Roger Cox. 1978. "The Aftermath of Divorce." In Joseph H. Stevens and Marilyn Matthews, eds., *Mother/Child, Father/Child Relationships*, pp. 149–76. Washington, D.C.: The National Association for the Education of Young Children.

Hirschman, Albert O. 1970. *Exit, Voice and Loyalty.* Cambridge: Harvard University Press.

Hirshleifer, Jack. 1977. "Economics from a Biological Viewpoint." *Journal of Law and Economics*, 20, (1): 1–52.

Hobbes, Thomas. 1968. *Leviathan.* Edited by C. B. Macpherson. Harmondsworth, England: Penguin. [Originally published 1651.]

Holmstrom, Bengt. 1979. "Moral Hazard and Observability." *Bell Journal of Economics*, 10, (1): 74–91.

Homans, George C. 1961. *Social Behavior: Its Elementary Forms.* New York: Harcourt Brace.

———. 1964. "Bringing Men Back In." *American Sociological Review*, 29, (6): 809–18.

———. 1965. "Effort, Supervision and Productivity." In Robert Dubin, ed., *Leadership and Productivity*, pp. 51–67. San Francisco: Chandler.

Hornstein, H. A., E. Fisch, and M. Holmes. 1968. "Influence of a Model's Feeling about His Behavior and His Relevance as a Comparison Other on Observers' Helping Behavior." *Journal of Personality and Social Psychology*, 10, (3): 222–26.

Horowitz, Helen Lefkowitz. 1984. *Alma Mater: Design and Experience in the Women's Colleges from Their Nineteenth Century Beginnings to the 1930s.* New York: Knopf.

Hoxie, Robert Franklin. 1915. *Scientific Management and Labor.* New York: D. Appleton.

Huitt, Ralph K. 1961. "The Outsider in the Senate: An Alternative Role." *American Political Science Review*, 55, (3): 566–75.

———. 1969. "Democratic Party Leadership in the Senate." In R. K. Huitt and R. L. Peabody, eds., *Congress: Two Decades of Analysis*, pp. 136–58. New York: Harper & Row.

Hursh, Steven R. 1980. "Economic Concepts for the Analysis of Behavior." *Journal of the Experimental Analysis of Behavior*, 34, (2): 219–38.

International Herald Tribune. 1984. "2 Sudan Thieves Lose Hands, Legs." 22 May: 4.

Iorizzo, Luciano J., and Salvatore Mondello. 1971. *The Italian-Americans.* New York: Twayne Publishers.

Jackman, Mary R., and Robert W. Jackman. 1983. *Class Awareness in the United States.* Berkeley: University of California Press.

Jackson, R. J. 1968. *Rebels and Whips: An Analysis of Dissension, Discipline and Cohesion in British Political Parties.* London: Macmillan.

Jacobson, Gary C. 1983. *The Politics of Congressional Elections.* Boston: Little, Brown.

Janowitz, Morris. 1978. *The Last Half-Century.* Chicago: University of Chicago Press.

Jensen, Michael C., and William H. Meckling. 1976. "Theory of the Firm: Managerial Behavior, Agency Costs and Ownership Structure." *Journal of Financial Economics,* 3, (4): 305–60.

Jones, Charles O. 1964. "Inter-Party Competition for Congressional Seats." *Western Political Quarterly,* 17, (3): 461–76.

———. 1968. "Joseph G. Cannon and Howard W. Smith: An Essay on the Limits of Leadership in the House of Representatives." *Journal of Politics,* 30, (3): 617–46.

Kahneman, Daniel, and Amos Tversky. 1979. "Prospect Theory: An Analysis of Decision Under Risk." *Econometrica,* 47, (2): 263–91.

Kalt, Joseph P., and Mark Z. Zupan. 1984. "Capture and Ideology in the Economic Theory of Politics." *American Economic Review,* 74, (3): 279–300.

Kanter, Rosabeth Moss. 1972. *Commitment and Community: Communes and Utopias in Sociological Perspective.* Cambridge: Harvard University Press.

Kapteyn, Arie, Tom Wansbeek, and Jeannine Buyze. 1980. "The Dynamics of Preference Formation." *Journal of Economic Behavior and Organization,* 1, (2): 123–57.

Kau, James B., and Paul H. Rubin. 1979. "Self-Interest, Ideology, and Logrolling in Congressional Voting." *Journal of Law and Economics,* 22, (2): 365–84.

Kaufman, Herbert. 1960. *The Forest Ranger: A Study in Administrative Behavior.* Baltimore: Johns Hopkins University Press (for Resources for the Future).

Kelley, John E. 1982. *Scientific Management, Job Redesign and Work Performance.* London: Academic Press.

Key, V. O., Jr. 1964. *Politics, Parties and Pressure Groups.* 5th ed. New York: Thomas Y. Crowell.

Keyserling, Mary Dublin. 1979. "Women's Stake in Full Employment: Their Disadvantaged Role in the Economy—Challenges to Action." In Ann Foote Cahn, ed., *Women in the U.S. Labor Force,* pp. 25–39. New York: Praeger.

Kiesler, Charles A., and Sara Kiesler. 1969. *Conformity.* Reading, Mass.: Addison-Wesley.

Kim, Oliver, and Mark Walker. 1984. "The Free Rider Problem: Experimental Evidence." *Public Choice,* 43, (1): 3–24.

Kingdon, John W. 1977. "Models of Legislative Voting." *The Journal of Politics*, 39, (3): 563–95.

Kip, Richard de Raismes. 1953. *Fraternal Life Insurance in America*. Philadelphia: College Offset Press.

Kohlberg, Lawrence. 1969. "Stage and Sequence: The Cognitive-Developmental Approach to Socialization." In David A. Goslin, ed., *Handbook of Socialization Theory and Research*, pp. 347–480. Chicago: Rand McNally.

Knight, Frank H. 1921. *Risk, Uncertainty, and Profit*. Boston: Houghton Mifflin.

Kolm, Serge-Christophe. 1983. "Altruism and Efficiency." *Ethics*, 94, (1): 18–65.

Kriegel, Annie. 1972. *The French Communists: Portrait of a People*. Chicago: University of Chicago Press.

Kropotkin, Petr. 1902. *Mutual Aid: A Factor of Evolution*. London: William Heinemann.

Kula, Witold. 1976. *An Economic Theory of the Feudal System*. London: NLB Books.

Kuper, H., and S. Kaplan. 1944. "Voluntary Associations in an Urban Township." *African Studies*, 3, (4): 178–86.

Kurtz, Donald V. 1973. "The Rotating Credit Association: An Adaptation to Poverty." *Human Organization*, 32, (1): 49–58.

Kurtz, Donald V., and Margaret Showman. 1978. "The Tanda: A Rotating Credit Association in Mexico." *Ethnology*, 17, (1): 65–74.

Landes, David S. 1969. *The Unbound Prometheus*. Cambridge: Cambridge University Press.

Laslett, Peter. 1984. *The World We Have Lost: England Before the Industrial Age*. 3d ed. New York: Scribner's.

Latané, B., and J. M. Darley. 1970. *The Unresponsive Bystander: Why Doesn't He Help?* New York: Appleton-Century-Crofts.

Laumann, Edward O. 1973. *Bonds of Pluralism*. New York: John Wiley.

Laver, Michael. 1981. *The Politics of Private Desires*. Harmondsworth, England: Penguin.

Lazear, Edward P. 1979. "Why Is There Mandatory Retirement?" *Journal of Political Economy*, 87, (6): 1261–84.

Leach, Edmund. 1962. Introduction: "What Should We Mean by Caste?" In E. Leach, ed., *Aspects of Caste in South India, Ceylon and North West Pakistan*, pp. 1–10. London: Cambridge University Press.

Le Bon, Gustave. 1960. *The Crowd: A Study of the Popular Mind*. New York: Viking. [Originally published 1895.]

Lefkowitz, M. R., R. Blake, and J. S. Mouton. 1955. "Status Factors in Pedestrian Violations of Traffic Signals." *Journal of Abnormal and Social Psychology*, 51, (3): 704–6.

Leibenstein, Harvey. 1975. "Aspects of the X-Efficiency Theory of the Firm." *Bell Journal of Economics*, 6, (2): 580–606.

Levi, Margaret. 1987. *Of Rule and Revenue*. Berkeley: University of California Press.

Lewis, David. 1969. *Convention: A Philosophical Study*. Cambridge: Harvard University Press.

Lifton, Robert J. 1961. *Thought Reform and the Psychology of Totalism*. New York: Norton.

Light, Ivan. 1972. *Ethnic Enterprise in America*. Berkeley: University of California Press.

Lindenberg, Siegwart. 1982. "Sharing Groups: Theory and Suggested Applications." *Journal of Mathematical Sociology*, 9, (1): 33–62.

————. 1983. "Utility and Morality." *Kyklos*, 36, (3): 450–68.

Loewenberg, Gerhard. 1967. *Parliament in the German Political System*. Ithaca, N.Y.: Cornell University Press.

Lowell, A. L. 1902. "The Influence of Party upon Legislation in England and America." In the *Annual Report* of the American Historical Association, pp. 321–542. Washington, D.C.: Government Printing Office.

Lucas, Robert E. B. 1979. "Sharing, Monitoring, and Incentives: Marshallian Misallocation Reassessed." *Journal of Political Economy*, 87, (3): 501–21.

Lyman, Stanford M. 1977. *The Asian in North America*. Santa Barbara, Calif.: ABC-Clio.

McCarthy, John D., and Mayer N. Zald. 1977. "Resource Mobilization and Social Movements: A Partial Theory." *American Journal of Sociology*, 82, (6): 1212–41.

McCloskey, Donald P. 1976. "English Open Fields as a Behavior Toward Risk." In P. Uselding, ed., *Research in Economic History*, vol. 1, pp. 124–70. Westport, Conn.: JAI Press.

McDonald, Glenn M. 1984. "New Directions in the Economic Theory of Agency." *Canadian Journal of Economics*, 17, (3): 415–40.

Machina, Mark J. 1983. "Generalized Expected Utility Analysis and the Nature of Observed Violations of the Independence Axiom." In B. P. Stigum and F. Wenstop, eds., *Foundations of Utility and Risk Theory with Applications*, pp. 263–93. Dordrecht: D. Reidel.

McManus, John C. 1975. "The Costs of Alternative Economic Organizations." *Canadian Journal of Economics*, 8, (3): 334–50.

MacRae, Duncan, Jr. 1958. *Dimensions of Congressional Voting*. Berkeley: University of California Press.

————. 1967. *Parliament, Parties, and Society in France, 1946–1958*. New York: St. Martin's.

Malinowski, Bronislaw. 1926. *Crime and Custom in Savage Society*. London: Routledge.

Marglin, Stephen A. 1974. "What Do Bosses Do? The Origins and Function of Hierarchy in Capitalist Production." *Review of Radical Political Economics*, 6, (2): 60–112.

Margolis, Howard. 1982. *Selfishness, Altruism, and Rationality*. Cambridge: Cambridge University Press.

Marsden, Peter V., and Nan Lin, eds. 1982. *Social Structure and Network Analysis*. Beverly Hills: Sage Publications.

Marwell, Gerald, and Ruth E. Ames. 1979. "Experiments on the Provision of Public Goods: I. Resources, Interest, Group Size and the Free-Rider Problem." *American Journal of Sociology*, 84, (6): 1335–60.

———. 1980. "Experiments on the Provision of Public Goods: II. Provision Points, Stakes, Experience, and the Free-Rider Problem." *American Journal of Sociology*, 85, (4): 926–37.

Marx, Karl. 1965. *Capital*. 3 volumes. Moscow: Progress Publishers. [Originally published 1867.]

———. 1972. "The German Ideology: Part I." In Robert C. Tucker, ed., *The Marx-Engels Reader*, 2d ed. New York: Norton. [Originally published 1932.]

———. 1975. *The Eighteenth Brumaire of Louis Bonaparte*. New York: International Publishers. [Originally published 1852.]

Matthews, Donald R. 1961. "United States Senators: A Collective Portrait." *International Social Science Journal*, 13, (4): 620–34.

Matthewson, Stanley B. 1931. *Restriction of Output Among Unorganized Workers*. New York: Viking.

Mayhew, David. 1966. *Party Loyalty Among Congressmen*. Cambridge: Harvard University Press.

———. 1974. *Congress: The Electoral Connection*. New Haven: Yale University Press.

Meade, J. E. 1972. "The Theory of Labour-Managed Firms and Profit Sharing." *The Economic Journal*, 82, (325s): 402–28.

Merry, Sally Engel. 1984. "Rethinking Gossip and Scandal." In Donald Black, ed., *Fundamentals*, vol. 1 of *Toward a General Theory of Social Control*, pp. 271–302. New York: Academic Press.

Merton, Robert K. 1967. *On Theoretical Sociology*. New York: Free Press.

———. 1973. *The Sociology of Science*. Chicago: University of Chicago Press.

Michels, Robert. 1962. *Political Parties: A Sociological Study of the Oligarchical Tendencies of Modern Democracy*. Translated by Eden Paul and Cedar Paul. New York: Free Press. [Originally published 1911.]

Miller, Clem. 1971. "Six Letters to Constituents." In Nelson W. Polsby, ed., *Congressional Behavior*, pp. 136–52. New York: Random House.

Miller, David. 1981. "Market Neutrality and the Failure of Cooperatives." *British Journal of Political Science*, 11, (3): 309–29.

Minor, W. 1978. "Deterrence Research: Problems of Theory and Method." In James A. Cramer, ed., *Preventing Crime*, pp. 21–46. Beverly Hills: Sage Publications.

Mitchell, Ann. 1985. *Children in the Middle*. New York: Tavistock Publications.

Mitford, Jessica. 1977. *A Fine Old Conflict.* New York: Knopf.

Moles, Oliver C. 1976. "Marital Dissolution and Public Assistance Payments: Variations among American States." *The Journal of Social Issues,* 32, (1): 87–102.

Morgenstern, Oskar. 1951. *On the Accuracy of Economic Observations.* Princeton: Princeton University Press.

Mueller, Dennis C. 1978. "Voting by Veto." *Journal of Public Economics,* 10, (1): 57–75.

———. 1979. *Public Choice.* Cambridge: Cambridge University Press.

Murakami, Yasusuke. 1984. "Ie Society as a Pattern of Civilization." Jackson School of International Studies, University of Washington. Mimeograph.

Murakami, Yasusuke, Shumpei Kumon, and Seizaburo Sato. 1979. *Bunmei toshiteno Ie Shakai* (*Ie Society as a Pattern of Civilization*). Tokyo: Chūōkōron Sha.

Nakane, Chie. 1970. *Japanese Society.* Berkeley: University of California Press.

Nelson, Daniel. 1975. *Managers and Workers.* Madison: University of Wisconsin Press.

———. 1980. *Frederick W. Taylor and the Rise of Scientific Management.* Madison: University of Wisconsin Press.

Newman, Graeme. 1978. *The Punishment Response.* Philadelphia: Lippincott.

Nisbet, Robert. 1966. *The Sociological Tradition.* New York: Basic Books.

Nordhoff, Charles. 1965. *The Communistic Societies of The United States: from Personal Visit and Observation.* New York: Schocken Books. [Originally published 1875.]

North, Douglass C. 1981. *Structure and Change in Economic History.* New York: Norton.

Norton, Thomas L. 1968. *Trade Union Policies in the Massachusetts Shoe Industry, 1919–1929.* New York: AMS Press. [Originally published 1932.]

Nozick, Robert. 1974. *Anarchy, State and Utopia.* New York: Basic Books.

Oberschall, Anthony. 1973. *Social Conflict and Social Movements.* Englewood Cliffs, N.J.: Prentice-Hall.

Oliver, Pamela. 1980. "Rewards and Punishments as Selective Incentives for Collective Action: Theoretical Investigations." *American Journal of Sociology,* 85, (6): 1356–75.

Olson, Mancur. 1965. *The Logic of Collective Action.* Cambridge: Harvard University Press.

Opp, Karl-Dieter. 1982. "The Evolutionary Emergence of Norms." *British Journal of Social Psychology,* 21, (2): 139–49.

Orwell, George. 1959. *Down and Out in Paris and London.* New York: Mentor.

Ostrogorski, Moisei. 1964. *The United States.* Vol. 2 of *Democracy and the*

Organization of Political Parties. New York: Anchor. [Originally published 1902.]

Ouchi, William G. 1981. *Theory Z*. Reading, Mass.: Addison-Wesley.

Ouchi, William G., and Mary Ann Maguire. 1975. "Organizational Control: Two Functions." *Administrative Science Quarterly*, 20, (4): 559–69.

Owen, Bruce M., and Ronald Breautigam. 1978. *The Regulation Game: Strategic Use of Administrative Process*. Cambridge, Mass.: Ballinger.

Oz, Amos. 1973. *Elsewhere, Perhaps*. Translated by Nicholas de Lange. New York: Harcourt Brace Jovanovich.

Ozbudun, Ergun. 1970. "Party Cohesion in Western Democracies: A Causal Analysis." *SAGE Comparative Politics Series*, (1): 303–388.

Paige, Jeffrey. 1975. *Agrarian Revolution*. New York: Free Press.

van Parijs, Phillipe. 1981. *Evolutionary Explanation in the Social Sciences: An Emerging Paradigm*. London: Tavistock Publications.

Parkin, Frank. 1979. *Marxism and Class Theory*. New York: Columbia University Press.

Parsons, Talcott. 1937. *The Structure of Social Action*. New York: McGraw-Hill.

———. 1958. *Social Structure and Personality*. New York: Free Press.

———. 1973. "Some Afterthoughts on *Gemeinschaft* and *Gesellschaft*." In W. J. Cahnman, ed., *Ferdinand Tönnies: A New Evaluation*, pp. 140–50. Leiden: Brill.

Pateman, Carole. 1970. *Participation and Democratic Theory*. Cambridge: Cambridge University Press.

Peltzman, Sam. 1984. "Constituent Interest and Congressional Voting." *Journal of Law and Economics*, 27, (1): 181–210.

Piaget, Jean. 1932. *The Moral Judgement of the Child*. London: Routledge & Kegan Paul.

Piliavin, I. M., J. Rodin, and J. A. Piliavin. 1969. "Good Samaritanism: An Underground Phenomenon?" *Journal of Personality and Social Psychology*, 13, (4): 289–99.

Polanyi, Karl. 1957. *The Great Transformation*. Boston: Beacon. [Originally published 1944.]

Polsby, Nelson W., Miriam Gallaher, and Barry S. Rundquist. 1971. "The Growth of the Seniority System in the U.S. House of Representatives." In N. W. Polsby, ed., *Congressional Behavior*, pp. 172–202. New York: Random House. [Originally in *The American Political Science Review*, 53, 3 (1969): 787–807.]

Popkin, Samuel L. 1979. *The Rational Peasant*. Berkeley: University of California Press.

Posner, Richard A. 1980. "A Theory of Primitive Society, with Special Reference to Law." *The Journal of Law and Economics*, 23, (1): 1–53.

Pratten, C. F. 1976. *Labour Productivity Differentials Within International Companies*. Cambridge: Cambridge University Press.

Rachlin, Howard. 1980. "Economics and Behavioral Psychology." In

J. E. R. Staddon, ed., *Limits to Action: The Allocation of Individual Behavior*, pp. 205–36. New York: Academic Press.

Ranney, A. 1968. "Candidate Selection and Party Cohesion in Britain and the United States." In W. J. Crotty, ed., *Approaches to the Study of Party Organization*, pp. 139–58. Boston: Allyn and Bacon.

Raub, Werner, ed. 1982. *Theoretical Models and Empirical Analyses: Contributions to the Explanation of Individual Actions and Collective Phenomena*. Utrecht, Netherlands: E. S.-Publications.

Reitz, Jeffrey G. 1980. *The Survival of Ethnic Groups*. Toronto: McGraw-Hill Ryerson.

Renkiewicz, Frank. 1980. "Polish Fraternalism and Beneficial Insurance in America." In Scott Cummings, ed., *Self-Help in Urban America: Patterns of Minority Business Enterprise*, pp. 113–30. Port Washington, N.Y.: Kennikat Press.

Rice, S. A. 1928. *Quantitative Methods in Politics*. New York: Knopf.

Rockwell, John. 1982. "The Berlin Philarmonic: What Makes it Great?" *The New York Times*, October 17, Section 2.

Rohlen, Thomas P. 1974. *For Harmony and Strength: White Collar Organization in Anthropological Perspective*. Berkeley: University of California Press.

Ross, E. A. 1901. *Social Control*. New York: Macmillan.

Ross, George. 1982. *Workers and Communists in France: From Popular Front to Eurocommunism*. Berkeley: University of California Press.

Ross, H. Lawrence, and I. V. Sawhill. 1975. *Time of Transition: The Growth of Families Headed by Women*. Washington, D.C.: Urban Institute.

Roy, Donald. 1952. "Quota Restriction and Goldbricking in a Machine Shop." *American Journal of Sociology*, 57, (5): 427–42.

Rushton, J. Philippe. 1980. *Altruism, Socialization, and Society*. Englewood Cliffs, N.J.: Prentice-Hall.

Rutter, Michael. 1971. "Parent-Child Separation: Psychological Effects on the Children." *Journal of Child Psychology and Psychiatry and Allied Disciplines*, 12, (4): 233–60.

Saive, Marie-Anne. 1980. "Mondragón: An Experiment with Co-Operative Development in the Industrial Sector." *Annals of Public and Cooperative Economics*, 51, (3): 223–55.

Sandler, Todd, and John T. Tschirhart. 1980. "The Economic Theory of Clubs: An Evaluative Survey." *Journal of Economic Literature*, 18, (4): 1481–1521.

Sasmore, Robert M. 1966. "Operant Conditioning of a Small-Scale Muscle Response." *Journal of the Experimental Analysis of Behavior*, 9, (1): 69–85.

Scarborough, William K. 1966. *The Overseer*. Baton Rouge: Louisiana State University Press.

Schafer, Roy. 1968. *Aspects of Internalization*. New York: International Universities Press.

————. 1976. *A New Language for Psychoanalysis*. New Haven: Yale University Press.

Schattschneider, E. E. 1942. *Party Government*. New York: Holt, Rinehart and Winston.

Schelling, Thomas C. 1978. *Micromotives and Macrobehavior*. New York: Norton.

Schofield, Norman. 1985. "Anarchy, Altruism and Cooperation." *Social Choice and Welfare*, 2, (3): 207–19.

Schotter, Andrew. 1981. *The Economic Theory of Social Institutions*. Cambridge: Cambridge University Press.

Schumpeter, Joseph A. 1950. *Capitalism, Socialism, and Democracy*. New York: Harper.

————. 1954. *History of Economic Analysis*. New York: Oxford University Press.

Schwarz, J. E. 1980. "Exploring a New Role in Policy Making: The British House of Commons in the 1970's." *American Political Science Review*, 74, (1): 23–37.

Schwarz, J. E., and L. E. Shaw. 1976. *The United States Congress in Comparative Perspective*. Hinsdale, Ill.: Dryden.

Scott, James C. 1976. *The Moral Economy of the Peasant*. New Haven: Yale University Press.

Scott, John Finley. 1971. *Internalization of Norms: A Sociological Theory of Moral Commitment*. Englewood Cliffs, N.J.: Prentice-Hall.

Selltiz, C., M. Jahoda, M. Deutsch, and S. W. Cook. 1959. *Research Methods in Social Relations*. New York: Holt, Rinehart and Winston.

Sen, Amartya, and Bernard Williams, eds. 1982. *Utilitarianism and Beyond*. Cambridge: Cambridge University Press.

Shambaugh, Bertha M. 1932. *Amana That Was and Amana That Is*. Iowa City: State Historical Society of Iowa.

Shannon, W. W. 1968. *Party, Constituency and Congressional Voting*. Baton Rouge: Louisiana State University Press.

Shepsle, Kenneth A. 1978. *The Giant Jigsaw Puzzle: Democratic Committee Assignments in the Modern House*. Chicago: University of Chicago Press.

Shirai, Taishiro. 1975. "Decision-Making in Japanese Labor Unions." In Ezra F. Vogel, ed., *Modern Japanese Organization and Decision-Making*, pp. 167–84. Berkeley: University of California Press.

Simmel, Georg. 1955. "The Web of Group Affiliations." Translated by Reinhard Bendix. In *Conflict and the Web of Group Affiliations*, pp. 125–95. New York: Free Press. [Originally published 1922.]

Simon, Herbert A. 1957. *Models of Man*. New York: John Wiley.

————. 1983. *Reason in Human Affairs*. Stanford, Calif.: Stanford University Press.

Smith, Adam. 1961. *The Wealth of Nations*. 2 volumes. London: University Paperbacks. [Originally published 1789.]

Smith, Robert J. 1983. *Japanese Society: Individual, Self and The Social Order*. Cambridge: Cambridge University Press.

Smith, Vernon. 1979. "An Experimental Comparison of Three Public Good Decision Mechanisms." *The Scandinavian Journal of Economics*, 81 (2): 198–215.

Snidal, Duncan. 1979. "Public Goods, Property Rights, and Political Organizations." *International Studies Quarterly*, 23 (4): 532–66.

Snow, David A., and Richard Machalek. 1984. "The Sociology of Conversion." *Annual Review of Sociology*, 10: 167–90.

Sombart, Werner. 1953. "Medieval and Modern Commerical Enterprise." In Frederick C. Lane and Jelle C. Riemersma, eds., *Enterprise and Secular Change*, pp. 25–40. Homewood, Ill.: R. D. Irwin.

Sorauf, F. J. 1964. *Political Parties in the American System*. Boston: Little, Brown.

Spiro, Melford E. 1956. *Kibbutz: Venture in Utopia*. Cambridge: Harvard University Press.

———. 1984. "Some Reflections on Cultural Determinism and Relativism with Special Reference to Emotion and Reason." In Richard A. Shweder and Robert A. LeVine, eds., *Culture Theory: Essays on Mind, Self, and Emotion*, pp. 328–346. Cambridge: Cambridge University Press.

Stalson, J. Owen. 1942. *Marketing Life Insurance: Its History in America*. Cambridge: Harvard University Press.

Stigler, George J. 1966. *The Theory of Price*. New York: Macmillan. [Originally published 1942.]

———. 1971. "Smith's Travels on the Ship of State." *History of Political Economy*, 3, (2): 265–77.

Stigler, George J., and Gary S. Becker. 1977. "De Gustibus Non Est Disputandum." *American Economic Review*, 67, (2): 76–90.

Stinchcombe, Arthur. 1965. "Social Structure and Organization." In J. G. March, ed., *Handbook of Organizations*, pp. 142–93. Chicago: Rand McNally.

———. 1968. *Constructing Social Theories*. New York: Harcourt and Brace.

Stolarik, M. Mark. 1980. "Slovak Fraternal-Benefit Societies." In Scott Cummings, ed., *Urban Self-Help in America*, pp. 130–45. Port Washington, N.Y.: Kennikat Press.

Stone, Katharine. 1974. "The Origins of Job Structures in the Steel Industry." *Review of Radical Political Economics*, 6, (2): 61–97.

Sweeney, J. 1973. "An Experimental Investigation of the Free Rider Problem." *Social Science Research*, 2, (3): 277–92.

Sweet, James A. 1973. *Women in the Labor Force*. New York: Seminar Press.

Sykes, Gresham M. 1958. *The Society of Captives*. Princeton: Princeton University Press.

Talmon, Yonina. 1972. *Family and Community in the Kibbutz*. Cambridge: Harvard University Press.

Taylor, Frederick W. 1947a. *Shop Management.* New York: Harper & Row. [Originally published 1903.]

———. 1947b. *The Principles of Scientific Management.* New York: Harper & Row. [Originally published 1911.]

Taylor, Michael. 1976. *Anarchy and Cooperation.* London: John Wiley.

———. 1982. *Community, Anarchy, and Liberty.* Cambridge: Cambridge University Press.

Thernstrom, Stephan, Ann Orlov, and Oscar Handlin, eds. 1980. *Harvard Encyclopedia of American Ethnic Groups.* Cambridge: Harvard University Press.

Thibaut, J. W., and H. H. Kelley. 1959. *The Social Psychology of Groups.* New York: John Wiley.

Thomas, Henk, and Chris Logan. 1982. *Mondragón: An Economic Analysis.* London: George Allen and Unwin.

Thompson, E. A. 1966. "A Pareto Optimal Group Decision Process." In Gordon Tullock, ed., *Papers on Non-market Decision Making,* pp. 133–40. Charlottesville: University of Virginia Press.

Tiebout, C. M. 1956. "A Pure Theory of Local Expenditures." *Journal of Political Economy,* 64, (5): 416–24.

Tilly, Charles. 1978. *From Mobilization to Revolution.* Reading, Mass.: Addison-Wesley.

Timberlake, W., and J. Allison. 1974. "Response Deprivation: An Empirical Approach to Instrumental Performance." *Psychological Review,* 81, (2): 146–64.

Titmuss, Richard. 1971. *The Gift Relationship: From Human Blood to Public Policy.* New York: Random House.

Tocqueville, Alexis de. 1951. *Democracy in America.* Edited by Phillips Bradley. New York: Knopf. [Originally published 1835.]

Tönnies, Ferdinand. 1957. *Community and Society.* Translated and edited by Charles P. Loomis. East Lansing: Michigan State University Press. [Originally published 1887.]

Trivers, Robert L. 1971. "The Evolution of Reciprocal Altruism." *Quarterly Review of Biology,* 46, (1): 35–57.

Truman, David. 1959. *The Congressional Party.* New York: Free Press.

Turner, Julius. 1951. *Party and Constituency: Pressures on Congress.* Baltimore: Johns Hopkins University Press.

Turner, Julius, and E. V. Schneier, Jr. 1970. *Party and Constituency: Pressures on Congress.* Rev. ed. Baltimore: Johns Hopkins University Press.

Tversky, Amos. 1975. "A Critique of Expected Utility Theory: Descriptive and Normative Considerations." *Erkenntnis,* 9, (2): 163–173.

Umbeck, John R. 1981. *A Theory of Property Rights with Application to the California Gold Rush.* Ames: Iowa State University Press.

United Nations (Department of Economic Affairs). 1951. *Labour Productivity of the Cotton Textile Industry in Five Latin-American Countries.* New York: United Nations.

Vallier, Ivan. 1959. *Production Imperatives in Communal Systems: A Comparative Study with Special Reference to the Kibbutz Crisis.* Ph.D. dissertation, Department of Social Relations. Harvard University.

Van Dyke, Vernon. 1977. "The Individual, the State, and Ethnic Communities in Political Theory." *World Politics,* 29, (3): 342–69.

Vélez-Ibáñez, Carlos G. 1983. *Bonds of Mutual Trust: The Cultural Systems of Rotating Credit Associations among Urban Mexicans and Chicanos.* New Brunswick, N.J.: Rutgers University Press.

Verberne, L. G. J. 1959. *De Nederlandse arbeidersbeweging in de negentiende eeuw (The Dutch Labor Movement in the Nineteenth Century).* Utrecht: Spectrum.

Verdon, Michel. 1981. "Kinship, Marriage and the Family: An Operational Approach." *American Journal of Sociology,* 86, (4): 796–818.

Vickrey, William. 1961. "Counterspeculation, Auctions, and Competitive Sealed Tenders." *Journal of Finance,* 16, (1): 8–37.

Vogel, Ezra F. 1979. *Japan as Number One.* Cambridge: Harvard University Press.

von Neumann, John, and Oskar Morgenstern. 1944. *Theory of Games and Economic Behavior.* Princeton: Princeton University Press.

Wade, L. L. 1985. "Tocqueville and Public Choice." *Public Choice,* 47, (3): 491–508.

Walford, Cornelius. 1871–80. *The Insurance Cyclopaedia.* 6 vols. London: C. and E. Layton.

Wallerstein, Immanuel. 1974. *The Modern World-System.* New York: Academic Press.

Ware, James R., trans. 1955. *The Sayings of Confucius.* New York: New American Library.

Webb, Eugene J., Donald T. Campbell, Richard D. Schwartz, and Lee Sechrest. 1969. *Unobtrusive Measures.* Chicago: Rand McNally.

Webb, Sidney, and Beatrice Webb. 1907. *The History of Trade Unionism.* London: Longmans, Green and Co.

Weber, Max. 1946a. "India: The Brahman and the Castes." In Hans Gerth and C. Wright Mills, eds., *From Max Weber: Essays in Sociology,* pp. 396–415. New York: Oxford University Press. [Originally published 1916–1917.]

———. 1946b. "The Meaning of Discipline." In Hans Gerth and C. Wright Mills, eds., *From Max Weber: Essays in Sociology,* pp. 253–64. New York: Oxford University Press. [Originally published 1922.]

———. 1958. *The Protestant Ethic and the Spirit of Capitalism,* translated by Talcott Parsons. New York: Scribner's. [Originally published 1904–5.]

———. 1968. *Economy and Society.* Edited by Guenther Roth and Claus Wittich. New York: Bedminster Press. [Originally published 1922.]

———. 1981. *General Economic History.* Translated by Frank H. Knight. New Brunswick, N.J.: Transaction Books. [Originally published 1924.]

von Weiszäcker, Carl Christian. 1971. "Notes on Endogenous Change of Tastes." *Journal of Economic Theory,* 3, (4): 345–72.

White, Harrison C., Scott A. Boorman, and Ronald L. Breiger. 1976. "Social Structure from Multiple Networks. I. Blockmodels of Roles and Positions." *American Journal of Sociology*, 81, (6): 730–80.

Whyte, William Foote. 1955. *Money and Motivation*. New York: Harper & Row.

Wilensky, Harold L. 1967. *Organizational Intelligence*. New York: Basic Books.

Williams, Aaron. 1866. *The Harmony Society at Economy, Pennsylvania*. Pittsburgh: W. S. Haven.

Williams, G. C. 1966. *Adaptation and Natural Selection*. Princeton: Princeton University Press.

Williams, Robin M., Jr. 1968. "The Concept of Norms." In the *International Encyclopedia of the Social Sciences*, vol. 11, pp. 204–8. New York: Macmillan.

Williamson, Oliver E. 1975. *Markets and Hierarchies*. New York: Free Press.

———. 1981. "The Economics of Organization: The Transaction Cost Approach." *American Journal of Sociology*, 87, (3): 548–77.

Wilson, E. O. 1975. *Sociobiology*. Cambridge: Harvard University Press.

Wilson, E. O., and Charles J. Lumsden. 1981. *Genes, Mind, and Culture: The Coevolutionary Process*. Cambridge: Harvard University Press.

Wilson, James Q. 1973. *Political Organizations*. New York: Basic Books.

———. 1983. "Raising Kids." *The Atlantic*, October: 45–56.

Wilson, James Q., and Richard J. Herrnstein. 1985. *Crime and Human Nature*. New York: Simon and Schuster.

Windmuller, John P. 1969. *Labor Relations in the Netherlands*. Ithaca, N.Y.: Cornell University Press.

Wittfogel, Karl. 1957. *Oriental Despotism*. New Haven: Yale University Press.

Woodward, Joan. 1965. *Industrial Organization: Theory and Practice*. London: Oxford University Press.

Wright, Erik Olin. 1985. *Classes*. London: Verso.

Wrong, Dennis. 1961. "The Oversocialized Conception of Man in Modern Sociology." *American Sociological Review*, 26, (1): 183–93.

Wu, David Y. H. 1973. "To Kill Three Birds with One Stone: The Rotating Credit Associations of the Papua New Guinea Chinese." *American Ethnologist*, 1, (3): 565–84.

Young, Oran. 1979. *Compliance and Public Authority*. Baltimore: Johns Hopkins University Press.

Zablocki, Benjamin. 1971. *The Joyful Community*. Baltimore: Penguin.

———. 1980. *Alienation and Charisma*. New York: Free Press.

INDEX

Abruzzi, Adam, 138, 140
Agency costs, 132
Agents: and institutional structures of groups, 52; as monitors, 130–33; and principals, 134 n; as providers of control, 52; of socialization, 68
Akerlof, George A., 136
Alchian, Armen, 24, 130, 136, 170–71
Allais, Maurice, 172 n
Altruism: and free riders, 60; and informal self-sustaining controls, 60; and neoclassical economic theory, 71; and rational egoism, 60; and selection processes, 60; and social interdependence, 71; and socialization, 60, 68
Altruistic behavior: and kin-selection, 70; and reciprocity, 70; and reproductive fitness, 70; and selection theories, 70; as self-interest, 70
Altruists: and corporate interest, 77; and information, 77
Amana colony, 151, 157, 161
Ames, William, 27 n, 61, 182
Ancient Law (Sir Henry Maine), 57
Anderson, Gary M., 169
Appelbaum-Maisel, Malka, 27
Ardener, Shirley, 107–8, 110
Arrington, Leonard, 44 n, 49 n
Arrow, Kenneth J., 33, 61, 61 n, 73
Axelrod, Robert, 74–75

Babbage, Charles, 135
Bandura, Albert, 66, 68

Bane, Mary Jo, 57
Banfield, Edward, 68
Banton, Michael, 6 n
Barth, Fredrik, 48
Baumol, William, 44 n
Becker, Gary S., 41, 57, 71–72, 184
Becker, Howard, 164
Bendix, Reinhard, 15 n, 139
Ben-Porath, Yoram, 171
Bentham, Jeremy, 136, 150, 162
Berkowitz, S. D., 25 n
Bernstein, Paul, 124, 139, 153 n
Berreman, G. D., 48
Blalock, Hubert, 7 n
Blau, Peter M., 6 n, 45
Blumstein, Phillip, 19
Bodnar, John, 115
Bohm, P., 27 n
Bonacich, Edna, 178
Bonnett, Aubrey, 109–10
Boudon, Raymond, 6 n
Bouglé, C., 48
Bradley, Keith, 154 n
Brady, David, 102
Braverman, Harry, 139 n
Breautigam, Ronald, 172
Brennan, Geoffrey, 45–46
Brenner, Reuven, 172 n
Breton, Albert, 119, 141, 178
British Liberal Party, 99
Broad, William: and monitoring scientific research, 135
Bruderhof, 41; and intentional communities, 152–53, 155, 159, 161
Buchanan, James, 33, 37, 45–46, 152
Burawoy, Michael, 141
Butterick, John, 131

211

Compositor: G & S Typesetters, Inc.
Text: 10/13 Plantin
Display: Plantin
Printer: Braun-Brumfield, Inc.
Binder: Braun-Brumfield, Inc.